THE TIGER TRIUMPHS

THE STORY OF
THREE GREAT DIVISIONS
IN ITALY

The Naval & Military Press Ltd

Published by

The Naval & Military Press Ltd
Unit 10 Ridgewood Industrial Park,
Uckfield, East Sussex,
TN22 5QE England

Tel: +44 (0) 1825 749494
Fax: +44 (0) 1825 765701

www.naval-military-press.com
www.military-genealogy.com

In reprinting in facsimile from the original, any imperfections are inevitably reproduced and the quality may fall short of modern type and cartographic standards.

A MAN'S DESTINATION IS HIS OWN VILLAGE,
HIS OWN FIRE AND HIS WIFE'S COOKING,
TO SIT IN FRONT OF HIS OWN DOOR AT SUNSET
AND SEE HIS GRANDSON AND HIS NEIGHBOURS' GRANDSON
PLAY IN THE DUST TOGETHER.

SCARRED BUT SECURE HE HAS MANY NARRATIVES
TO REPEAT AT THE HOUR OF CONVERSATION
(THE WARM, OR THE COOL HOUR, ACCORDING TO THE CLIMATE)
OF FOREIGN MEN, WHO FOUGHT IN FOREIGN PLACES,
FOREIGN TO EACH OTHER.

THIS WAS NOT YOUR LAND OR OURS : BUT A VILLAGE IN THE
    MIDLANDS
AND ONE IN THE FIVE RIVERS, MAY HAVE THE SAME MEMORIES.
LET THOSE WHO GO HOME TELL THE SAME STORY OF YOU—
OF ACTION WITH A COMMON PURPOSE, ACTION
NONE THE LESS FRUITFUL IF NEITHER YOU NOR I
KNOW UNTIL THE JUDGEMENT AFTER DEATH,
WHAT IS THE FRUIT OF ACTION.

By kind permission of Mr. T. S. Eliot's publishers.

I HAVE HAD THE DISTINCTION OF HAVING UNDER MY COMMAND A TRIO OF GREAT INDIAN DIVISIONS—THE FOURTH, EIGHTH AND TENTH —WHOSE FIGHTING RECORD IN ITALY IS A SPLENDID ONE.

"The achievements in combat of these Indian soldiers are noteworthy. They have carried on successfully in grim and bloody fighting against a tenacious enemy helped by terrain particularly favourable for defence. No obstacle has succeeded in delaying these Indian troops for long or in lowering their high morale or fighting spirit.

"They are well led, these Three Divisions. Each of the Divisional Commanders at one time commanded a battalion of an Indian Infantry Regiment in combat. These Divisional Commanders came up the hard way.

"Your 'Jawan' and 'Tommy Atkins' and 'Jock' and other soldiers of this international 15th Army Group have established firm bonds of friendship and respect born in action against a tough enemy. The bravery of Indian troops is attested by the Battle Honours and Decorations awarded.

"The Fourth, Eighth and Tenth Indian Divisions will forever be associated with the fighting for Cassino, the capture of Rome, the Arno Valley, the liberation of Florence and the breaking of the Gothic Line.

"I salute the brave soldiers of these Three Great Indian Divisions."

Mark W. Clark.

FEBRUARY 27TH, 1945. FIFTEENTH ARMY GROUP, ITALY.

CONTENTS

CHAPTER		PAGE
	SECTION ONE. THE LOWER ADRIATIC	
I.	THE NEW CAMPAIGN	1
II.	EIGHTH DIVISION ADVANCES	7
III.	MOZZAGROGNA AND VILLA GRANDE	19
IV.	WINTER AND SPRING	31
	SECTION TWO. CASSINO—THE EPIC	
V.	THE FIRST ASSAULT FAILS	39
VI.	THE SECOND ASSAULT FAILS	49
VII.	EIGHTH DIVISION PUNCHES THE HOLE	65
	SECTION THREE. CENTRAL ITALY	
VIII.	EIGHTH DIVISION IN PURSUIT	81
IX.	TENTH DIVISION IN THE TIBER VALLEY	87
X.	FOURTH DIVISION IN THE ARNO VALLEY	103
XI.	EIGHTH DIVISION CLEARS FLORENCE	113
	SECTION FOUR. THE GOTHIC LINE	
XII.	THE ENEMY AT BAY	119
XIII.	FOURTH DIVISION OPENS THE BATTLE	122
XIV.	GURKHA LORRIED BRIGADE ENTERS THE FRAY	135
XV.	TENTH INDIAN DIVISION ON THE GOTHIC LINE	141
XVI.	EIGHTH DIVISION—FIFTH ARMY'S FLYING SQUAD	151
	SECTION FIVE. THE LAST CAMPAIGN	
XVII.	THE FLOODBANKED RIVERS	173
XVIII.	TENTH DIVISION CLEARS THE WAY	176
XIX.	EIGHTH DIVISION PUNCHES THE HOLE AGAIN	183
XX.	THE LAST PHASE	194
	POSTSCRIPT	
XXI.	MACEDONIA AND THE JULIAN MARCHES	202

LIST OF ILLUSTRATIONS

FRONTISPIECE

Between pages 10 *and* 11

BULLDOZER	BAILEY BRIDGE
DELAYED SIGNAL	PRINCIPAL ENEMY
BOGGED DOWN	BLOCKED ROAD
OPEN FRONT—C.I.H. RAIDERS	PUNJABIS MOVE UP

Facing page 27

DIVISIONAL COMMANDERS

Between pages 60 *and* 61

THE BATTLEFIELD

Reproduced by kind permission of Margaret Bourke-White and the publishers of "Life."

PANORAMA OF CASSINO

From the painting by Capt. Hogg and Capt. Henshaw

JUNCTION RAPIDO AND LIRI VALLEYS

MONASTERY BOMBARDMENT	VESUVIUS BOMBARDMENT
FROM SNAKE'S HEAD	FROM POINT 445
AIR DROPPING—HANGMAN'S HILL	CASSINO SHAMBLES

Between pages 92 *and* 93

VILLAGE PATROL	PICKUP VAN
ADVANCE THROUGH THE WHEAT	CARRIERS LEAD THE WAY
ENEMY HOLDS WHITE HOUSE	PIFFERS CLIMB
KING'S OWN—COVERING FIRE	ENEMY IN SIGHT

LIST OF ILLUSTRATIONS Cont.

Between pages 140 *and* 141

BALUCHI TOMMYGUNNER . FORWARD MORTAR TEAM
TAVOLETO BURNS . SAN MARINO CITY STATE
FOR SUPREME VALOUR
CAMERONS CLOSE ON SAN MARINO
6TH LANCERS MOP UP . . . THEIR HAUL
MAHRATTAS AT MONTE VERRUCA

Between pages 172 *and* 173

HIGH APENNINES . . . GURKHA SNOW PATROL
SIKH RAIDERS . . . . JAIPUR GUNNERS
GURKHA SIGNALMAN . . . . SIKH SKI-MAN
SAPPERS AND MINERS—LAMONE RIVER . HARDY MUSSALMANS
MAHRATTAS STORM FLOOD BANK . ARK BRIDGE
RAIDERS UNDER ARTIFICIAL MOONLIGHT
DUKWS LOAD GUNS
GUNS ACROSS . . . . . JEEPS ACROSS
DIAGRAM OF SENIO RIVER DEFENCES

Facing page 189

COMMANDER-IN-CHIEF'S THANKS . HISTORIC MOMENT

End of Book

NAIK AND BRIGADIER . . EVERYBODY HAPPY
GENERAL FREYBERG'S FAREWELL . HOMEWARD BOUND

MAPS AND DIAGRAMS

INDIAN BATTLEFIELDS IN ITALY	*Page* 6
LOWER ADRIATIC SECTOR	*Facing page* 26
MONASTERY HILL MASSIF AND CASSINO TOWN . .	*Page* 40
EIGHTH INDIAN DIVISION IN PURSUIT	,, 82
GOTHIC LINE BATTLEFIELD IN THE HIGH APENNINES	,, 118
THE BREAK-THROUGH ON THE RIVER LINES .	*Facing page* 188

1. THE LOWER ADRIATIC

CHAPTER ONE

THE NEW CAMPAIGN

TWO EARLIER VOLUMES* have revealed how faithfully India bore her share of Great Britain's heavy commitments in Middle East and in the great deserts during the first four years of war.

During that period Italy's East African empire toppled into ruins. Iran, Iraq and Syria were made secure. In Western Desert, the tide of advantage ebbed and flowed, but the Mediterranean campaign steadily became a heavier drain not only on Italian but on German resources. Finally the United Nations mustered their strength, and in a great drive destroyed the last vestiges of Axis power in Africa. The Indian troops who at one time had been the only infantry division in Middle East, remained in the van of the battle for three years, and it was justice that at the finish in Tunisia they should have added to their already remarkable bag the German Commander-in-Chief, and many thousands of his men.

With the war in Africa over, Fourth Indian Division withdrew from Tunis to Tripoli. There the King Emperor came to thank his men in person. The Indians moved eastwards across a score of familiar battlefields, and concentrated during the summer of 1943 at Alexandria. The sepoys took their ease, knowing well that when the battle mounted in vehemence, the call again would come to them.

Near at hand comrades likewise were waiting for the word. Eighth Indian Division, which had lost a brigade at El Alamein, was again at full strength, and eager for employment. Tenth Indian Division, which had swept through three little wars in Iran and Iraq only to meet unmerited disaster in Western Desert, had trained earnestly in Cyprus and Syria for more than a year against the campaign to come. Further east, Sixth Indian Division and Thirty-First Indian Armoured Division, in garrison in Iran and Iraq, hopefully scanned the west, seeking some portent of battle. Thus five Indian Divisions stood waiting for the call—no small contribution to the war against Germany at a time when the Japs stood at the gateways of Bengal.

It was quite impossible that all these fine troops should be employed in Europe. Indeed, in the summer of 1943 many believed the services of Indian forces in the Western theatres to be at an end. Although Middle East and the deserts were tranquil, garrison requirements there continued to be substantial. Moreover, Burma was India's chief anxiety, and it seemed probable that the tough seasoned veterans

---

* NOTE.—*The Tiger Strikes*—the narrative of the Eritrean campaign, the battle of Sidi Barrani, and the Syrian campaign. *The Tiger Kills*—Western Desert from 1941 onwards, and the Tunisian campaign.

of Western Desert would be redeployed against the still unshaken Japs. There was another important consideration. Day by day the conflict had become more and more a technician's war. Every new weapon bred a new defence. Specialist cadres multiplied. To win battles against the Germans the private soldier must not only know something about a great many subjects, but he must supplement his courage and determination with exceptional adaptability and resource. In such a war, thought some wiseacres, the Indian soldier, in spite of his unmatched bravery and discipline, would be too greatly handicapped. On this account the supreme test of the European theatre would be denied him.

Such speculation betokened ignorance of much that had happened in the first four years of war. The sepoy, although no longer recruited exclusively from the so-called "martial races", still for the most part came out of the Indian countryside, and brought with him the ryot's limited horizon. The limits were those of opportunity rather than of intelligence, for when once the Indian recruit stepped into the outside world, he speedily caught the ferment in the air, and responded to the stimuli of new ideas. By 1943, Indian troops were singularly well informed, not only regarding the business of battle, but also concerning the world at large. As an illustration, their Army newspapers now appeared in eleven languages, instead of two as in peace time. Even the impassive Gurkhas had their Gurkhali news sheet, which they read with avidity. The increase in general knowledge, induced by the sight of new lands, contacts with diverse peoples, training in new routines, was reflected in the alacrity with which Indian troops became adept in the latest devices of war. Over and over again, in the course of this narrative, episodes will supply illustrations of the quickness of mind and ingenuity of Indian soldiers on critical occasions. Mastery of new weapons challenged, but did not impede, the progress of their education. Under stress of necessity the sepoys learned the new trades of warfare easily and thoroughly, in a manner which astonished their mentors.

Nor was this quick-mindedness only characteristic of the fighting troops. In the long array of ancillary services essential to modern warfare, Indian units undertook new duties with enthusiasm and ability. As far back as 1941, New Zealand engineers, building a standard gauge line in Western Desert, undertook to teach two companies of Indian Sappers and Miners the routine of railway construction. Within three months, to the joy of their Kiwi instructors, the Indians were laying daily yardages of track equal and even superior to those of the New Zealanders themselves. Under similar circumstances, in the three thousand miles between Teheran and Tunis, hundreds of miscellaneous Indian units had skilled themselves in new occupations. No less than 224 of these formations followed the Indian divisions to Italy, and if their names do not appear prominently in this story, it is because of the exigencies of narrative, and not because they did not make a full contribution to the final victory.

Whatever the speculations of clubs and messes, Field-Marshal Alexander knew the facts. Soon after the fall of Tunis he let it be known that he proposed to employ Indian troops in Europe. The Anglo-American thrust, in Mr. Churchill's phrase, into "the soft under-belly of the Axis", opened with a landing in Sicily in July. 3/10 Baluch Regiment, 3/12 Frontier Force Regiment, and certain pioneer companies, participated in these landings, as elements in the administrative "Brick" which controlled the beachheads. The invasion swept northwards and cleared Sicily; with scarcely a pause Eighth Army leapt the narrow straits into the toe of Calabria. In early September Fifth Army stormed ashore at Salerno, to the south of Naples. Here under Beachmasters Command went the Jodhpur Sardar Light Infantry, a fine State Forces unit, whose services in this tricky enterprise were recognized by a D.S.O. for Major Ram Singh and five other awards—the first decorations for Indian troops in Europe in this war.

Two armies abreast, the advance up Italy began. The Italians surrendered, and at first it seemed possible that rather than maintain a battle line with two seaward flanks, the enemy would abandon the Kingdom and would withdraw to main defensive positions along the great wall of the Alps. This hope was unfulfilled. Fresh German formations rushed south to reinforce the stubborn rearguards which slowed down the Allied advance. A captured document gave the following succinct reasons for the decision of the Germans to turn Italy into a battlefield :

(1) It was best for Germans to fight as far as possible from the Fatherland.

(2) The United Nations should be denied the use of Itálian airfields from which fighter-bombers might attack the Reich.

(3) The United Nations should be denied the use of the ports of Genoa, Trieste and Venice, which would continue to be used as German bases for harrying the sea supply lines of the Mediterranean.

(4) Germany should continue to draw plentiful supplies of war material from Italian factories. The German Army could live on the Italian countryside, and could even export food to Germany.

(5) Italy was the first and last member of the Axis in Europe, and could not be abandoned without loss of prestige.

It seems possible that these excellent reasons were implemented in the minds of the German General Staff by a further pertinent consideration. Much of Italy consisted of terrain which lent itself to military defence. On such battlefields resolute garrisons might sell ground at an extortionate price in blood. The flat narrow peninsula of Calabria offered few obstacles to invaders, but eighty miles north of the Gulf of

Taranto, where the ankle of Italy begins to swell into a calf, a mountain chain emerged in the centre of the Kingdom. These mountains created watersheds which directed the Italian rivers to the east and to the west, into the Adriatic and Tyrrhenian seas. Scores of such rivers on each coast lay across the path of any invader from the south, and each of these watercourses offers an individual obstacle to mechanized forces.

As the Italian peninsula widened, the central mountain spine thickened and increased in substance, until it towered into the Sierra-like ridges and lofty crests of the High Apennines. This mighty natural fortress commanded both the eastern and the western littorals of Italy. Beyond the Apennines lay the flat fruitful plains of Emilia and Lombardy, but here likewise the water barriers continued; instead of brawling torrents in gashed ravines, great rivers, of which the Po is the mightiest, wound across the land between artificial dykes raised above the plain. These fertile provinces grew much food, and in the midst of their rich fields stood the arsenal cities of Milan and Turin, where behind blued windows the machines roared for twenty-four hours daily, shaping the tools of war. Italian agriculture and industry alike made handsome contributions to the German war machine. It was inconceivable that such resources should be surrendered without a struggle.

Enemy strategy, therefore, was based on the possibility of bleeding the Allies white at low cost to Germany. Every advantage of terrain would be exploited to the full, and enemy forces would be committed to decisive battle only in key positions. Such positions would be covered by new fortifications in the rear. The entire Italian peninsula would be transformed into a fortress which would engulf as many Allied formations as possible, pinning down large bodies of troops which otherwise might be free to strike elsewhere.

Such strategy, however, imposed two necessities on the enemy. A large body of troops must be kept available not only in order to man the battle lines but also to garrison successive reserve positions. Comparatively few of these troops at any one time would be in action. The German plan required a great many men, and it likewise required the presence of high class shock troops; for if men are to be thin upon a battlefield they must be both competent and indomitable. Field-Marshal Alexander revealed long afterwards, that there were always more enemy than Allied troops in Italy, and a comparatively high percentage of such troops consisted of the flower of the German Army—paratroopers, Panzer Grenadier divisions and other specialist formations.

Faced by such concentration and such quality of opponents, a stern task awaited the soldiers of the United Nations in Italy. On the other hand, their mounting labours were lightened by new tools of battle. Gone were the days when emergencies must be met by improvisations out of the scrap of battlefields. Behind the Allied armies now stood the greatest industrial mobilization the world has ever seen. A vast array of scientists, technicians, organizers and craftsmen, sensitive to the vagaries, instant to the necessities of battle, built and delivered a spate of equipment and machines for the new campaign. Among a thousand devices, two were of such paramount importance as to make the difference between defeat and victory. Bulldozers, long the envy of commanders in the desert, multiplied their functions to meet a hundred emergencies. These great scoops and their crews became integral elements of every battlefield. Whatever the malice of the enemy or the whim of nature, if earth and stone could repair the damage the bulldozers speedily would open the way. A brigade of artillery or a heavy concentration of bombers might wreak fantastic destruction on a vital target. Yet in a matter of hours a half-dozen grimy drivers with chugging caterpillars would mend and make workable. The bulldozer was surgeon-on-the-spot to all wounded terrain.

As the bulldozers served with solid earth, so the Bailey Bridge served with unstable water. The simple magic of these Meccano-like frames and sections ranks only behind Radar and the atomic bomb as the greatest development of the war. Neither enemies nor Allies possessed comparable equipment. A bridge of any length and height, of any tensile strength or carrying power, would grow to completion in a few short hours. The versatility of this equipment equalled its simplicity, and as a result, in the heroic chronicle of the Italian campaign, the bulldozer-driver and the bridge-sapper stand with the infantryman, the gunner and the airman in the front rank of those who made victory possible.

To Indian soldiers the Italian campaign came as a fresh challenge. After bitter ordeals among the saw-toothed peaks of Eritrea, under the thirsty glare of the desert, in the steaming swamps of Burma, a greater strain, a more complicated enterprise awaited them. This book will tell how they met the challenge.

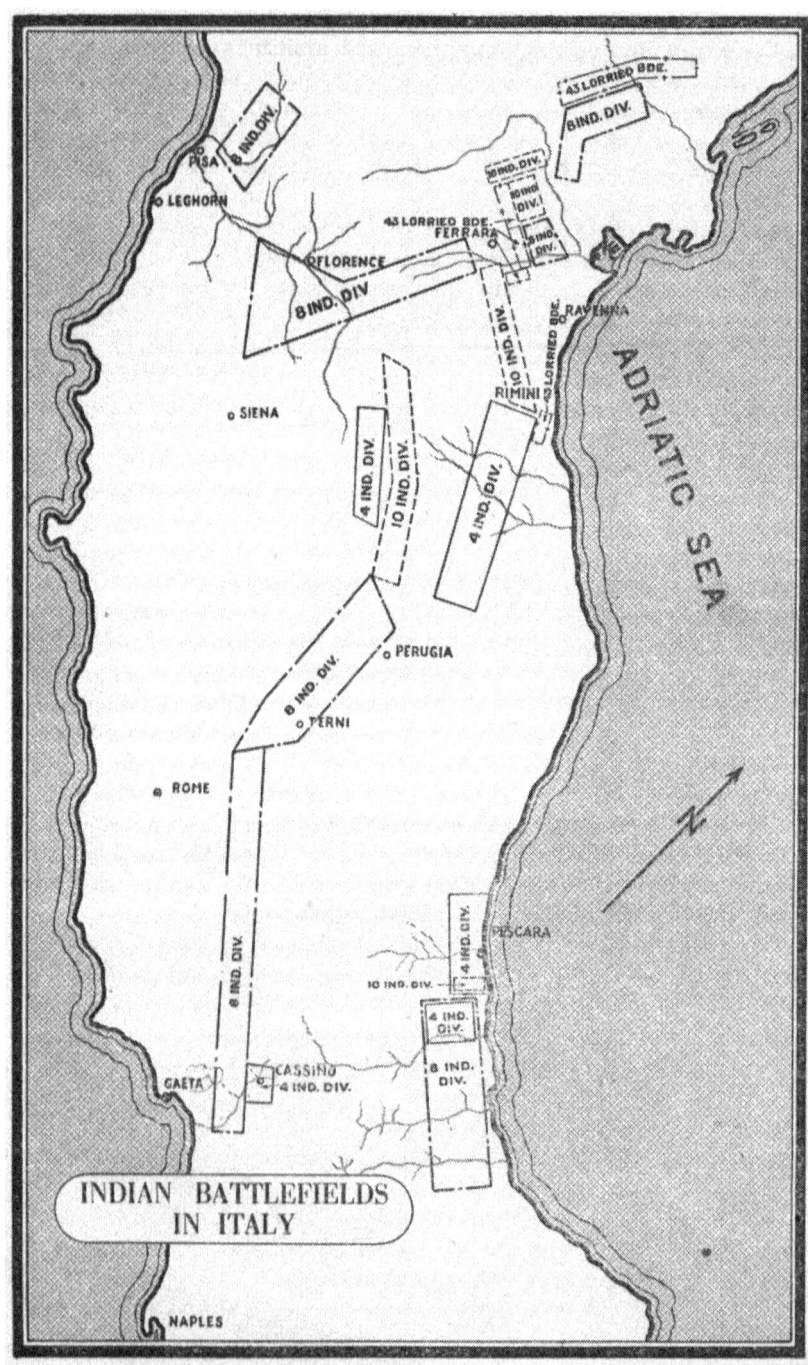

CHAPTER TWO

EIGHTH DIVISION ADVANCES

AT DAWN ON SEPTEMBER 19TH, 1943, six liners entered Taranto harbour, in the instep of the foot of Italy. This convoy bore Eighth Indian Division, whose battle order on arrival was as follows:—

G.O.C. *Major-General Dudley Russell, C.B.E., D.S.O., M.C.*

(*Brigadier C. H. Boucher, C.B.E., D.S.O.*)
17*th Infantry Brigade*
1st Royal Fusiliers
1/12 Frontier Force Regiment
1/5 Royal Gurkha Rifles

(*Brigadier T. S. Dobree, D.S.O., M.C.*)
19*th Indian Infantry Brigade*
1/5th Essex Regiment
3/8 Punjab Regiment
6/13 Royal Frontier Force Rifles

(*Brigadier B. S. Mould, D.S.O., O.B.E., M.C.*)
21*st Indian Infantry Brigade*
5th Royal West Kent Regiment
1/5 Mahratta Light Infantry
3/15 Punjab Regiment

Machine Gunners
5/5 Royal Mahratta (Machine Gun Battalion), Mahratta Light Infantry

Reconnaissance Regiment
6 D.C.O. (Bengal) Lancers

Artillery
3 Field Regiment R.A.
52 Field Regiment R.A.
53 Field Regiment R.A.
4 Mahratta Anti-tank Regiment I.A.
26 Light Anti-Aircraft Regiment R.A.

Engineers
7 Field Company
66 Field Company
69 Field Company
47 Field Park Company
(All Bengal Sappers and Miners)

Medical Services
29 Field Ambulance
31 Field Ambulance
33 Field Ambulance

The Division possessed a leavening of veteran units. Royal Fusiliers had been engaged in the first Jebel Campaign in 1940, and afterwards against the Vichy French in Syria, 6/13 Frontier Force Rifles had fought in Eritrea, 3/15 Punjabis in Somaliland, 1/3 Mahrattas and the Royal West Kents, together with 3 and 53 Field Regiments, had been blooded in Western Desert as part of 8th Army.

Major-General Dudley Russell had had a distinguished career. After commanding the battalion of Frontier Force Rifles which now served under him, he had completed the East African campaign as a staff officer with Fifth Indian Division. In the autumn of 1941 he took over command of 5th Indian Infantry Brigade, and became known in Western Desert as a tenacious and resourceful leader. "Pasha" was a man of immense energy, with a highly retentive memory and a flair for organization. His men knew him by his broad-brimmed slouch hat, his long staff, and by his contempt for danger. Like many Desert leaders he dressed to please himself; only in the coldest weather were shorts, grey shirt and chaplies replaced by battle dress. Those who knew him intimately found him to be a charming personality, with a wide knowledge of the world and a rare fund of military experience.

Eighth Indian Division concentrated to the east of Taranto and immediately began to follow north in the path of Eighth Army. A screen of rearguards had confronted General Montgomery's men as they pushed northwards through Calabria, Basilica and Puglia. These provinces comprise the foot and ankle of Italy, where the land is flat. The rivers tend to empty into the south, and so constitute no obstacle to troops advancing from that direction. One hundred and forty miles north of Taranto the broken land begins. Thereafter, for many miles along the Adriatic, rolling ridges and valley bottoms succeed in monotonous procession. Where spurs from the central mountain spine approach the coast, the ridges are sharper and more irregular, the valleys narrower and more abrupt. Twenty miles west of the mouth of the river Sangro, the Maiella massif abuts into the lowlands; the countryside between the sea and the mountains increases in ruggedness. The ridges are high, hog-backed, and even razor-backed; the water-courses are deep-cut and steep-banked. The roads are of secondary class, and usually traverse the crests of the ridges, in exposed positions. The countryside is intensively cultivated, even steep rocky hillsides being terraced for garden patches and vines; the ditches and terrace walls are lined with pollarded willows and larches. On stony and sparse ground unfit for cultivation, thick clumps of scrub and bramble grow. The tightly clustered houses of the villages stand on the crests of the higher ridges. These hamlets offered excellent observation points, and afforded cover for men and guns.

It was in such countryside that the enemy elected to make his first stand. A flexible defensive zone had been created, which the Germans called the Gustav Line. Its positions began on the Adriatic coast near the mouth of the Sangro river, south of the port of Pescara. The zone traversed the valley of the Sangro to the southern slopes of Monte Greco. Thereafter the fortifications followed the line of the Volturno Valley through Central Italy, thence through the Mignano Gap to Monte Camino, and on down to the Tyrrhenian coast.

Eighth Army confronted the Gustav positions between the Maiella mountains and the sea with three corps in forward positions. Eighth Indian Division went forward to join 5 Corps under Lieut.-General C. W. Allfrey, C.B., D.S.O., M.C., who had made acquaintance with Indian troops in the last stages of the Tunisian Campaign. Seventy-eighth British Division, with an unsurpassed record in the North Africa fighting, Fourth Army Tank Brigade and Special Service Brigade comprised the other troops in Fifth Corps. Prior to the arrival of Eighth Indian Division the Corps had been harassing the retreating Germans vigorously in the Termoli area, where the River Biferno interposed a water barrier across the path of the advance. The enemy was sufficiently sensitive to this pressure to bring up a fresh division from reserve.

This new division was of less concern to General Montgomery than that age-old enemy of the offensive, bleak winter. The weather had broken; autumnal rains filled the valleys and softened the hillsides. Placid streams became brawling torrents overnight. Sodden roads crumbled under the unaccustomed traffic and retaining walls slid from under along steep hillsides. The fields and pastures churned into mud, so that lorries skated on their way, or skidded into the ditches with wheels spinning helplessly. All bridges had been systematically destroyed and the approaches to fords and to likely diversions had been heavily mined. Every resource of military science had been enlisted to impede advancing troops, to expose them to fire, and to shelter the defenders.

Battlefields more unlike the open ranges of Western Desert could not have been imagined. Distances now must be measured by hours rather than by miles. Traffic was pinned to a few highways. Moreover, secrets could not be kept. The countryside swarmed with civilians, homeless and vagrant, giving enemy agents cover for their activities. Surprise, like speed of movement, was impossible to attain. The battle therefore had to be fought the hard way. The enemy must be found and destroyed in his strength.

On October 18th, 17th Indian Infantry Brigade relieved a British brigade at Larino, four miles south-east of the Biferno. Fifteen miles beyond the Biferno the river Trigno, a more substantial stream, runs parallel to Route 86, one of the main roads from Central Italy. The advance from the Biferno was resumed with Seventy-eighth British Division in the coastal sector, moving on the right flank of the Indians, and Fifth British Division keeping pace on the left of 17th Brigade.

On the night of October 20th the Divisional Artillery fired its first rounds in Italy. That same night two companies of Royal Fusiliers crossed the Biferno and seized high ground to the north of the river. For the next three days patrols worked forward through the rolling countryside towards the Trigno. Except for skirmishes with similar enemy patrols, no opposition was encountered. On the night of October 24th 1/12 Frontier Force and 1/5 Gurkhas passed through the Royal Fusiliers and took up the running. 17th Brigade now widened its front, with the 6th Lancers in touch with Seventy-eighth Division, and the Gurkhas linked up with First Canadian Division on the left. Five miles short of the Trigno, 19th Brigade passed through 17th Brigade, with 1/5th Essex and 3/8 Punjabis leading. An ominous portent was the identification of First German Parachute Division on the front, one of the most skilful and belligerent of German formations. Nevertheless, only sharp skirmishes ensued when 19th Brigade took a firm grip on the south bank of the Trigno through occupation of Monte Mitro and Montefalcone.

In this neighbourhood the Trigno ran between steep escarpments, whose crests stood fifteen hundred feet above the bottom of the valley. In many places the banks were sheer. The river was one hundred yards wide and in full view of the enemy on the ridges to the north. Ordinarily no more than two feet deep, the stream had risen sharply as a result of the autumnal rains. All bridges were blown, and all approaches mined. The arrival of 13th and 34th Indian Mule Companies, those ubiquitous carriers of yesterday who have justified their survival over and over again in the present war, solved the immediate supply problem. 19th Brigade (Brigadier T. S. Dobree, D.S.O., M.C.) immediately prepared to force the Trigno, in order to seize Tufillo Village and Monte Ferrano on the high ground. Intelligence reported the positions to be defended by paratroopers, who were fully aware of the purpose of the Indians.

For three days before the attack, heavy rains hampered preparations. Tracks deteriorated into quagmires. The roads had been so thoroughly destroyed that it was necessary for bulldozers to work upon by-passes and diversions, often in full view of the enemy. Under lowering skies, pelted by cold rains, the infantry waited dourly. By the end of October the approaches to the Trigno were organized, and at 0345 hours on November 2nd, 6/13 Frontier Force Rifles silently defiled into the icy stream and began to cross. The supporting barrage burst on the ridge

BULLDOZER

BAILEY BRIDGE

DELAYED SIGNAL

PRINCIPAL ENEMY

BOGGED DOWN

BLOCKED ROAD

OPEN FRONT—C.I.H. RAIDERS

PUNJABIS MOVE UP

ahead of them, and Eighth Indian Division was committed to its first action in Europe.

Frontier Force Rifles, though out of timing with the barrage, surged up the spur for nearly 2,000 yards, and by 0800 hours had mustered on their start line for the attack on Tufillo Village. The Frontiersmen's assault was launched against a typical German "hedgehog" position. All approaches were mined and booby-trapped. A curtain of mortar bombs covered the minefield. Every house held a sniper. Attempts to close were met with showers of grenades. Quick savage sallies were flung against any ground won. Eventually the battalion was held up, a few hundred yards short of its objective.

On the left of the Frontier Force Rifles, when dawn broke, the Essex began to cross the Trigno. Enemy artillery laid down an accurate shoot on the line of the river. The leading companies pushed through the barrage and up the hillside under murderous machine-gun fire from front and flanks. The convex curve of the slope prevented Frontier Force Rifles from aiding their British comrades as they strove to come up into line. The forward companies pushed on manfully, and reached their first objective. Mounting casualties, however, made the position untenable, and the Essex withdrew to the north bank of the Trigno, taking their wounded with them.

This success stimulated the enemy, and throughout the day Frontier Force Rifles, pinned down on the approaches to Tufillo, remained under heavy, harassing fire as prelude to counter-attack. In the late afternoon a strong force of paratroopers, making good use of natural cover, assembled close to "D" Company on the right fringe of the village. This possibility had been foreseen, and the Divisional Artillery were standing to, hands on lanyards. As the paratroopers dashed to the attack, the range flashed back—the exact yardage to "D" Company's outpost line. Subedar Sawar Khan, commanding the forward platoon, cannily realized that the Germans in the open must suffer more than his own men in their foxholes; so he had shouted over his radio for defensive fire to fall on his own positions. As the shoot came down, the attack faltered and the enemy fled.

That night 3/8 Punjabis joined Frontier Force Rifles in a new assault upon Tufillo. The attack went in on a crescent around the front and right flanks of the village. Two companies were caught in cross fire and lost heavily. Dense darkness made communications difficult. Nevertheless the attack was gallantly pressed home, until German tracer fired haystacks and silhouetted the Indians as they advanced. This ruse revealed to the enemy how few continued the assault. The paratroopers counter-attacked at once, forcing the Punjabis and Frontiersmen back to their start lines.

On November 3rd/4th, for the third night in succession, the same two gallant battalions struck for Tufillo. On this occasion each battalion was reinforced by a company of Mahratta machine-gunners. Enemy concentration shoots swept down on the outskirts to the village, and in the darkness companies scattered and lost touch. The same defensive fire caught the mule trains carrying consolidation weapons and ammunition. The consequent disorganization rather than the enemy impeded the advance, for the recurrent assaults had had their effect, and the Germans were already retiring to their main battle positions. It was not until the following night that the patrols discovered that Tufillo was empty, and that the front was open.

During the fighting, 21st Brigade (Brigadier B. S. Mould, D.S.O., O.B.E., M.C.) had been moving up in support. (While passing through Montefalcone 3/15 Punjabis detected an enemy agent signalling by means of peals on the church bells.) By November 5th the two brigades were abreast, and in the next forty-eight hours they pushed forward for several miles beyond the Trigno. The Divisional problem no longer was to eject the enemy, but to maintain the troops on the move. Sapper and transport services laboured for twenty-four hours daily at the task of preparing roads and of passing supplies forward. On the main Divisional route Montefalcone exhibited a museum piece in road construction. A flight of steps on a steep hillside had been levelled off with concrete to form a skidway on which vehicles were winched up and lined down. A senior officer who visited Eighth Indian Division refused to believe that the forward Brigades could be maintained over such improvisations, but within forty-eight hours of the evacuation of Tufillo, Divisional communications were sufficiently stable to warrant intensified pursuit of the enemy.

During this advance, 6th Lancers on the left of the Divisional front ferreted deeply in enemy territory. A detachment of the Cavalrymen rushed the village of Castello behind the enemy's lines. The patrol seized prisoners, only to be charged by motor-cycle combinations armed with machine-guns. The alacrity with which the enemy struck back on such occasions was characteristic of the perfect training and exuberant morale of the German troops who confronted Eighth Army.

On November 7th, 17th Brigade, which had been serving under Seventy-eighth British Division, returned to the fold, and on the same day 166th Newfoundland Field Regiment joined Eighth Indian Division—another of those contacts with far-flung parts of the Commonwealth which this war has made memorable. 17th Brigade came into the line on the right flank of the Division, and Royal Fusiliers, with a quick rush, captured a valuable bridge over the Senello ravine. Demolition charges were already in place, and the crossing was deemed of sufficient importance for a German engineer patrol to return next night in the hope of discovering careless sentries. This party was destroyed. 1/5 Gurkhas passed through, and under severe shell fire seized a dominating knoll near the river Osento. The hamlet of Atessa stood on still higher ground, sheer above the river. When night fell the Gurkhas advanced to attack the village with three companies in line, reached the enemy's outposts without being discovered, and went in with the bayonet. In a lively account their commander, Major Morland-Hughes, described the assault.

"It was a nightmare trying to call the lads to heel and to point them in the right direction. They were having the time of their lives winkling fat Jerries out of barns and hotting up the less mobile ones with bursts from their tommy-guns. All through the night I kept encountering Jemadar Pitragh Pun (later killed near Caldari), as he roved in the hunt with his revolver in one hand, a grenade in the other, and his kukri between his teeth."

By 2100 hours the Gurkhas had overrun the village and were digging in. A fierce counter-attack was repulsed by the expenditure of nearly all small arms ammunition. Signallers, artillery officers, and the transport services worked feverishly to establish communications and to get supplies forward. With only scattered clips of ammunition remaining, the dauntless Gurkhas awaited the next assault. At midnight a strong enemy force, covered by flanking machine-gun fire, tried to crash through "C" Company. As the Germans closed, the Gurkhas countercharged with kukris. Their knives took a terrible toll, and the enemy fled in disorder, sped upon their way by Rifleman Okel Gurung, who had snatched a machine-gun from his first victim, instantly to bring it into play upon its former owners. Among the bodies found next morning was that of a much-decorated officer.

(It is sad to record that Rifleman Gurung, a most courageous youngster, who afterwards won both the Indian Order of Merit and the Military Medal, was killed in the final battle of the Italian campaign.)

Next morning Gurkha patrols exploited beyond Atessa without contacting the enemy. The way to the Sangro was open. 19th Brigade passed through 17th Brigade and spread out across the countryside to the north-west. This extension of the Divisional front was designed to screen the New Zealanders, who had recently landed in Italy and were coming into the line on the left of the Indians. 3/8 Punjabis turned directly into the west and attacked Pirano with tanks in close support. After some bickering the enemy withdrew. Concurrently 6/13 Frontier Force Rifles moved almost due south on Archi, a small town on a cone-shaped mound about 2,000 yards south of the Sangro. Before dawn on November 18th a carrier patrol explored the outskirts of the town without encountering opposition. Unfortunately the troops sent to seize and to consolidate approached the village by a different road, and bumped into a last-stand rearguard dug in among the tombstones of the village cemetery. Brisk fighting ensued, in which Captain Whitehouse, commander of the Sikh company, was killed. It was not until next day that the town was cleared, and patrols of the Essex passed through the Punjabis to explore the swollen Sangro in search of crossings. The position at Archi gave excellent observation over the valley as far as the river mouth twelve miles away.

(The Sangro sometimes flows east and west, sometimes north and south, and sometimes in between. As the general axis of advance lay into the north, to avoid confusion this narrative will refer only to the north or south bank of this river.)

The comparative ease of the early advances of Eighth Indian Division did not deceive anyone as to the rigours to come. It was obvious that with the first spurs of the Maiellas extruding only 15 miles from the coast, and with a substantial river like the Sangro thrown as a moat across these miles, the enemy would stand stubbornly in such a position. Detailed reconnaissance revealed, as one officer put it, "the lie of the land to be distinctly Boche". South of the river a high ridge breaks sharply into the valley bottom. On the northern bank, half a mile beyond the bed of the stream, a well-defined escarpment rises, covered with stunted trees and slashed by gullies. This escarpment gradually mounts for a further 1,000 yards, where a series of humpy knolls mark the highest ground of all. Upon these knolls stand the villages of Fossacesia, San Maria, Mozzagrogna, Romagnoli and Andrioli. These scattered hamlets on the crest of the escarpment provided ideal sites for characteristic German defensive positions, and they had been "hedgehogged" as the anchor strongholds of the eastern flank of the Gustav Line.

From look-outs on this high ground the enemy had complete observation over the southern approaches to the Sangro. Any attempt to close up on the river could be instantly detected. The villages had been transformed into fortresses, with shelters 20 feet deep, machine-gun nests and connecting tunnels proofed against the heaviest shelling. Houses in key positions had been reinforced with concrete. Pill-boxes had been built. Often different floors or different rooms in the same building were converted into separate strongpoints, so that if assailants broke into one side of the house, the other side still could be defended. Escape tunnels connected the houses, and the storming of one strong point usually left the victors under fire from a nearby redoubt.

Before the villages could be reached, it was necessary to traverse deadly ground seeded thickly with anti-tank and anti-personnel mines. Minefields in aprons and belts covered all approaches, and constituted an even greater impediment than the pillboxes and weapon pits of the villages. In the two years since the land mine became a specialized weapon, the enemy had continued to improve his types and sowing technique, until these devilish devices were a fearful obstacle in the path of every advance. No longer could mine detectors guarantee clean ground, as the enemy used mine-cases of wood, pressed paper, plastic and other non-metallic materials, which gave no response to the sweep. The little Schu-mine, of cheap manufacture yet powerful enough to shear off the feet of anyone luckless enough to tread upon it, was broadcast in millions, not only on tracks and possible diversions, but at random over the countryside. This abominable machine inflicted more casualties on troops in attack than any other weapon. Delayed action mines, which absorbed a number of pressures before exploding, added new terrors on tracks and highways. No braver acts have been performed in this war than the rescue of men trapped or wounded on minefields. It was felt by many to be invidious that a distinction should be made and that the Victoria Cross and other usual military decorations should be withheld for outstanding heroism on minefields. No battlefield afforded greater risks or evoked colder courage.

The plan of battle for assault on the Gustav Line by Fifth Corps called for heavy concentrations on narrow sectors. The Corps front extended fifteen miles inland from the Adriatic coast, and was held from right to left by Seventy-eighth British Division, Eighth Indian Division, and Second New Zealand Division. An elaborate deception plan was employed to conceal the focal point of attack. On the adjoining Thirteenth Corps front a false picture was built up by aggressive patrolling, dummy guns and false dumps, together with a fictitious Army Sending Station which continuously filled the air with pseudo-signals.

The attack would be opened by Seventy-eighth Division in the coastal sector. When a bridgehead had been established, Eighth Indian Division would break into the main defensive positions on the crest of Mozzagrogna—San Maria ridge. Simultaneously, on the left of the battlefield, the New Zealanders would strike with a double thrust, to the north-west with Chieti as objective, and to the south-west down Route 5, to cut German lines of communications east of the Maiella mountains.

This ambitious plan had been adopted in spite of one incalculable obstacle—the weather. The winter rains had set in, and no reprieve from bitter cold, swollen streams, and sodden earth could be expected. The Sangro in spate averaged five feet in depth, and was of such turbulence that patrols on more than one occasion had been drowned. The infantry bivouacked miserably in boggy fields under pelting showers. Transport speedily churned the water-logged earth into mud soup; vehicles slithered and skidded uncontrollably on the greasy tracks. Heavy transport and guns were winched and manhandled into position by their shivering, mud-soaked crews. Sappers and transport services toiled unceasingly to keep the roads open, and to get supplies through to the advanced positions. The Provost Corps—those battle-masters whose names so seldom appear in the record—manned their posts for twenty-four hours in the day, clearing traffic jams, sorting out priorities, and keeping the tide of vehicles flowing. By herculean efforts preparations for the assault were completed, and in the dense darkness of 0415 hours on November 20th, troops of Seventy-eighth British Division, whose patrols for some days had dominated the northern bank of the Sangro, attacked in the coastal sector. By first light a bridgehead had been established. The enemy chose not to fight back, but to stand at bay in the midst of his maze of defences among the villages on the crest of the ridge.

No sooner had the attack began than rain poured in torrents. The Sangro rose and spread across its valley. Vehicles were unable to traverse the morass, and vital bridging material could not be brought to the launching sites. Without bridges Eighth Indian Division dared not attempt a frontal assault on such a heavily fortified position, since without consolidation weapons and materials gains could not be held. It was necessary therefore to postpone the Indian attack, and the operation opened inauspiciously with one brigade of Seventy-Eighth marooned in a shallow bridgehead on the north bank of the Sangro. The commander of the British Division felt that at all costs he must thicken his troops on the enemy's side of the river. In the next night a second brigade forded the Sangro and dug in on the rising ground under the escarpment.

For thirty-six hours the Sappers toiled without ceasing on the vital bridges. The quagmire approaches greedily sucked down every type of revetting material—road rail, road metal, logs, faggots, fascines and railway sleepers. Many tons of every type of reinforcement were hammered in to assure firm abutments. By the morning of November 22nd, the first bridge was ready for vehicles. That afternoon three crossings were available. All night tanks and anti-tank guns rumbled over, and came up into close support of the infantry. November 23rd was fine and one hundred fighter bombers battered the villages on the crest of the ridge. No deception could conceal the imminence of a major operation, and Field-Marshal Kesselring, who visited the front on November 22nd, ordered another Panzer Grenadier Division to reinforce the Adriatic sector with all haste.

The next stroke, however, came from General November. A fair day on the coast coincided with a cloudburst in the Maiella mountains. Storm water came surging down, and by the evening of November 23rd the bridges were awash and the spate had undermined the approaches and abutments. One bridge collapsed, the others were unusable. The two brigades north of the Sangro were still marooned, and short of supplies essential to battle. If their predicament were detected, the enemy was in a position to destroy them.

To British forces a river may be a barrier, but an ocean, never. Two detachments of DUKWS, those queer amphibious carriers, appeared out of nowhere, and began to ferry supplies and ammunition from the southern to the northern beaches adjoining the mouth of the Sangro. They worked without ceasing for forty-eight hours, and transported two thousand tons of supplies. No sooner had this ferry service been established than the Sangro subsided as rapidly as it had risen. Damage to the bridge approaches, however, held up the movement of troops on the Indian front, and it was not until the night of November 24/25th that 3/15 Punjabis of 21st Infantry Brigade crossed the stream and relieved a battalion of Seventy-eighth Division in the gully below Mozzagrogna.

A fine day on the 25th gave the dive-bombers a second outing. British and Indian troops in reserved seats on the edge of the escarpment observed the display with the utmost satisfaction. That night, 1/12 Frontier Force Regiment and part of 1/5 Mahrattas, came up on the left of the Punjabis. By dawn, thirty-six hours later, all of 17th and 21st Brigades were across the river, with mule transport trains busily establishing dumps of equipment and supplies. It was boldly decided to use the bridges by day, in full view of the enemy. The Germans shelled the crossings continuously, but the flow of vehicles and tanks was unimpeded. The shallow bridgehead was now crowded to bursting with the troops, supplies, and supporting arms of two divisions.

While these preparations were in hand, the battle had opened elsewhere. It will be remembered that 19th Brigade had spread out on a wide front on the left of the corps sector, in order to screen the deployment and advance of the New Zealanders. It was decided to use this screen to establish a bridgehead at Calvario, eight miles inland from Mozzagrogna. At 0300 hours on the morning of November 23rd 3/8 Punjabis advanced to force the Sangro in a silent attack, and to seize a high, wooded knoll on the north bank of the river.

In the darkness, "C" Company under Captain Gardhari Singh, led the way, wading through turbulent floods up to the men's chests. Wet and shivering, the Punjabis emerged and began to clamber towards their objective. Other companies of the battalion followed in close support. One hundred yards short of the crest the alarm was given, and enemy machine-guns and tanks opened fire. Alert New Zealand gunners instantly pinpointed the flashes from the tank guns, and sent the panzers scurrying with salvoes of well-placed shells. The leading Punjabi sections, undeterred by the traversing spandaus, stalked the machine-gun posts and destroyed them. The crest was won.

Behind the Punjabis, 1/5 Essex followed across the river in pouring rain. New Zealand engineers had stretched a rope from bank to bank, and two Sappers stood in the bed of the stream for hours, pinioning it against the current in order that the waders might have a steady guideline. By dawn the Essex were mustered on the far bank, and at the height of the storm launched an attack on a three-company front on the right of the Calvario knoll. The Home County men were met by withering machine-gun fire. In spite of heavy casualties they gallantly forged ahead and established themselves in houses on the fringe of Calvario village. A clump of Germans dashed to the counter-attack at the moment when Private Bishop, an Essex machine-gunner, appeared with his weapon at an upper window. The bulk target was a marksman's dream, and Bishop broke the rush single-handed.

When day came Punjabis and Essex clung to their positions in a shallow crescent around the precarious bridgehead. Once again the malice of the weather intervened. The Sangro suddenly rose four feet, and made the fords impassable for wheels. Mule trains were rushed up, but the animals were swept off their feet and carried down the river. Several wounded were drowned when attempts were made to evacuate them in mule litters. Detecting the difficulties the enemy concentrated a heavy shoot on the crossings and threw in a strong counter-attack. On the right flank a company of the Essex was forced back to the river bank. The Punjabis smashed three similar assaults in quick succession. Most of the officers were down, one company losing three commanders before noon. In the late afternoon Jemadar Sumerze Ram took command of the 12 remaining men of one Punjabi company, and beat off a fourth attempt to overrun the position.

That evening Essex and Punjabis were so thin on the ground that the forward companies were withdrawn from the positions which they had won at such a heavy cost. Captain Gardhari Singh, however, having led the attack, felt a proprietary interest in Calvario, and withdrew unwillingly. Next morning he signalled to the brigade commander that the enemy could be in no better case than themselves. He was sure, he said, that the Boche had been fought to a standstill. He asked permission with his handful of gallant survivors to attempt to reoccupy Calvario. Permission granted, he advanced without opposition—the enemy was gone. The Essex and remaining Punjabis came forward and consolidated the objectives which they had abandoned a few hours before. A bridgehead across the Sangro had been established for the New Zealanders.

Its task completed, 19th Brigade moved back to join Eighth Indian Division in the Mozzagrogna area. Before its arrival the main attack had begun.

CHAPTER THREE

MOZZAGROGNA AND VILLA GRANDE

AT MIDNIGHT ON NOVEMBER 27th, 1/5 Gurkhas advanced through the inevitable rainstorm towards the outskirts of Mozzagrogna. A concentration shoot crashed down on the village, but as it lifted enemy machine-guns clattered, sweeping the greasy slopes up which the Gurkhas scrambled to the close. Two companies penetrated the outpost line covering the village, and began to mop up house by house. In this grim game of night fighting, of surprise and sudden death, there are no finer soldiers in the world than the little hillmen from Nepal.

Bedlam broke loose. Above the crash of exploding mines and bombs, the staccato rattle of machine-guns and the screams of the wounded, the high voices of the Gurkhas could be heard guiding each other from quarry to quarry. One large house at the corner of the village was held in strength. Deadly hand-to-hand fighting ensued as the Gurkhas came leaping out of the darkness. Fifteen German dead were picked up in or around this building.

Moving up in close support of the Gurkhas, Royal Fusiliers were strung out along the track between the river and the village. They had been ordered to pass through Mozzagrogna before turning north-east along the main ridge to attack San Maria. They waited for the word in most uncomfortable surroundings, for they were in the midst of a minefield. The road and its verges were heavily sown, and enemy shell fire, searching the track, caused the mule trains to stampede. Many animals blew up on box mines. It was impossible to move bodies from the road without detonating other mines, and when Fusiliers dived into the ditches to avoid shells, death often awaited them. Half-way between the river and the ridge a giant crater blocked the road. This obstacle was ringed by a curtain of mortar fire. On either side the ground was stiff with mines, and every diversion fraught with mortal risk. After nightmare hours the order to advance was received with utmost relief. But the plan had been changed. The enemy in Mozzagrogna had proven too strong for a single battalion. Instead of attacking San Maria, Royal Fusiliers were ordered to move to the aid of the Gurkhas.

As the British troops approached the village, the battle grew about them. A leading Fusilier section spotted a German mortar crew crawling along a wall to man their weapon, well in the rear of the Gurkha positions. A quick traverse by a Bren gunner tumbled six dead Germans on to the ground. As they entered the village enemies appeared everywhere. Every alley or upper window held a sniper or machine-gunner. Tanks could be heard milling about on the northern outskirts of the village. After the Gurkhas had passed, other enemies had reoccupied strong points and weapon pits, and the battle resolved itself into a vicious and confused hurly-burly in which small groups hunted each other to the death.

Major Morland Hughes had established battle headquarters in the church in the main square. A first-aid post was set up in the shelter of the altar. The roar of enemy tanks grew louder, and Fusiliers took station at the doors with limpet bombs to meet the panzers, should they endeavour to break in. Major Morland Hughes climbed to the belfry to reconnoitre. At that moment two enemy tanks, a flamethrower and a Mark Four, lurched into the square and bore against the church. The flamethrower hosed the walls with blazing oil. Across the square Major Warner of Royal Fusiliers swiftly swung a PIAT by rope to a roof top. The first well-aimed bomb blew off the flamethrower's turret. As its commander climbed out, Major Morland Hughes shot him. Detecting the sniper high overhead the Mark Four sprayed the belfry with its light guns, missing the marksman but hitting the peal of bells. The carillon rang wildly as Major Morland Hughes climbed down in some haste. Before the Fusiliers' PIAT could score again the second panzer withdrew and no equivalent liberties were attempted thereafter. The battle reverted to a man to man struggle.

Jemadar Ram Singh Rana, Intelligence Officer of the Gurkhas, heard noises in his cellar. Dropping map boards and pencils, he and his draughtsmen leapt downstairs with their kukris, killing nine Germans. While establishing quarters in another building, the Jemadar again heard noises. Quietly he stepped into the adjoining room, to discover an enemy observation post manned by two signalmen. One he slew with the knife as the other sprang screaming through the window.

At broad daylight, although Gurkhas and Fusiliers held half the village, the situation remained fluid. No sooner would an area be mopped up than paratroopers would emerge from undetected hideouts to kill or to be killed. Above the rattle and crash of artillery and small arms, the roar of bulldozers could be heard fighting the second and no less vital battle of communications. Enemy tanks and self-propelled guns could enter Mozzagrogna freely from the north, whereas the tracks forward from the Sangro were still blocked. No diminution of enemy strength and will to resist could be discerned, and as the forenoon passed it became evident that if the Germans struck in strength they could regain Mozzagrogna before 17th Brigade's consolidation groups arrived. Towards noon it was decided to withdraw the Gurkhas and Fusiliers to positions south of the village. The fracas by now was of such a confused nature that some groups never received the order. Other parties were so deeply engrossed in individual stalking matches that they ignored it. In the centre of the village, however, where a cohesive battle still raged, Gurkhas and Fusiliers argued as to who should withdraw first. The Fusiliers insisted upon the honour of covering the retirement. "Run, Johnny!" they shouted. On the word the Gurkhas in groups of four or five sprinted across the open square, while their British comrades pinned down the spandau teams with fusillades. The Fusiliers slipped away leaving the church and square to the enemy, but elsewhere bitter fighting continued throughout the day. The count of survivors was not complete until late that afternoon when 100 Gurkhas returned, bringing their wounded with them, and expressing deep satisfaction with the morning's work in the village.

Throughout the day the Sappers had laboured unceasingly on the track leading up from the Sangro. By nightfall repairs had progressed to a point when it seemed probable that 50th Royal Tank Regiment, which was standing by, would be able to reach Mozzagrogna within a few hours. General Russell thereupon ordered a fresh assault that evening. Corps artillery was concentrated for a terrific shoot on the village, and at 2100 hours 1/12 Frontier Force Regiment moved forward to attack. It is perhaps worth recording that some of the Royal Fusiliers, who had survived the ordeal of the previous night, and who now had been detailed to cover Sapper working parties along the road, deserted their comparatively safe tasks and joined the Frontiersmen as they went by to Mozzagrogna.

Once again the bombardment held the enemy garrison in the deep dug-outs, and once again as it lifted the Germans rushed to their surface posts. Again the battle resolved into dozens of sudden deadly encounters in cellars, on roof-tops, in alleys, and behind the angles of broken walls. In a crypt a number of Germans who had taken refuge in the wine vats were despatched. A platoon of Dogras passed a house cleared shortly before. A shot rang out. As the Dogras burst in, 22 Germans including an officer threw up their hands. Every now and then a squat, cheerful Gurkha would emerge from hiding and join the hunt. One had killed his guard after capture. Another had leapt on a flame-throwing tank with no other weapon but his kukri, and had cut down its observer. The hours of night passed, and the grim game went on until the streak of dawn showed in the east. In the first light a roar from the south of the village drowned the chatter of small arms fire. The road from Sangro was open, and the British tanks were crowding through. The leading troop had been given a pin-point on three enemy tanks which had shelled the Sappers during the night. The troop commander searched them out and came upon them at point blank range with their guns facing the wrong way. They were destroyed in a twinkling.

With the arrival of British armour the defences of Mozzagrogna collapsed. As the battered but triumphant survivors of 17th Brigade mopped up the village, a special message of congratulation came in from Field-Marshal Montgomery. Unfortunately delayed-action mines on the road between the river and the village continued to take toll. Lieut.-Colonel G. E. Russell of 50th Royal Tank Regiment had been killed earlier in the day when his jeep went up. Seven sweepings were necessary before the tracks and verges were clean.

During the Mozzagrogna fighting, Seventy-eighth British Division had been heavily engaged on the right of 17th Brigade, where it had taken over and completed the original task of Royal Fusiliers, the capture of San Maria. The armoured brigade supporting the British Division could only advance through the Indian front, and in order to clear the way, 17th Brigade was instructed to secure an essential crossroads to the north-west of Mozzagrogna. On the night of November 29th the tough team of Gurkhas and Royal Fusiliers pushed forward, seized this position and effected a link-up with Seventy-eighth Division. At 1030 hours next morning the enemy struck at the junction with infantry and self-propelled guns. Fortunately a counter-attack had been foreseen, and all arms stood ready. For fifty minutes artillery, planes and armour plastered the approach area, severely mauling the enemy. The British tanks came through and the way was open for the battle to swing into the east, pinning the Germans against the sea. All anchor positions of the Gustav Line were now in British hands. One thousand prisoners had been taken, and a number of German units had been decimated. That evening Field-Marshal Kesselring ordered additional fresh divisions from Northern Italy to hasten to the Adriatic sector.

Nevertheless Allied High Command believed it possible to sustain the momentum of the advance. 21st Indian Infantry Brigade turned west from Mozzagrogna along the top of the ridge with Romagnoli, the next hedgehog position, as objective. 5th Royal West Kents led the advance, and came under heavy fire as they approached the hamlet. The two leading companies lost 3 officers and 85 men killed or wounded within ten minutes of opening the assault. Major Stocker brought up the reserve company and laid a heavy mortar shoot upon a line of trenches concealed behind hedges on the outskirts of the village. Pinning down the defenders he attacked from both flanks in the rear of the entrenched position, and stormed the village. Three counter-attacks, shattered in quick succession with the aid of close support from the fighter-bomber "cab-rank", convinced the enemy that Romagnoli could not be regained.

Simultaneously 1/5 Mahrattas, with two troops of tanks in close support, endeavoured to seize the Redecoppe feature which barred advance on the important centre of Lanciano. Once again heavy fire swept the front as the Mahrattas dashed forward. Lieut-Colonel W. R. Thompson, M.C., fell mortally wounded, with many of his gallant men about him. When night fell the Mahrattas were still short of their objective, and it was necessary to consolidate before attempting to advance further.

On December 2nd, 3/15 Punjabis passed through the Mahrattas and reached the road junction a few hundred yards south-east of Lanciano. Simultaneously Royal West Kents attacked into the north, to ease the flank pressure on Seventy-eighth Division. Tanks of the 1st Canadian Armoured Brigade supported the Kentish men, and good team work forced the Germans out of Treglio. On the opposite flank of the division, 6th Lancers probed until they found a comparatively open road into Lanciano, along which the armoured cars bowled merrily until they turned a last corner to come face to face with a German tank. The cavalrymen withdrew hurriedly, but established and held a road block cutting off Lanciano from the west. The town was now closely invested on three sides. That night the enemy made a virtue of necessity and cleared out. "D" Company of 3/15 Punjabis entered next morning and received a rousing welcome from the liberated civilians.

Roads from north, south, east and west met at Lanciano. Exploring and mopping up gave 6th Lancers much to do. The enemy had prepared many bridges and culverts for demolition, but had failed to blow them. The armoured cars raced along the roads to surprise numerous stragglers and rearguard groups. If resistance stiffened, Canadian tanks were on call close at hand. In such fashion the ground up to the river Moro was speedily cleared of the enemy.

Under the original plan, the rôle of Eighth Indian Division in these operations was now completed. First Canadian Infantry Division on the sea coast had relieved the valiant Seventy-eighth British Division, which went out to rest after having suffered over 7,000 casualties in less than six months. The two fresh divisions, Canadians and New Zealanders, were briefed for the next attack, with the Eighth Indian Division in the centre in a more or less static role. The New Zealanders had been probing in the broken ground beyond the Sangro. Their advanced elements reached Orsogna, but fell back before a panzer attack. (In a scuffle the Kiwis took a few prisoners, and found them to be men from Nineteenth Panzer Grenadier Division, a re-constituted version of Ninetieth Light Division, which had refused to surrender to anyone except the New Zealanders in Tunisia.) On December 7th, in shocking weather which limited air and armour support, the Kiwis attacked Orsogna with two brigades, and fought their way into the centre of the town. Once again German armour massed against the invaders, and forced a withdrawal.

The situation on the left flank of the Indians, therefore, was stalemate. On the right flank the Canadians likewise were in trouble. They had established bridgeheads over the Moro, but could make little headway in the difficult ground to the north of the river. In order to concentrate their strength, the Canadians asked Eighth Indian Division to take over the left sector of their front. On December 7th, 21st Indian Brigade moved up to Frisa, about two miles north of Lanciano, to relieve a Canadian brigade. The Indians were not intended to enter the battle, but were instructed to demonstrate and to employ deception tactics in order to draw German reserves from the Canadian and New Zealand fronts.

It has already been noted that deception had become highly organised. In order to convince the enemy, tangible deceits had to be provided. General Russell decided that a convincing deception would be to build a bridge over the Moro on his front, and to build it at such a place and in such a manner that the enemy could not choose but believe it to be meant for use. A reconnaissance of the Moro banks revealed a point at which a right-angled bend in the road made it an impossible site from which to launch a bridge from the south bank. But, argued Lieut.-Colonel C. M. MacLachlan, O.B.E., commander of the Divisional sappers, if it is impossible to build a bridge from the near bank, why not build it backwards from the enemy's bank? Thereafter, if the Germans discover it, they will be certain that we needed this crossing badly. If they do not discover it, we might surprise them by using it.

(There is an ecclesiastical flavour about this reasoning which suggests dominies among Colonel MacLachlan's ancestors.)

Thus originated the project which became famous as "Impossible Bridge". The area surrounding the bridge site was extremely active. German fighting patrols often crossed to the south bank of the Moro looking for trouble. While the bridge remained no more than a project, the forward companies of Mahrattas and Royal West Kents endured a series of savage counter-attacks. One such assault broke into the Indian positions from the rear. The situation remained critical until the artillery intervened and a squadron of tanks rushed up and ejected the enemy.

On the morning of December 8th, the Canadians in the coastal sector launched a major assault. Bitter fighting ensued and progress was slow. Simultaneously the New Zealand Division had renewed the attack on Orsogna. Here likewise the going was heavy. With both flanks more or less pinned down, Eighth Indian Division entered the Corps attack. 21st Indian Brigade was ordered to seize Caldari, on the extreme right of the Divisional position. With no crossing available for this sector, Colonel MacLachlan's shrewd project now became an urgent necessity: "Impossible Bridge" must be rushed to completion for immediate use. On the night of December 8/9th, Sappers of 69th

Indian Field Company crossed the river, swept the approaches for mines, and cut steps in the bank. When day broke, 4th Mahratta Anti-tank Regiment and 50th Royal Tank Regiment moved up to cover the Sappers, who worked steadily under the noses of the enemy. The bridge was completed by day, and that night 3/15 Punjabis, with one company of 5th Royal Mahratta Machine-Gunners, and other supporting arms, crossed the Moro to establish a bridgehead.

The Germans reacted violently to this incursion. From patrol clashes the fighting mounted into a tense struggle. The Punjabis went forward to clear a strong-point with the bayonet. The mules bearing the Mahratta machine-guns had strayed, and Jemadar Rajwam Sowant was in no mood to wait for his weapons. He ordered his machine-gunners to fix bayonets and to charge beside the Punjabis. That night, "Impossible Bridge" was strengthened, and next morning British tanks crossed to come up in close support of the Punjabis and Mahrattas. Mopping up continued, but the area remained unhealthy with enemy snipers and mortar teams infiltrating audaciously. In destroying these pests a number of cat-eyed, soft-footed Indians compiled remarkable individual bags. Havildar Badlu Ram of the Punjabis slew sixteen Germans, and others were not far behind his total. The ground was cleansed and a firm bridgehead established.

On the night of December 9/10th there was thunder on the right when the Canadians struck in great strength against San Leonardo on the road to Ortona. Once again the enemy confined the advance by desperate resistance. In order to allow the Canadians to regroup, a second Indian brigade was ordered into the battle: but before entry it was necessary to enlarge the bridgehead. On the night of December 12/13th, a composite force of 1/5 Mahrattas, Royal Mahratta Machine-Gunners and 50th Royal Tank Regiment, passed through the Punjabi outposts and probed the enemy positions to the west. When this force cut the lateral road east of Consalvi, a number of German lorries, laden with rations, obligingly drove into the trap. Closing up on a pin-pointed German position, the air was rent by the Mahratta war cry, "Shivaji Maharaj Ki Jai", as two companies charged. The outpost line of trenches and weapon pits were overrun, but in a number of houses and fortified emplacements the enemy held out and threw back the attack. British tanks roared up, asking for targets. Captain H. J. M. Pettingell, M.C., instructed his men to indicate enemy strongholds by tracer fire. Wherever flights marked centres of resistance the tanks bored in to destroy the defenders. This co-operation saved many Mahratta casualties, broke down resistance, and cleared the strongpoint with a bag of sixty prisoners.

The enemy was in no mood to accept this reverse. At 1700 hours on the next afternoon a fierce artillery shoot swept over the Mahratta position. Panzers approached along the lateral road from the west, and by clever use of dead ground avoided retaliation from British support weapons. Night closed over a noisy scene. Almost twelve hours of harassing fire and "softening-up" prepared for the infantry assault. Just before dawn a company of Panzer Grenadiers supported by seven tanks smashed at the position. The Mahrattas were waiting unshaken, and hurled back their assailants. No further attempts were made to retake this ground.

Adjoining the Canadians on the right of "Impossible Bridge", the Royal West Kents were similarly tested. On four successive nights they stood off determined counter-attacks. Until "Impossible Bridge" was opened, this battalion was isolated. Casualties were substantial, but the Kentish men remained in good heart, and gave the hard-fighting Canadians a firm flank. Everywhere 21st Brigade had taken the shock, had enlarged the bridgehead, and had made its gains secure.

Eighth Indian Division was now ready to move to the assault. On the night of December 13/14th, 17th Brigade, under command of Brigadier J. Scott-Elliott, D.S.O., M.C., advanced against Caldari. Royal Fusiliers stormed the village after a wild night's fighting. Forty German dead were found among the ruins. 1/5 Gurkha Rifles seized Point 198 and beat off every attempt to oust them. On the next afternoon a troop of Panzers appeared out of nowhere and assailed the Gurkha position. PIAT mortars blew a leading tank to pieces, and the others withdrew. That evening 1/12 Frontier Force Regiment worked up on the left of the Gurkhas and seized positions along the lateral road which ran parallel to the Moro about 1,000 yards north of "Impossible Bridge". An enemy tank force which included flame-throwers charged the consolidation groups and cut off the Dogra Company. British tanks hurried up. At dawn the Sikh and Dogra companies of Frontiersmen hurled back the enemy in headlong flight, and captured two disabled tanks. On the following evening, 1/5 Essex of 19th Brigade relieved the Royal West Kents, who moved at once to attack on the left flank of the Frontier Force Regiment. The British infantry swept forward in great style, overrunning a number of enemy positions for a bag of 36 prisoners and 4 Mark IV tanks. Twenty-four hours later, 3/15 Punjabis passed through the Mahrattas and seized fresh positions along the lateral road.

The Indians were now firmly embedded in the main German defences. From December 14th onwards the crescendo of battle steadily rose. The New Zealanders slogged their way up to the lateral highway. Day after day the Canadians smashed for small and hard-won gains. Attack and counter-attack followed in quick succession. Toe to toe the adversaries battered each other, refusing to yield ground. By December 15th no less than seven heavy Canadian attacks had failed to storm a key position. On both flanks of the battlefield the great

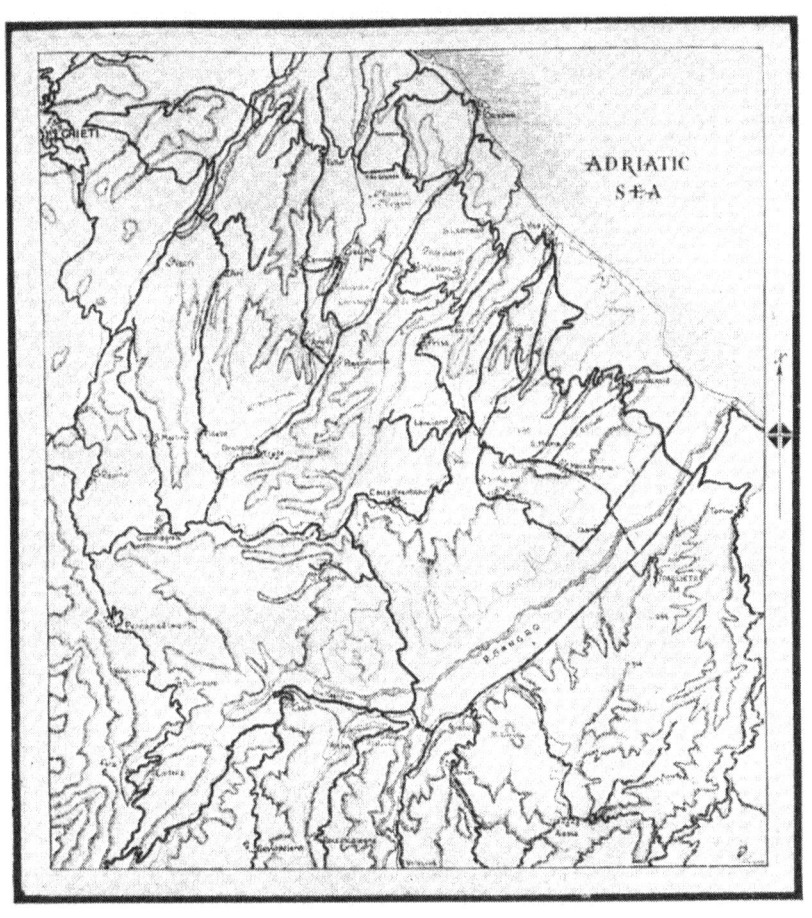

LOWER ADRIATIC SECTOR

Major-General Dudley Russell, C.B., C.B.E., D.S.O., M.C., Eighth Indian Division

Major-General F. I. S. Tuker, C.B., D.S.O., O.B.E., Fourth Indian Division

DIVISIONAL COMMANDERS

Major-General Denys Reid, C.B., D.S.O., M.C., Tenth Indian Division

Major-General A. W. W. Holworthy, D.S.O., M.C., Fourth Indian Division

fighting men from the Dominions found it necessary to fight for every yard. A swift break-through was impossible.

In the Indian sector the front was more fluid, and General Russell decided to exploit his advantage. He brought up his reserves from 19th Brigade and threw them into the fray. 6/13 Frontier Force Rifles, with 50th Royal Tank Regiment and Mahratta anti-tank gunners in close support, pushed across the lateral highway and commenced to work towards Tollo, two and a half miles to the north-west. Such an advance would have gouged a deep salient in the German defence system at its most sensitive spot, for the heavily fortified hamlet of Villa Grande, half-way to Tollo, served as the hinge upon which the defences of the coastal sector swung. To bring still greater weight to bear, 13th Corps returned Fifth British Infantry Division, which now came into the line between the Indians and the New Zealanders. The new troops took over a sector from 21st Indian Infantry Brigade on the left, and General Russell was thus able to concentrate his three brigades on the key point of Villa Grande.

Between December 17th and 21st the battlefield was tidied for a decisive trial at arms. Food, ammunition, equipment, and consolidation weapons were assembled in close support of the fighting line. On December 18th the indomitable Canadians renewed their attacks, and after two days' bitter fighting crashed into Ortona. In the broken streets of the seaport ferocious battles ensued. For seven days the men from the Dominion grappled with paratroopers in a death struggle. The hour had struck when the full weight of Eighth Army should be brought to bear. 19th Brigade was ordered to mount an immediate attack against Villa Grande, and to exploit any gains as far as the line of the Arielli river, which wandered southwards from the Adriatic through Tollo.

In the early hours of December 22nd, 1/5th Essex of 19th Brigade mustered on a start line south of Villa Grande, with "C" Squadron 50th Royal Tank Regiment in close support. It was a night of bitter frost. Infantry, tank-men and gunners had much ado to keep warm, and to keep their weapons serviceable. They walked up and down in little groups, stamping their chilled feet and swinging their arms. At 0530 hours, hundreds of guns crashed in a fearful concentration on Villa Grande. Flashes ringed and stabbed the southern horizon. Ankle-deep in freezing mud, the Essex waited until the barrage lifted. The leading company swept up to the southern edge of the village and plunged into the murk of smoke and fumes, in an endeavour to pin down the defenders before they could man their emplacements.

In their dug-outs and tunnels, the paratroopers had waited alertly for the instant when the storm of shell lifted. They sprang up the stairways and into the open with weapons blazing. Fierce and deadly fighting raged along the fringe of broken houses. On one or two positions where the Essex had overrun strong-points, quick counter-attacks forestalled every attempt at consolidation. The Home County men were obliged to relinquish their precarious footholds. The attack on Villa Grande had failed.

Twenty-four hours later to the minute, this same gallant battalion once more threw themselves at the village. With the waves of infantry came the tanks, and when the Germans clambered from their deep shelters, bombs and cannon shells greeted them. Dawn broke with the outskirts of Villa Grande firmly held. At noon the Essex formed up for a fresh advance. As the infantry deployed, German artillery and nebelwerfers intervened with a heavy shoot which blasted the British positions. Close behind the barrage the paratroopers counter-attacked. A blaze of fire greeted them, and the assault was shattered. The Essex immediately advanced to mop up the remainder of the village.

Then followed a second Mozzagrogna, in which from house to house, from cellar to loft, from one rubble pile to the next, the Essex and the paratroopers hunted each other to the death. Quick, deadly encounters marked every yard of progress. A British section races for the shelter of a blind wall. Bren gunners edge cautiously round the corner to the door. A kick shoots it open; tommy guns spray the hall and stairs; the remainder of the section spring to the windows, and roll grenades over the sills. On the blast of the bombs the tommy gunners charge inside to the close. In the cellar, on the stairs, under the eaves, Germans are dead and dying. With all speed the British section mans observation posts from which to rake the next house, and to cover their own approaches. Often they are too late. Paratroopers emerge from a near-by hide-out, and crawl stealthily into the shelter of the blind wall. Once again the battered door bursts in. Bullets hose the hall and stairway, and the house rocks with the shock of grenades. Over the sprawled bodies of British and Germans, the paratroopers feverishly mount their weapons to meet the next assault, which may be only minutes away.

A score of such small deadly battles marked the progress of the Essex as they extended their hold on Villa Grande. All day the crash of artillery and mortar bombs, the sudden chatter of tommy guns, and the springing boom of grenades, bespoke the ebb and flow of the fighting. The grim struggle spread. That morning, 3/15 Punjabis, also with tank support, had thrown the enemy out of Vezzano, half a mile south of Villa Grande. Before the consolidation groups could link up with the Essex, a counter-attack penetrated the Punjabi position, inflicting forty casualties. With equal speed, however, a reserve company raced forward and flung back the intruders. A continuous brigade line was established.

December 24th passed with thrust and counter-thrust which occasionally flared into heavy fighting. The Essex found the area around the village church to be infested with paratroopers, who clung to their broken burrows and fought fanatically until the last. Brigadier Dobree sent 3/8 Punjabis forward on the right of the Home County men, to threaten the village from that flank.

Christmas morning was heralded by intense artillery bombardments along the entire Eighth Army front. The Canadians were finishing off the enemy in Ortona. The Indians were softening up the German positions for a new thrust. In the west Fifth British Division and the New Zealanders were pounding the obstinate defenders who still barred the way into Orsogna. That afternoon 3/8 Punjabis struck at Villa Grande from the east. On the outskirts of the village, enemy machine gunners who had reoccupied weapon-pits and dug-outs previously cleared by the Essex, opened heavy fire. Without hesitation the leading Punjabi company changed direction and swept to flank to deal with this menace. The Mussalman company then resumed its attack on its original objective, only to be pinned by cross fire. Advance against this deadly sleet was impossible. Major Gardhari Singh spotted some haystacks, and the wind lay in the right quarter. Three captured German machine-guns with tracer ammunition were trained on them, and within a few minutes the sodden ricks emitted dense smoke which drifted across the front, cloaking the village. Behind this screen the Punjabis raced for the nearest houses and seized two of them. Paratroopers closed from all sides; a gangster's battle, from window to window, from door to door, ensued. Ammunition began to run low. A mule laden with grenades had tried to reach the houses, only to be shot down thirty yards away. Every yard was swept by spandau fire at point-blank range. Darkness promised to bring the inevitable counter-attack, against which grenades would be indispensable. But how to get them? To Lance Naik Allah Dad the situation presented no problem. "Why are you worrying, Sahib?" he said to his Company Commander. "This is a simple matter. I shall run to the mules and fetch the grenades."

He sprang across the open amid the crackle of bullets, and flung himself behind the shelter of the dead mule. His astounded comrades saw him rise, not with one but with four boxes of grenades—a mule's load—on his back. He bore a charmed life, and reached shelter exhausted but unhurt. With ammunition replenished the Punjabis held their ground, and that night made contact with the Essex on the southern perimeter of the village. The Royal West Kents likewise began to press in from the south-east. The ring around Villa Grande tightened.

Fighting continued throughout Boxing Day. The ground had dried, and British tanks were able to come forward. Riding on the outside of the leading tank, Major Gardhari Singh pointed out enemy posts. As high explosive and armour-piercing shells crashed into the emplacements, the paratroopers bolted into the open. As they ran, machine-guns brought them down. On the northern fringe of the village a few last-stand covering parties stuck it until mopped up. Otherwise the battle for Villa Grande was over.

The Indians entered the village to find a shambles, with dead Germans sprawled on the rubble heaps, in the entrances to dug-outs, or floating in water-filled slit trenches. Villa Grande, as one correspondent put it, looked "as though a giant had trodden on a child's box of blocks". Out of this desolation emerged men, women and children—the villagers who had cowered in cellars and crypts while the battle raged above them. They stared unbelievingly at the insane tangle of wreckage which was all that remained of their homes. A simple community had been threshed under the flail of war.

As the year drew to its close, the Germans on the Adriatic front were reeling from the mighty buffets of Eighth Army. In the coastal sector the Canadians having cleared Ortona were probing towards Pescara. On the Indian front the bastions of the Gustav Line had been stormed. On the left the Germans flinched under the resounding blows of the New Zealanders and Fifth British Division. Now was the time to intensify the assault. But as fresh formations moved up to take over the battle, and with their added weight to strike the mortal blow, winter supervened. On the last day of the year a blizzard swept in from the Adriatic, with biting cold winds, drifting snow and driving sleet. Visibility and ceiling fell to nil, controlled movement was impossible. Communications failed; men floundered and lost themselves between company and company. Long lines of frost-bound vehicles stood starkly immobile by the roadside. Before the wrack of the weather the offensive slowed to a standstill.

The end of the year, and the end of the active campaign, also saw the end of a memorable association. General Montgomery left the men whom he had led from El Alamein. The memory of that small bereted figure, its highly individual clothes, its pungent speech, will remain with soldiers of the Eighth Army as long as they live.

CHAPTER FOUR
WINTER AND SPRING

WITH THE ADRIATIC FRONT gripped by winter, Allied High Command proceeded with plans on the other side of Italy. Preparations were made for a landing at Anzio, 30 miles south of Rome, in conjunction with a drive up the Pontine Marshes along the Tyrrhenian Sea. For this operation, Fifth Army was strengthened at the expense of Eighth Army, and certain formations took the roads to the west. Eighth Army in turn drew from other theatres. Early in January a new but very well-known divisional flash appeared in the Adriatic sector. Fourth Indian Division had arrived from Egypt and had moved up to enter the line near Orsogna.

This veteran formation, the victors of Sidi Barrani, Keren, and a score of battles in Western Desert and Tunisia, had earned world fame. In four years the Red Eagle Division had suffered 25,000 casualties, had taken over 100,000 prisoners, and had travelled more than 10,000 miles. Certain of the older units had disappeared, but it was pleasing to note on arrival in Italy that 11th Indian Infantry Brigade, which had been destroyed at Tobruk, had been reconstituted and that the long-standing association with British gunners remained unchanged. The battle order of the Division was as follows:—

G. O. C. Major-General F. S. Tuker, C.B., D.S.O., O.B.E.

5*th Indian Infantry Brigade,* *(Brigadier D. R. Bateman,* *D.S.O., O.B.E.)*	1/4th Essex Regiment. 1/6 Rajputana Rifles. 1/9 Gurkha Rifles.
7*th Indian Infantry Brigade,* *(Brigadier Q. de T. Lovett,* *D.S.O.)*	1st Royal Sussex. 4/16 Punjab Regiment. 1/2 Gurkha Rifles.
11*th Indian Infantry Brigade* *(Brigadier V. C. Griffin)*	2nd Cameron Highlanders. 4/6 Rajputana Rifles. 2/7 Gurkha Rifles.
Divisional Reconnaissance Regiment	Central India Horse.
Machine Gun Battalion	5th Machine Gun Battalion Rajputana Rifles.
Artillery	1st Field Regiment R.A. 11th Field Regiment R.A. 31st Field Regiment R.A. 149th Anti-Tank Regiment R.A. 57th Light A.A. Regiment R.A.

Engineers	4th, 12th and 21st Field Companies (Sappers and Miners).
	11th Field Park Company.
	5th Bridging Platoon.
Medical Services	17th, 26th and 32nd Field Ambulances.
	15th Indian Field Hygiene Section.

The Orsogna battlefield, where Fourth Division relieved the New Zealanders between January 15th and 17th, had yielded little gains after months of heavy fighting. Orsogna stood on a high ridge above the river Moro, with the main road from Central Italy to the Adriatic running along the crest. The town had been fortified to fortress strength, and had thwarted the utmost efforts of the New Zealanders to secure it. When Fourth Indian Division faced this formidable position, it was in anticipation of a stern struggle. High Command however willed otherwise. After a fortnight's seasoning in the forward positions, during which 4/16 Punjabis of 7th Brigade showed that they had lost nothing of their old art of worrying the enemy, Fourth Division was relieved and warned for transfer to Fifth Army.

Eighth Indian Division, which had had little more than a glimpse of its famous comrades, continued to man a two-brigade sector in the centre of Eighth Army. The front was static, but the monotonous B.B.C. announcement, "Little to report from the Adriatic sector. Patrolling continues", often did less than justice to the situation. Nearly every night fighting flared up, as patrols clashed or raiding parties overran outposts. The following despatch from an Indian Army Observer describes routine conditions:

"Most of our front-line troops—British, Indian and Gurkhas—live in farmhouses on the hillsides. When dusk comes, patrols go out to investigate houses opposite, where movement has been seen during the day. Many small bitter encounters occur in the darkness when our men surround suspected enemy strongholds, sometimes only a few hundred yards from our line. A number of prisoners have been taken in this nerve-racking business. The operations are reminiscent of the 'No Man's Land' patrols of the last war in Flanders. Since the enemy operates in much the same manner as ourselves, houses on our side of the line are constantly guarded against German 'rustlers', who swoop out of the darkness to snatch prisoners. Several such 'cutting-out' parties have been beaten off with loss.

"Two of the stealthiest peoples in the world—both expert woodsmen and trackers—roam nightly in No Man's Land, giving the Germans the jitters. They are Gurkhas and North American Indians from the Canadian Rockies. The other night two patrols went out together. The Gurkha hillmen carried tommy guns and their dreaded kukris.

The Canadian scout patrol, consisting of four trappers, two cowpunchers and two North-American Indians, were armed with automatic weapons and hunting knives. One of the North-American Indians—who looked very like a Gurkha himself except that he was taller—said to me in a broad Canadian accent: 'This is the first time that we have seen the Gurkhas, and boy, are they good? I thought I knew a bit about tracking, but I can't teach those boys anything. I'm mighty proud to be associated with them.'

"So near to one another are the German and Indian troops in this sector that they have taken to conversations. The other evening a German called out, 'Hallo, Indians! Why don't you go home?' An enraged V.C.O., who spoke English, shouted back, 'I did not come all the way from El Alamein to go home. It is you who will go!' The Germans went next day, driven back by this Subedar and his men."

Upon the departure of Fourth Indian Division, Fifth Canadian Armoured Division assumed control of the Orsogna front. This contact developed into one of the warmest associations of the war. For months to come Canadian armour served with Indian Infantry, until the sepoys boasted of Canadian tank regiments with as great pride as they showed in their own battalions. Language imposed no handicap. A *lingua franca* of which Italian was the base was supplemented by English and Hindustani phrases. Joint training familiarized tank men and infantrymen with each other's problems, and such knowledge evoked the warmest admiration for each other's craft and courage. Co-operation became so close that on one occasion, when supplied with other armour, a Mahratta battalion complained. "Why can we not have our own tanks?" they asked. When a questionnaire requested Indian units to choose British regiments for post-war affiliation, a Punjabi battalion voted unanimously for the 14th (Calgary) Armoured Regiment. Nor was this admiration one-sided. A young Canadian tank officer, decorated for courage and resource in action, summed up the feeling of his men when he said: "When they tell us we are going to be fighting with the Indians we are happy as hell. I hope they feel the same way about us."

Early in February, Eighth Indian Division side-slipped to the left and spread out over a front of nearly twenty miles between Orsogna and the Maiella mountains. The line ran nearly due north and south; its southern flank, which rested against the high spurs of the range, was open. 6th Lancers, the Divisional Reconnaissance Regiment, was made flank guard and given patrol and intelligence responsibilities over the gaps in the line. The first of the Italian partisan detachments to serve under Divisional Command arrived, and made themselves very useful in bushwhacking expeditions across the wild and broken mountain sides. During the next two months the Lancers and Mahratta Anti-tank Gunners embarked on a number of similar expeditions. Observation posts and local guards were shot up, prisoners snatched and communications interrupted. The Indians made such nuisances of themselves that the German Commander in this sector issued a series of exhortations in routine orders. He besought his men to be more alert, to be more offensive-minded, to frustrate the pestiferous Indians at all costs. It seems probable that he made representations further afield, for in March a new German formation, the Three Hundred and Thirty-Fourth Division, entered this sector. The new troops were highly aggressive and thereafter the sepoys had it less their own way. During March a series of grim scuffles occurred, in which both sides took punishment. In one or two ambitious attempts to isolate Indian detachments, as much as a company of the enemy was employed. On one occasion, near the village of Fallascose, a clash led to a fire-fight which lasted for eight hours. In a fierce night encounter, 1/5 Mahrattas taught a German force a sharp lesson with no losses to themselves.

In spite of foul weather and frequently interrupted communications, all divisional services continued to function admirably. Perhaps the most noteworthy if unspectacular achievement was that of the Indian Medical Services. Troops who had never known extreme cold now fought in frozen foxholes, patrolled in a slush and sleet, waded icy rivers, slept in snowdrifts, bivouacked in blizzards. Yet such hardihood had been achieved through adaptability and training that serious illnesses fell to vanishing point, and the general health of the sepoys was so good that an Indian ADMS was able to boast, "If the general health of India was equal to that of our men in Italy, we should be the mightiest nation in the world ".

The long tour of Eighth Indian Division on the Adriatic drew to a close. On the night of April 7/8, Fourth Indian Division returned from Central Italy and relieved their comrades between Orsogna and the Maiellas. Next day, German artillery fired broadsheets into Fourth Division's lines, which read, "It wasn't much of a rest you had, was it? You need not think you will be allowed to complete your rest in this sector, although you may have been told that it was quiet here." This rapid identification illustrates the difficulty of maintaining field security in a countryside lately liberated from the enemy.

Three Hundred and Thirty-Fourth Division continued to be cocky. On Hitler's birthday (April 20th) they dressed Orsogna with flags and bunting, and displayed arrogant notice-boards which invited the Indians to participate in the celebration. As if further to mark the day, ten Focke-Wulfes bombed an Indian dressing station in Lanciano, causing 180 casualties. It is hoped that a reprisal shoot on Orsogna interfered to some degree with the celebration. A more potent response to the enemy challenge was the arrival (also on Hitler's birthday) of a new Indian formation, which began to relieve the Canadians in the coastal sector. Tenth Indian Division had landed in Italy late in March with the following battle order:

G.O.C. Major-General Denys Reid, C.B., C.B.E., D.S.O., M.C.

10th Indian Infantry Brigade (Brigadier T. N. Smith, O.B.E.)	1/2 Punjabis. 4/10 Baluch Regiment. 2/4 Gurkha Rifles.
20th Indian Infantry Brigade, (Brigadier J. B. McDonald, O.B.E.)	8th Manchester Regiment. 3/5 Mahratta Light Infantry. 2/3 Gurkha Rifles.
25th Indian Infantry Brigade (Brigadier Eustace Arderne, D.S.O.)	1st King's Own Regiment. 3/1 Punjab Regiment. 3/18 Royal Garhwal Rifles.
Reconnaissance Regiment	Skinners' Horse.
Machine Gun Battalion	1st Royal Northumberland Fusiliers.
Artillery	68th, 97th, and 154th Field Regiments R.A. 13th Anti-Tank Regiment R.A. 30th Light A.A. Regiment R.A.
Engineers	5th, 10th and 61st Field Companies. Sappers and Miners. 41st Field Park Company.
Medical Services	14th, 21st and 30th Field Ambulances. 14th Field Hygiene Section.

Major-General Reid, who won three decorations in his 'teens in the last war, had been a highly regarded commander in the African campaign. From a battalion of Mahrattas in Eritrea, he became Brigadier of the 29th Indian Infantry Brigade in Fifth Indian Division. He commanded the mixed force of Indians and South Africans which captured the Libyan oases of Giarabub and Jalo in 1941. During Rommel's offensive in 1942, after holding El Adem box and fighting a brilliant delaying action over two hundred miles of desert, he was captured just before reaching safety at El Alamein. He escaped through the German lines near Cassino in November 1943, and thereafter assumed command of Tenth Indian Division. A shrewd Scot of imposing physique, with a keen sense of humour, he had proved to be an aggressive, popular and able leader.

On April 22nd, when the relief of the Canadians had been completed, Fourth and Tenth Indian Divisions held the entire Adriatic front between the sea and the Maiellas, a distance of 30 miles. All six brigades were in the line. The left flank of Fourth Division rested on the haunches of Monte Amore, whose snow-covered summits and even contours gave the mountain the appearance of an inverted pudding basin. Here Central India Horse was the chief component of Dawnay Force, a detached group whose mission was to patrol the uplands and to worry the Germans. Dawnay Force entered fully into the spirit of this enterprise, and established itself in the ruins of a number of XVth century robbers' castles on commanding crests. It sallied out to rieve the countryside in a manner not unlike that of the original owners of these habitations. An incident early in April recalled classical history, when a detachment of German ski troops cut off an Indian patrol on the lip of Monte Fara Gorge. Using their greatcoats as the Romans once used their shields, the Indians tobogganed to safety at the bottom of the canyon.

On Tenth Division's front it was not until May 4th, nearly a fortnight after coming into the lines, that the German broadsheets of welcome arrived. Either the enemy's intelligence or his printer had been tardy. General Reid had his own ideas of welcome. He offered a reward of £5 for each prisoner taken. (His A.D.C., a Scots banker in civilian life, was appalled by this commitment, and when £60 had been earned, summarily terminated the offer on the grounds of a technicality.) Although the snow still lingered in the Maiellas, spring had come over the land. With fair weather the Adriatic front wakened from its winter sleep. A correspondent with the forward troops sends an interesting picture of conditions on this thinly-manned front:

"The bleak-looking farmhouses, which dot the countryside, are the scene of many quick, murderous encounters. Both Indian and German detachments live in much the same fashion. Downstairs, in the toolsheds and cattle stalls, the infantry platoons are quartered. The cellar serves as a bolt-hole in emergency. The upper storeys, reached by outside staircases, which give excellent observation, house the machine-gunners, signallers, and other specialists. Everyone moves discreetly during the day to avoid unwelcome attention from enemy guns. When darkness falls, the danger mounts. These farmhouses nearly all have blind walls, behind which a raiding party may approach unseen. Throughout the night, therefore, sentries are stationed on all sides in slit trenches. Alarm wires are strung and likely approaches are mined or booby-trapped. The technique of surprise, like the precautions against it, demand courage and resourcefulness of a high order, as well as skill in battle tactics which are a mixture of gangster and Red Indian practices."

From May onwards, raids and "cutting-out" parties were features of the day's work on all sectors of the Indian front. At first the enemy was in the ascendant. During the first week in May, 2/4 Gurkhas of 10th Brigade were attacked twice. On the second occasion two platoons were overrun. A counter-attack by their neighbours, 1/2 Punjabis, chased back the enemy. Next night 2/3 Gurkhas on 20th Brigade front, were similarly raided. Stubborn hand-to-hand fighting ensued before the Germans withdrew. On Fourth Division's front, 1/9 Gurkhas and 3/10 Baluchis likewise were attacked. The assault on the Gurkhas was particularly severe, the raiders being estimated at the strength of a half-battalion. At dawn on May 14th a sharp shoot descended on 11th Brigade's front between Arielli and Orsogna, where the right forward company of 3/12 Frontier Force Regiment was stationed on a neck of land between three convergent valleys. Emerging from these valleys, a substantial German force, supported by tanks, overran the Frontiersmen. A counter-attack by a reserve company failed to eject the enemy, and it was not until evening that the intervention of the 2nd Camerons restored the situation. In this fighting, 11th Brigade suffered 150 casualties.

To these assaults the Indians reacted with characteristic vigour. On Tenth Division's front, 1/2 Punjabis crossed a stream, and in a wild Donnybrook in the dark, destroyed an enemy post and took prisoners. On the next night, 3/18 Garhwalis raided with equal success. Fighting patrols from the King's Own and Mahrattas stalked and scuppered enemy outposts on successive evenings. At midnight on May 23rd a company of 2/3 Gurkhas, in a sudden onset at Lone House, depleted the ranks of Two Hundred and Seventy-Eighth German Division by 20 killed and 3 prisoners. 8th Manchesters about the same time bumped an enemy patrol and inflicted casualties.

Under this pummelling the aggressiveness oozed out of the enemy. Intelligence reports showed German commanders to be jumpy. Wireless intercepts from isolated posts were couched in plaintive key. British and Indian soldiers, in the idiom of the battlefield, told each other that there was a flap on over the way. An officer in an Indian observation post sent this characteristic message:

"A white flag has been seen waving frantically in the area C 279134. Later a man began to crawl towards our lines. He has not yet arrived, but tea for fifty had been laid on."

In view of the possibility of an enemy withdrawal on the Adriatic front, both Indian divisions undertook to pin down their adversaries and to keep them under strict observation. During the last days of May, heavy German transport movements to the north were reported. Attempts to explore enemy positions, however, led to clashes which proved the enemy still to be holding in force. A combined patrol of Manchesters and Central India Horse was cut up on a risky expedition among the foothills of the Maiellas. Royal Sussex, on 7th Brigade's front, and both Camerons and Frontier Force Regiment on 11th Brigade's front, ran into trouble when they attempted to probe too intimately.

At the end of May, a regrouping of forces in the Adriatic sector occurred. The Italian Utili Division arrived to relieve Fourth Indian Division on the Orsogna front. Their advance parties came forward with bands playing and with flags flying. The German artillery greeted such advertisement of intentions with a heavy shoot which interfered to some extent with the relief. Fourth Indian Division side-slipped on to the coastal sector, and on June 4th relieved Tenth Indian Division, which left at once for Central Italy. Fourth Divisional Artillery remained behind Orsogna in support of the Italians, while the guns of the Third Carpathian Division covered the Indians on the coast. A few of the old hands still remained who remembered the Carpathian Brigade which served beside them on the drive into Cyrenaica in 1941.

On June 7th a deserter from Two Hundred and Seventy-Eighth German Division revealed an enemy withdrawal to be imminent. At dawn next morning a Baluchi patrol reported Germans to be marching out of their positions carrying full equipment. At 0800 hours pursuit groups on all three brigade fronts advanced on the trail of the enemy. Simultaneously the Italians on the left discovered their sectors to be open and took up the chase.

Except for minefields along the river Arielli, no obstacles were encountered in the first stages of the pursuit. On the outskirts of Polo, 1/2 Gurkhas mopped up an enemy strong point which included the rather unusual defence of dug-in flamethrowers. Next morning the same battalion drew an enemy counter-attack when the hillmen pressed too closely in the chase. The Germans suffered a number of casualties in this futile enterprise. Thereafter the pace of the advance quickened. The partisans were up all over the countryside, and on more than one occasion these avenging irregulars chased Germans into the arms of the Indians. The Utili Division on the left kept edging across into the east, constricting the communications of Fourth Division until something like a bottle-neck resulted. With only two main roads on which to advance, 7th Brigade covered the entire Divisional front, and 11th Brigade were pushed on to the beaches. There amphibious craft awaited them. 2nd Camerons, with detachments of pioneers were ferried up the coast and landed north of Francavilla.

On June 10th, 1/2 Gurkhas entered Chieti, a sizable market town, where they received a delirious welcome. Here 7th Brigade received the news that 11th Brigade, having taken to the water, might claim the exciting prize of Pescara. Two Cameron officers had set off on bicycles in order to add this important seaport to their 'game book'. 7th Brigade countered by despatching its reconnaissance squadron and a Sherman tank, with instructions to hurry. The result of the race was close, and is still a matter of dispute. Pescara was found to be looted and deserted.

The last of the Indian divisions now prepared to leave the Adriatic front. On June 13th, Third Carpathian Division took over from the Fourth Indian Division, which withdrew to a training area at Campobasso in preparation for transfer to Central Italy.

2. CASSINO—THE EPIC

CHAPTER FIVE

THE FIRST ASSAULT FAILS

FROM TIME TO TIME, divisions were relieved on the Adriatic coast and disappeared. All took the roads to Central Italy, where in turn they were committed to the epic struggle for Cassino.

This battle stands in the heroic category of Dunkirk, Stalingrad and Caen. Despite staggering losses the men of the United Nations strove for months to break the German defences at their strongest point. This narrative deals only with the fortunes of the Indian Divisions. It must not be forgotten that other troops shared in full measure the same disasters and contributed equally to the victory. Fourth Indian Division was not the only division to be well-nigh destroyed at Cassino, nor Eighth Indian Division the only formation to smash through. The story of Cassino is a saga of valour and endurance shared by all.

On the Adriatic coast the Gustav Line, based on a succession of ridges and rivers, constituted a flexible zone of defence. When it entered the mountains it became rigid. The key, the arch-essential bastion of these fixed positions, lay in the spacious valley of the Liri, some sixty miles south-east of Rome. Here a great abrupt buttress of the Matesi mountains towers above the countryside, commanding all approaches from east, south and west. Its crest is Monte Cairo, a huge cone rising five thousand feet above the valley. From this eminence a spade-shaped promontory of high ground thrusts down for ten miles to end in a high and almost sheer tip, which overlooks the valley of the Rapido to the east, and the valley of the Liri to the north-west. This is Monastery Hill. The little town of Cassino snuggles around its haunches. Route 6, one of the main roads linking Rome and Naples, comes up from the south, crosses the Rapido and swings through Cassino Town before turning to the north-west along the eastern slope of the Liri valley.

A second road to Rome traverses the reclaimed Pontine marshes along the Tyrrhenian coast. This road had been heavily damaged by bombing. Moreover, its low-lying water meadows, checkerboarded with drainage rhines, offered serious obstacles to mechanized advance. These circumstances accentuated the importance of the Liri thoroughfare.

The river Liri follows the western or opposite wall of the valley, and does not approach Cassino. Its principal tributary, the Gari, rises in the mountains a few miles behind the town. Before the Gari reaches Cassino it is joined by a substantial stream from the north-east which

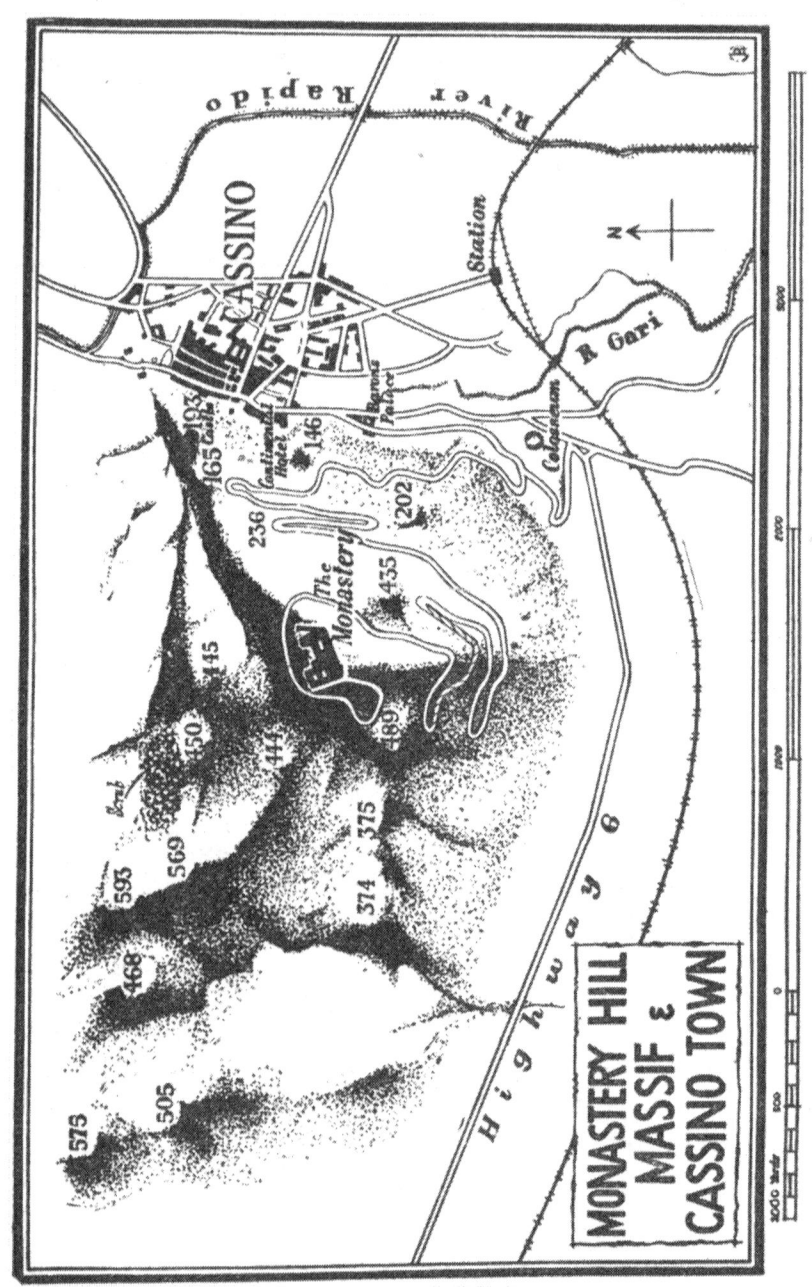

is known as the Rapido. After the Rapido flows into the Liri, another change of name occurs, and the river is known as the Garigliano. Lest these different names confuse, in this narrative the river will be known as the Rapido, and the valley as the Liri.

Soldiers have been no uncommon sight on the streets of Cassino. Year by year staff officers have come to lecture and to arrange exercises on a site which was familiar to military scholars as a model of impregnable terrain. Of this set piece battlefield, Monastery Hill is the key. Monte Cairo is imposing, even awesome to the eye, but although its crest commands a vast area of countryside, it can be by-passed and neutralized if its slopes are beleaguered. But nothing can traverse the Liri or Gari-Rapido valleys save by consent of Cassino. If the Allies wished to strike for Rome by way of the main highway, they must first secure the heights with the Monastery upon its crest. Towering above precipitous slopes, as if in middle air, the great Benedictine hospice had been converted into a fortress during the nineteenth century. Even in the days of unlimited high explosive this lofty keep constituted a formidable obstacle. An imposing gate set in arches of stone thirty feet thick offered the only entrance. The walls were fifteen feet high, ten feet thick at their bases, loop-holed and tesselated. They were unscaleable and proof against any weapons which infantry might bring to bear.

In January the first battle for Cassino had been mounted on a grand scale. Three corps struck from three sides, while a fourth corps endeavoured to turn the position by a sea landing at Anzio. On the extreme left of a battlefront of more than twenty miles, Tenth British Corps attacked below the junction of the Gari and Liri rivers, seeking to bypass Cassino. In the centre U.S. Second Corps launched a frontal assault across the Rapido towards the high escarpments between Monte Cairo and Monastery Hill. On the right French Expeditionary Corps drove from the north-east in an endeavour to infiltrate behind Monte Cairo, and to amputate the enemy's mountain defences in entirety.

The centre failed to win home, and without success in the centre gains on the flank meant nothing. The American attack was thwarted by the unshakable grip of the enemy on the ridges and spurs above the valley of the Rapido. Murderous fire took a fearful toll. Foiled in their first assault the Americans mounted their next attack further to the north. After terrific fighting they forced their way across the Rapido and seized high ground in the rear of the main Cassino position. On January 29th they opened a third offensive with a double thrust, one division attacking southwards along the bottom of the Rapido valley, another along the crest of the escarpments above it. Six days of fluctuating fighting followed. A great effort hurled the enemy from Monte Castellone. By working down a long crest, afterwards known from its shape on the contour map as Snake's Head Ridge, advanced assault troops fought to within a few hundred yards of Monastery Hill. Here they were pinned down by fire from three sides. Within bow shot of the Monastery walls progress became impossible. The Americans had battled with dourness and gallantry beyond all praise, but they were fought out. It was time for others to take over.

Across the mountains from Eighth Army came two great divisions whose names had been a by-word throughout years of hard fighting in Africa. It is doubtful if two military formations composed of men of different race and culture ever achieved a closer association and a more comprehensive understanding than the Second New Zealand and Fourth Indian Divisions. They had been partners in hazardous enterprises from the beginning. Far back in 1940, before the New Zealand Division had reached Middle East, Kiwi lorry drivers accompanied Fourth Indian Division in the battle of Sidi Barrani. They raced their vehicles to within 150 yards of the walls of Tummar, and leapt down to charge beside the sepoys who stormed the camp. In the autumn offensive of 1941 the two Divisions served each other faithfully in the fighting along the Libyan escarpment. In Tunisia they had assailed the Mareth Line and the Enfidaville positions together. They had never failed each other. Year by year mutual understanding and appreciation increased. As fighting men they were of one piece—the warp and woof of an unsurpassed military fabric. Others boasted for them that they were the two finest Divisions in the Allied Armies.

This happy relationship was confirmed by the personal friendship of Lieut.-General Sir Bernard Freyburg and Major-General F. S. Tuker. To General Freyburg's great battle knowledge, General Tuker added outstanding comprehension of the fundamental problems of modern warfare. A military commentator once declared: "General Tuker's skill and training of infantry for war, and their leading in battle, is of such an original yet practical kind as to border on genius." Mountain warfare was his speciality. His etcher's eye (he is an artist of standing) for fine gradations of perspective, enabled him to master, as few commanders, the lie of a battlefield. In this new grim operation he promised to prove an exceedingly able lieutenant to an old colleague, and the long-standing illness which forced him into hospital just before the battle begun was not the least of the misfortunes of Indian troops in this ill-fated enterprise.

For the attack on Cassino General Freyburg became commander of the New Zealand Corps, which included his own Division, Fourth Indian Division with additional armour, artillery and ancillary troops. The plan for the new battle was in effect a continuation of the operation undertaken by Second U.S. Corps. Twin assaults would be mounted simultaneously on the high ground above the Rapido and along the bottom of the valley into Cassino Town. Fourth Indian

Division would attack on the crests of the ridges, reaching for Monastery Hill from the north. The New Zealanders would advance from the east, crossing the Rapido for a frontal assault on the town. As prelude to this attack 7th Indian Brigade would relieve troops of Thirty-fourth U.S. Division on Point 593, the highest ground on Snake's Head Ridge. This saddle-back ran into the west about one thousand yards in the rear of the Monastery. The ridge was twelve hundred yards in length, a narrow crest with deep ravines on either side. It was approached by a ford over the Rapido, and by a mountain track which climbed its slopes some distance north of Cassino Town.

Seen from afar the Monte Cairo or Cassino massif appears bare and smooth, with little natural cover. Closer inspection reveals it to comprise rough and broken ground with ridges, knolls and hollows everywhere. Thick scrub affords ample cover in many places. The ridges have precipitous slopes and razor-backed crests bestrewn with giant boulders. Indeed every resource of nature seemed designed to protect the defenders and to harass and to hinder their assailants. German engineers had exploited these advantages of terrain. Every nook and cranny of the dead ground held weapon pits. Emplacements had been blasted out of solid rock; pillboxes of steel and concrete had been built in. Outposts were connected by tunnels and covered by aprons of mines. These minefields in turn were commanded by machine-gun nests approximately fifty yards apart. Between these nests storm troopers waited in foxholes, each with an automatic weapon and a basket of bombs, to deal with any attempt to infiltrate into the position.

Fifteenth Panzer Grenadier Division held Cassino Town, Monastery Hill and Snake's Head Ridge. These men were tough veterans of a dozen battlefields. Their commander, Major-General Baade, was one of the younger German senior officers. His instructions came direct from Hitler and were unequivocal. Political as well as military considerations dictated that Cassino must be held, whatever the cost.

The men of Fourth Indian Division were well aware of the gravity of the task which confronted them. On his initial reconnaissance Brigadier Lovett of 7th Brigade had noted the extreme exhaustion of American troops, and on his return had recommended that their relief should be expedited. Isolated, frozen, battered by night and by day, handfuls of indomitable men clung to positions which they had clawed from the grip of the enemy. Six American regiments—eighteen battalions in all—were distributed between Monte Castellone and Cassino Town. These units had lost eighty per cent. of their effectives. The regiment on Snakes Head Ridge had only four hundred men standing. Here the enemy held the ruins of an old fort on the high western tip, and from this lookout brought fire to bear on every yard of the crest of the ridge. The only cover consisted of shallow saucers scraped out among the rocks, and two-man sangars of the type common on the North-West Frontier of India. These exposed positions had seen continuous and heavy fighting for some days before the Indians arrived. Numerous German counter-attacks sought to prise the Americans from their hard-won ground. More than 150 dead on one company front testified to the bitterness of the struggle.

The relief of the Americans was scheduled for the night of February 12th. For some days previously Fourth Indian Division had been organizing on a mule pack basis. In addition to the Indian mule companies, a heterogeneous assemblage of French, American and Italian mules of diverse training, habits and temper had been recruited: the Divisional transport services will not readily forget those days. A first attempt to open a way forward through the lines of the famous 133rd Japanese-American Regiment, on the left of the Divisional front, failed because not even mules could negotiate the terrain, and porter companies were not yet available. The approach therefore was shifted into the north, by way of Cairo village in the Rapido valley. Less than three miles from this hamlet, Monte Castellone was proving a soft spot in the Allied lines. Strong enemy fighting patrols had infiltrated, and it became necessary to deploy two battalions of 7th Brigade as a covering force until the Americans could deal with the intruders. The relief of Snake's Head therefore was postponed for twenty-four hours until the situation around Monte Castellone had stabilized.

On February 13th 7th Brigade's assembly area came under long-range artillery fire and casualties resulted. After nightfall the Indians moved off over the only available route, a rough mountain track which had deteriorated under heavy use. The enemy was alert, and the relief was shelled and mortared from the time it crossed the Rapido. Cautiously the Royal Sussex filtered platoons forward until they reached the shoulders of the ridge below Point 593. Here the outpost lines were only a few yards apart. The much enduring American garrison was relieved. It was necessary to carry out the last fifty men on stretchers. On the left of the Sussex 4/16 Punjabis groped forward to occupy the southern slopes of the ridge. When the inclement dawn broke 7th Brigade represented a spearhead thrust into the heart of the Monastery defences. The Sussex and the Punjabis formed the point of the spear, Thirty-Sixth U.S. Division to the north and Thirty-Fourth U.S. Division to the south, its blade and haft.

Across the Valley of the Rapido, five to six thousand yards south-east of Cassino, strong groups of artillery prepared for action. In the neighbourhood of Monte Croce, a peak capped with an ancient castle, guns were massed in a manner reminiscent of the wheel-to-wheel concentrations of the Great War. A battery commander describes his position thus:

"At least my battery is not in full view of Monastery Hill as are the other batteries. It shares a gully with New Zealand gunners and with a battery of 11 Field Regiment. Over the road are six U.S. 155s. Just behind us is a battery of American 105s and some British mediums."

This artillery target encouraged the enemy to risk his aircraft in a series of tip-and-run raids. These sudden exciting sorties did little damage, but they gave 57 L.A.A. Regiment an opportunity to prove that their shooting had not deteriorated since Western Desert days, when the sepoys credited this fine unit with marksmanship bordering on the miraculous. Seven aircraft destroyed over the Rapido valley within a week brought the Regiment's bag for the war to 103 victims counted on the ground, as well as more than 300 planes damaged in the air. These gunners had engaged enemy tanks over open sights near Benghazi in 1942. It is believed that their total kill exceeds that of any other anti-aircraft unit in the war.

The Air Forces likewise concentrated for the battle. Until now the Benedictine Monastery had been spared. The Germans declared no fighting formations to be in garrison and that the buildings housed only refugees from Cassino Town. Whatever the truth of such claim, it was apparent that the Monastery served as the enemy's main observation post. Warnings were dropped that aerial bombardment was imminent, and large groups of British and American aircraft were briefed for the operation.

The attack was originally planned to begin on the night of February 12/13th. Delays in relief and incessantly foul weather necessitated adjournment. The flooding of air-strips grounded many of the bomber groups, and the New Zealand Armoured Brigade, which was to support the assault on Cassino Town, was bogged down in the Rapido Valley. Some of the objectives of the Kiwis were under water. It was not until February 15th that the weather improved sufficiently for the battle to open.

At 0800 hours on that day the first of fifteen waves of aircraft bombed Monastery Hill. During the morning and afternoon 351 tons of bombs were dropped. Visibility was low, and stray bombs fell on the Indian positions on Snake's Head Ridge, inflicting 24 casualties. Forward posts were withdrawn to avoid additional losses. Observing this movement, the enemy in an intercepted wireless message exulted rather prematurely in the retirement of "Indian troops with turbans". The air bombardment inflicted great damage on the Monastery buildings without impairing their value as fortifications and observation posts. Nowhere were the breaches in the walls complete. Except in the case of direct hits, pillboxes and concrete emplacements remained unscathed. Nor could the artillery intervene effectively in direct support of the assault troops. Indian positions were so close to those of the enemy that a barrage programme was impossible and the fire plan had to be restricted to counter-battery work and concentration shoots on forming-up areas. These handicaps imposed a grim necessity. The Infantry must do the job single-handed.

A further and equally ominous circumstance was that the naked slopes of Snake's Head Ridge prevented reconnaissance and investigation of the enemy's positions. From the forward posts only rocky hillsides and patches of scrub could be seen. The Germans might hold the summit of Point 593 in battalion or platoon strength; his forces could only be estimated in terms of supply possibilities. It was this uncertainty which led to a conference summoned by the Divisional Commander at 7th Brigade Headquarters on the morning of February 15th. All intelligence submitted at that meeting suggested the impossibility of carrying Point 593 and Monastery Hill in a single operation. Point 593 was therefore declared a preliminary objective and the Royal Sussex were ordered to secure complete possession that night. The main attack on the Monastery would be launched twenty-four hours later.

During their forty-eight hours on the exposed crest of Snake's Head Ridge, the Sussex had been unable to make other than the simplest preparations for the assault. They were blind by day, since any movement drew intense fire. After darkness, the lie of the ground was so difficult that patrols brought only confused and hazy reports. Uncertainty as to the enemy's strength was linked to the impossibility of deploying substantial forces on a narrow and exposed start line. The first attack therefore was little more than a try-out. On the night of February 15th, one company moved forward. The German outposts were on the alert. Heavy and accurate machine-gun and mortar fire swept the forming-up area. The men who had carried Libyan Omar by storm dourly charged uphill. Seventy yards ahead they encountered an impassable palisade of boulders. Intense fire searched the darkness, pinning the South-Countrymen to the ground. After several unsuccessful attempts to outflank and to by-pass this obstacle the Sussex withdrew, having suffered twenty casualties.

On the following night the entire battalion mustered for the attack. By 2200 hours the forward company had found its way around the obstacle of the previous night, and had gained a footing on the approaches to Point 593. From behind boulders and from foxholes dug under rocky ledges the panzer grenadiers buffeted the advance with bursts of automatic fire and with showers of grenades. A second company pushed up to thicken the line. A magnificent charge headed by Lieut. Dennis Cox won home, and the Sussex caught their breath amid the ruins of the small fort. Then came a fatal misunderstanding —an enemy signal flare was interpreted as instructions to withdraw. Before dawn the Sussex abandoned this key position, which was never regained. Such unhappy errors had profound effects. Before the battle was resumed on February 17th it had become a Divisional instead of a

Brigade operation. With increased resources the plan reverted to the original conception—a non-stop drive to the summit of Monastery Hill. For this assault 4/6 Rajputanas and 1/9 Gurkhas were placed under command of 7th Brigade.

At midnight on February 17th 4/6 Rajputana Rifles, with three companies of the Sussex, were ordered to destroy the enemy on Point 593, and thereafter to seize Point 445, within 800 yards of the rear of the Monastery. Two hours later, 1/2 and 1/9 Gurkhas would smash through to storm the Monastery itself, thereafter advancing down the hillside to establish contact with the New Zealanders. The remaining battalions of 5th Indian Brigade (1/4 Essex and 1/6 Rajputana Rifles) would wait a success signal from the Monastery before moving to an attack on Cassino Town from the north. The other battalions of 11th Brigade —2/7 Gurkhas and 2nd Camerons—would supply porters and support companies for the assault groups. Simultaneously the New Zealand Division would launch an all-out attack on Cassino Town from the south-east.

This plan subjected the German positions to the shock of heavy forces from three sides. Nevertheless the key to the battle lay in the hands of the two Gurkha battalions. Should the agile hillmen win to the summit, as at Fatnassa and Djebel Garci, success was certain. Should they fail, there could be no victory. As midnight struck on February 17th, 4/6 Rajputana Rifles, heroes of a dozen desperate encounters, flung themselves in a fierce onslaught at Point 593. Yard by yard they closed upon their enemies. Once again a blaze of fire raked the slopes, and held the gallant Indians from the close. Major Markham Lee with a handful of men reached the crest and died there. By 0330 hours the attack was at a standstill. Nevertheless "B" and "C" Companies of 1/2 Gurkhas came forward, formed up on the left and began to work downhill towards Point 445.

A patch of scrub such as abounded on the ridges loomed in the darkness ahead. There had been no opportunity to reconnoitre this undergrowth, but since it was thin elsewhere and no impediment to free movement, it had not been considered a serious obstacle. A strong body of Germans had crept up and established themselves undetected in this covert within a stone's throw of the Indian positions. A thick seeding of mines with tripwires skirted the approaches; hidden in the scrub the storm troopers waited with tommyguns at the ready. As the Gurkhas attempted to worm through the copse, the leading platoon blew up on the mines almost to a man. A hail of bullets and grenades followed. Lieut.-Colonel Showers fell seriously wounded. Two-thirds of the leading companies were struck down within five minutes, yet the hillmen continued to bore in, reaching for their enemies. Naik Bir Bahadur Thapa although wounded in a dozen places emerged on the enemy's side of the copse with a few survivors and established a foothold. It was to no avail; in that deadly undergrowth dozens lay dead, many with four or more tripwires around their legs. Only a handful remained to be recalled to defensive positions at dawn. Stretcher-Bearer Sher Bahadur Thapa traversed this fearful undergrowth no less than sixteen times in order to bring out wounded comrades. (He was killed soon afterwards.)

Concurrently "A" and "D" Companies, with companies from 1/9 battalion in close support, picked their way around the left flank of the holocaust in the scrub, and worked steadily forward in the darkness towards the Monastery. Shortly before dawn "B" Company managed to effect a lodgement on Point 445. Eight hundred yards away a dark defiant height marked the supreme prize. Three companies of 1/9 Gurkhas closed up. They stood in the midst of a ring of enemies, embedded in the heart of the defences. Fire rained on them from three sides. Enemy sources afterwards reported an attack repulsed from the Monastery walls, and months later a colonel of paratroopers, captured near Florence, declared that he had led the counter-attack which had destroyed Gurkhas who had penetrated into the fortress itself. He was a pompous conceited man, who probably lied : but there are reasons to believe that a small great-hearted group, seven against a city, continued to seek the enemy until death closed on them.

At daybreak bitter fighting still raged around the key position of the old fort on Point 593. Attack after attack took toll until the enemy succeeded in winning back part of the crest. A fourth company of Rajputanas had been thrown in at 0430 hours but had failed to regain the summit. Indians and Sussex dug in together on the reverse slopes, with the enemy in mastery above them. A thousand yards beyond, the breaking light found the Gurkhas endeavouring to scratch meagre cover on the scrabbly summit of Point 445. To continue the advance by day would have been suicidal, and until Point 593 was cleared of the last enemies, it was impossible for supplies to pass forward. There was no alternative therefore but to withdraw from Point 445 under cover of darkness. As always in the Cassino fighting, gains of ground meant little; it was the Monastery or nothing. An assault mounted with consummate gallantry had failed to win home. The task was too great.

During this bleak winter night, when the ridges and hilltops spurted flame and re-echoed with the crash of bombs, in the valley of the Rapido and on the approaches to Cassino Town the New Zealanders had thrown in a great attack. Everywhere they encountered the same bitter unyielding resistance as their comrades on the heights above them. A precarious bridgehead across the Rapido was established through which the Kiwis advanced to their assault upon the town. A Maori battalion under intense mortar and machine-gun fire dashed across a minefield, slashed its way through belts of wire, and stormed Cassino railway station. If this position could have been held, the enemy garrison in Cassino would have been in jeopardy. Unfortunately dawn came too soon; in spite of herculean efforts New Zealand sappers had been unable to bridge the Rapido, and essential support arms, particularly tanks and anti-tank guns, could not reach the forward infantry. After continuous bombardments throughout the morning, a strong enemy counter-attack with tanks in the van retook the railway station. The Maori garrison was overrun. The remainder of the New Zealand infantry then withdrew across the river. Except for an attempt on the night of February 28th on the part of 4/16 Punjabis and 2/7 Gurkhas to improve their positions on the southern slopes of Snake's Head Ridge, the first assault on Cassino had ended.

CHAPTER SIX

THE SECOND ASSAULT FAILS

IT WOULD BE UNJUST to gloss the failure of the New Zealand and Indian divisions in their first attack upon Cassino. In fighting as intense, as heroic as any in history, two veteran formations had smashed without gain against this well-nigh impregnable position. Every variation of plan of battle led into a *cul de sac*, with enemies on all sides. There appeared to be particularly pertinent objections to continuing the attack on the high ground. The operations on the hilltops accentuated the difficulty of striking a balance between what the battle demanded, and what it was possible to supply. It obviously required more than one brigade to storm Monastery Hill; yet on Snake's Head Ridge it was impossible to deploy even a brigade. Moreover, it was only by the efforts of the remainder of the Division that a single brigade could be maintained in these forward positions. All supplies were fetched over a single track to the ford on the Rapido, under direct observation by the enemy. An officer wrote of "the eerie feeling of crossing miles of open ground with the eyes of enemies watching you from above." In the Cairo village concentration area the Divisional vehicles bogged down hopelessly before reaching the forward dumps; only the loan of six wheeled American lorries kept the supply line open. A single train to Snake's Head Ridge absorbed five companies of porters and 800 mules. The stormy winter weather added a final and almost decisive complication. Every journey forward became a nightmare which strained the maintenance services to the utmost. Further responsibilities would have incurred the risk of breakdown.

Nevertheless, neither Allied High Command nor the battered New Zealand and Indian divisions were prepared to accept a first failure as final. As soon as positions were consolidated, the planning of another battle began. The new scheme began by recognizing the enemy positions to be mutually supporting. Either they must be stormed simultaneously, or overrun consecutively. In the first battle the sharp thrust at the heart had failed. It was now decided to begin at the northern limits of the Cassino position and to roll up the defences one by one until Monastery Hill alone remained. Except for a diversionary feint the high ground to the rear of the Monastery would be disregarded. The New Zealanders would move down the Rapido Valley and force an entrance into Cassino Town from the north. When they had effected a foothold, Fourth Indian Division would advance on the right flank of the Kiwis, reducing the fortifications of the hillside above the town. When the attack had won around the shoulder of the Monastery glacis onto its western flanks, an assault upwards to seize Hangman's Hill would be launched.

On paper the new operation looked tidier than its predecessor. Indian and New Zealand troops would be attacking on parallel rather than on convergent axes. Gains either in Cassino Town or on the hillside above it would react to mutual advantage. The chief drawback to the scheme was the bottleneck between the escarpment and the town through which the Indians would enter the battle. A knoll about four hundred feet in height, bearing a castle on its crest, stood above the town like a preacher above his congregation. There was no entrance onto the slopes of Monastery Hill except through this pulpit. Below it, the fringes of the town lapped up to the Castle walls; on the upper side a deep gorge offered an impassable approach. Further to the south, and likewise standing on the hillside above the town, the Continental Hotel had been converted into a strong point covering east, west and south. The road from Cassino Town to the Monastery wound up the hillside in a series of sharp switchbacks. Each of its hairpin bends had been strongly fortified. Should an attack on the lower levels secure the Castle and Continental Hotel, the switchback strong points would continue to bar any advance up the slopes.

Above the switchbacks, and only two hundred yards below the crest from which the walls of the Monastery rose sheerly, a second pulpit, a rocky platform bearing the concrete pylon of an aerial ropeway, abutted from the mountain side. The gibbet-like structure gave this protuberant pimple the ominous name of Hangman's Hill. It was sufficiently close to the summit to be in part dead ground.

As preliminary to the major battle a New Zealand brigade undertook to storm Castle Hill. Through this corridor the Indians would sally on to the hillside, working along the slopes southward and upwards to secure Hangman's Hill as the jump-off position for the final assault upon the Monastery.

5th Indian Brigade was briefed to open the new battle. Those battalions which had been operating under 7th Brigade command on Snake's Head Ridge were withdrawn for a brief period of rest and preparation. 7th Brigade reinforced by 2/7 Gurkhas and 2nd Camerons assumed command of the Divisional front. The operation was planned for February 24th, but before it could be launched, winter struck with all the violence of a fresh foe. Rain froze into sleet, sleet turned to snow, snow to blizzards followed by high winds and torrential downpours. "The wind," wrote an officer, " holds up everything except the men's tents." Again the sodden air strips grounded the bombers, and in the valley bottoms tanks and vehicles churned the fields into mud sloughs. For 7th Brigade in their naked sangars on Snake's Head Ridge life was nearly unbearable. The enemy was less than 40 yards from the forward positions, and any movement drew retributory fire. Until the elements abated it was out of the question either to improve positions or to launch a fresh attack. Day by day the assault was postponed for upwards of three weeks. During these weeks, the hazard of their positions cost 7th Brigade sixty casualties daily. Never has a severer task confronted Indian troops, and never have they borne hardships and dangers with greater fortitude.

In the second week of March conditions began to improve, and plans for the resumption of the offensive were completed. The new scheme was elaborate and intensive. For three and a half hours before the infantry went in, the strongest air attack yet assembled in Italy would pound Cassino and Monastery Hill. Immediately after the air programme, an equally formidable array of artillery would lay down a four-hour shoot to cover the assault upon Cassino Town. 610 guns of all calibres were enrolled in the concentration which would cast 1,200 tons of shell upon the objectives. Thereafter, 6th New Zealand Infantry Brigade, with an armoured regiment in support, would storm Castle Hill, thrusting downwards into Cassino Town. 5th Indian Infantry Brigade would take over on Castle Hill, and would fan out on to the slopes of Monastery Hill, working along the outskirts of Cassino Town until in position to strike upwards for Hangman's Hill. Thereafter a final surge would carry the attack into the breaches of the Monastery.

Simultaneously, 7th Indian Brigade was ordered to undertake an audacious diversionary operation. The main supply route from Cairo Village had been improved from a trail to a track, and was now passable for tanks. Between Snake's Head Ridge and the next high ground to the west, a narrow valley led down past Point 569 and Point 444 almost to the rear walls of the Monastery. It was planned to send 7th

Brigade's Reconnaissance Squadron and a troop of American tanks through this gap as a filibuster with intent to cause confusion. Should the surprise be complete, it might even be possible for the tanks to make their way into the Monastery by the back door at a time when the defenders were fully occupied with 5th Brigade's frontal attack.

The enemy was well aware of the massive nature of the assault to come. After the February fighting, Fifteenth Panzer Grenadier Division had been withdrawn, to be replaced by the pride of the German Army, First German Parachute Division. These troops represented the élite of fanatical Nazi manhood. They had been trained never to lose cohesiveness nor the will to resist. If isolated or abandoned, man by man they fought to the death. They were Hitler's chosen warriors, imbued with outstanding *esprit de corps* and energy.

Their commander, General Richard Heidrich, was an intensified counterpart of his men. Of great physical courage, he was ruthless and not overnice in observing the usages of war. In an order before arrival at Cassino, Heidrich announced that he would hold commanding officers "personally responsible" for the success of the defence. His treatment of senior commanders who did not please him was sufficiently severe to endear him to the rank and file. Not that their lives mattered to him. An ambiguously worded but grim order, issued soon after arrival, implied that his men must regard themselves as more expendable than their mules, since a shortage of animals existed.

Seven battalions of paratroopers held Monastery Hill and Cassino Town, with the other three battalions in reserve at Monte Castellone. One hundred and eighty enemy guns covered this narrow front. High angle weapons were sown thickly in the hills behind the Monastery, including a number of "Nebelwerfers", devilish multiple mortars operated by remote control. The Luftwaffe was on tentacle, should the defence require air support.

On March 14th the German intercept service may have been puzzled by a pick-up. "Bradman will be batting to-morrow," it said. That night New Zealanders withdrew from Cassino Town. At 0830 hours next morning, the air attack went in. Three hundred and thirty-eight heavy bombers and one hundred and seventy-six mediums dropped one thousand one hundred tons of bombs. Cassino town crumbled under the devastating hail. A battalion of Third Parachute Regiment is believed to have died almost to a man under the ruins. On the stroke of noon the air onslaught ceased, and massed artillery crashed into action. Behind the barrage 6th New Zealand Infantry Brigade moved to the assault.

Four hours later, after bitter and fluctuating fighting, Castle Hill was captured. The New Zealanders continued down the slopes into Cassino Town. As dusk fell, 1/4 Essex, leading 5th Indian Brigade, took over from the Kiwis on Castle Hill and began to fan out on the hillside above the town. One company reached and secured Point 165, the first hairpin bend in the road which climbed to the Monastery. A sapper officer and his sergeant on reconnaissance penetrated as far as the rear of the Continental Hotel strongpoint, and after a series of gangster shooting matches returned with information which suggested that enemy defences on the hill were anything but airtight. The battle had opened auspiciously.

Behind the fighting line, however, fortune had failed the Indians. 1/6 Rajputana Rifles were pressing forward to support the Essex when enemy defensive fire caught them, inflicting many casualties. The night was impenetrably dark, with a thin, soaking rain. Except for the crash of shells on Cassino Town there was little guide to direction. The Rajputanas reached the outskirts to find that under the air bombardment the streets had disappeared. Only masses of rubble and tottering walls stood where a town had been; from deep hide-outs snipers and tommy-gunners crept to blaze at the passing sections from point-blank range. Two companies of Rajputanas made their way through the Castle and joined the Essex at Point 165. The other two companies had been dispersed and were withdrawn from action. An unlucky shell crashed into battalion headquarters and all officers present, including Colonel West and his adjutant, became casualties. Next morning the two forward companies which had reached the Castle, under Major Scaife, were merged into the 4/6 battalion under Colonel Scott.

At 0130 hours Colonel Nangle, commanding 1/9 Gurkhas, came forward to ascertain the position. Finding the Rajputanas to be short of their objectives, he sent two companies to reinforce the attack. Before reaching the Castle, "D" company bumped an enemy group armed with automatic weapons, and lost 15 men within a minute. "C" Company under Captain Drinkall was luckier, reached the Castle, passed through and disappeared across the hillside into the night, seeking the battle.

Thus of the three battalions of 5th Brigade, only two companies of Essex (the other companies being part of the garrison of the Castle), two companies of Rajputanas, and one company of Gurkhas managed to reach the battlefield. Having helped the Essex to consolidate at Point 165, the Rajputanas at 0245 hours moved against Point 236, the next hairpin bend higher up the hillside. Much hung on the capture of this position. Except for the Monastery it was the last strongpoint which gave observation on to the roads to the north along which the attacking troops must advance. It dominated the slopes of Monastery Hill in both directions and could bring flanking fire to bear on any forces which endeavoured to pass below or to climb above it. This valuable position was found to be strongly held. When the Rajputanas had closed to within 150 yards, a blaze of small arms fire swept the slope. The attack broke down and it was necessary to withdraw to the Castle and to reorganize before renewing the assault.

Dawn broke on a wild scene. The New Zealanders, like the Indians, found the air bombardment to have been too thorough. Huge craters had filled with rainwater, and with the streets obliterated the Kiwi armour could not break in to mop up. Those paratroopers who had lived through emerged from their shelters full of fight. A battle on the Stalingrad model developed. Bombers and snipers laboriously cleared a few yards at a time. On the hillside above the town the Essex and Rajputana Rifles experienced equal difficulty in establishing a perimeter around Castle Hill. Every shattered wall, every cellar window, harboured a paratrooper. Of "C" company of the Gurkhas there was neither sight nor sound. They had gone into the blue and were off the map. It seemed fantastic that a complete company could disappear on a few acres of hillside.

Full daylight revealed the paramount importance of Point 236, the upper hairpin bend. At 0830 hours the Rajputanas drew together for a second try for this key position. The artillery laid down a smokescreen, and the gallant Indians dashed uphill. Once again the attack broke down in the face of overwhelming fire. Fate was against this fine battalion which had fought with conspicuous success from Eritrea onwards.

Throughout the morning, both in Cassino Town and on the hillside, sudden gusts of fighting broke out from time to time, as New Zealanders and Indians, seeking to consolidate their positions, stumbled on stubborn pockets of resistance. Progress was slow, and the battle seemed to drag, when shortly after noon came electrifying news. Corps artillery had asked if it was safe to lay a shoot on Hangman's Hill. The New Zealanders reported that they could see figures around the outcrop, and a little later a faint wireless message came through. The lost company of 1/9 Gurkhas was firmly established on the crest. By one of those freaks of fortune which so often altered history, Captain Drinkall and his men had threaded their way past two battles in the darkness, passing along the narrowest of corridors between the fighting at the hairpin bends and the strong point of Continental Hotel. Across the rocky slopes the Gurkhas worked steadily forward, clambering silently and weaving their way through a maze of defences. They were unsupported and alone in the midst of the enemy. An hour before dawn they scrambled up the last few hundred yards, flung themselves at the crest, and secured only a less prize than the Monastery itself.

This exciting success made it imperative that whatever the risk this gallant company must be supplied and reinforced. Three principal obstacles stood in the way—the northern hairpin bends which the Rajputanas had twice failed to take, the Continental Hotel strongpoint above Cassino Town, and Point 202, a kopje-like knoll near the lowest southern switchback. For supplies to traverse the hillside, they must pass within one hundred and fifty yards of the first two positions before turning directly up the hillside with Point 202 on the flank. It was essential to neutralize these menaces before the lower slopes of Monastery Hill could be controlled.

The New Zealanders undertook to stage an attack that would keep the garrison of Continental Hotel out of the picture. The other obstacles were to be Indian responsibilities. Two companies of Rajputana Rifles would sally from the Castle for the third attack on the upper hairpin bend. The other two companies, with the remaining three companies of 1/9 Gurkhas, would head for Hangman's Hill. Approaching Point 202, the Rajputanas would be detached either to storm or to mask that strongpoint, while the Gurkhas passed through to their objective.

At 1900 hours the evening erupted in smoke and flame as the Indians above and the New Zealanders below swept to the assault. After three hours of stiff fighting, the Rajputanas had carried the upper hairpin bend, although a redoubt above it still held out. Similarly the New Zealand thrust, while not securing Continental Hotel, had engrossed its defenders. At 2000 hours the Gurkhas and the remaining Rajputana companies debouched from the Castle on their perilous passage. With heavy fighting within three hundred yards on either side the Indians gingerly picked their way forward. A bright moon gave a feeling of nakedness to the men who ventured between the crocodile's jaws. As the Gurkhas passed below Point 165 they came under fire from ground supposedly cleansed of the enemy—probably from an enemy party seeking to infiltrate around the flanks of the Rajputanas' assault higher up the slopes. Continental Hotel was negotiated safely, but after turning up the hillside, the Rajputanas lost touch. The Gurkhas plodded steadily upwards, and before dawn reached their comrades of "C" company on the crest of Hangman's Hill. Here they deployed, and only just in time; for as they spread out with "B" Company on the right, "C" and "D" companies on the platform around the gallows, and "A" Company astride the road on the left, a sharp unheralded counter-attack swept down from the Monastery. Fortunately it struck at the centre of the position. The paratroopers charged into a cone of fire, and fell back in disorder.

Similarly at first light a strong force of Germans came leaping down the hillside upon the newly won upper hairpin bend. These reinforcements threw the hard-fighting Rajputanas back on the lower switchback at Point 165. The morning "sitrep" (situation report) therefore was the customary compound of good and bad. None of the three obstacles had been neutralized, but three additional companies of Gurkhas had filtered through to provide a substantial garrison for Hangman's Hill.

The immediate problem was to supply this garrison. It was now forty-eight hours since "C" company had arrived on Hangman's Hill with a day's rations and filled waterbottles. There was no sign of lessening resistance in Cassino Town: on the contrary, there was evidence that the German commander had now charted the course of the attack, and had recognized the Castle Hill re-entrant to be the critical sector of the battlefield. During the forenoon of March 18th an obstinate series of enemy infiltrations began to establish a cordon around Castle Hill. From broken houses on the upper fringe of the town these groups blazed at any parties which endeavoured to sally from the Castle or to traverse the hillside. Every supply column must run the gauntlet. Even the Castle gate was brought under harassing fire. A state of siege began.

That evening a field company of Sappers and Miners with an Indian pioneer company as porters assembled behind Castle Hill laden with supplies. A strong escort of 4/6 Rajputana Rifles covered the carriers. Soon after leaving the forward dumps the supply column came under fire. It was midnight when the Castle was reached. Ahead the hillside was awake and bickering. It was too risky to take porters further, so the Rajputanas shouldered as many loads as possible and set off across the fire-swept slopes. Well aware of what was under way, the enemy threw a strong raid at Point 165, only two hundred yards above the line of passage of the supply party. Two companies of 1/6 Rajputanas broke up this incursion while their comrades trudged past below them. The tail of the carrier column was caught in a mortar concentration, badly mauled and disorganized, losing a portion of the supplies. The remainder doggedly plodded on to reach Hangman's Hill shortly before dawn. It was impossible to return during daylight, so the Rajputanas settled down among the Gurkhas in an exposed position, intensifying the shortage of supplies and overcrowding the limited expanse of dead ground.

March 18th passed sullenly, with venomous outbursts of fighting among Cassino rubble heaps and along the Rapido. The gunners had swathed the base of Monastery Hill in a mantle of smoke, to assist the New Zealand sappers who laboured on the bridge sites. Enemy mortar fire was incessant, with occasional salvos from heavy guns, probably eight-inch howitzers. The area below the Castle became more and more thickly infested with enemy snipers and bomb squads. From a strong point in a conspicuous twin towered building, the paratroopers worked upwards to constrict the bottleneck and to cut the flow of men and supplies on to the hillside. (It seems probable that while the Gurkhas were feeling their way through the German defences on the previous night, paratroopers had crept down in similar fashion from the Monastery by way of a ravine to the north of Castle Hill, and had reinforced the pestiferous pockets along the outskirts of the town).

THE SECOND ASSAULT FAILS

With the Castle closely invested, arrangements were made for an air dropping on Hangman's Hill. On the afternoon of March 19th forty-eight aircraft delivered containers of food, water and ammunition. The mark was so small and the slopes so steep that although the dropping was accurate, many of the containers bounced down the hillside out of reach of the Gurkhas. Sufficient supplies were retrieved to support the garrison on restricted rations.

At nightfall the battle reopened in Castle Hill area. The Essex prepared to extend the perimeter, supported by New Zealand tanks. Unfortunately the angle of fire resulted in a number of "overs" from the tank cannon which crashed through the walls of the Castle, burying Home Countymen who had formed up for the attack. From hideouts along the hillside fixed weapons constantly hosed the Castle gateway with small arms fire, so that the Essex could only move in and out singly and at the double. In spite of such difficulties preparations for renewal of the assault continued. A company of the Machine Gun Battalion of Rajputana Rifles made a trip to Hangman's Hill unmolested. The company of 1/6 Rajputanas which had spent the day with the Gurkhas returned to the Castle carrying wounded and bore back a load of supplies. Towards midnight 4/6 Rajputanas arrived to relieve the Essex, who were ordered to proceed before dawn to stiffen 1/9 Gurkhas for the final assault on the Monastery summit. In the last hours of darkness two companies of the British battalion began to move across the hillside while the third and fourth companies were in process of being relieved at the lower hairpin bend and in the Castle.

In retrospect the optimism of these plans appears surprising. With perfect observation the enemy could scarcely fail to follow the Indian moves. The situation around Castle Hill was steadily deteriorating. The Germans waited for the right moment, and as night thinned in the east, a battalion of First German Parachute Regiment doubled down the spur from the Monastery, lunging for Castle Hill. The companies of Rajputanas and Essex, engaged in relief at the hairpin bend, were overrun and destroyed. The attack swept on against the Castle itself and reached the walls. Quick and resolute action by the garrison companies stemmed the rush. Major Beckett of the Essex, although twice wounded, and Major Oswald of 1 Field Regiment, like knightly defenders of old, lined the walls with their men, exchanging showers of grenades and bursts of tommygun fire at point blank range. A paratroop prisoner in the castle courtyard watched this exciting clash with a professional eye. When his comrades fell back baffled he congratulated Major Beckett on a most soldierly performance and in token of his appreciation presented the Essex officer with his fur-lined paratrooper gauntlets. For once the enemy's timing was faulty. Apparently the Germans had planned to attack simultaneously from above and below, but the paratroopers were late on their start line in the outskirts of the town. By 0800 hours the assault from above had been driven to ground, while the threat from below did not develop until an hour later. Confused fighting followed with the Castle garrison imprisoned by enemy fire control of the gateway. Another section of the Castle wall collapsed, burying twenty men and two officers. An equal misfortune was the loss of Colonel Noble, who had led the Essex throughout years of hard fighting in Western Desert and Tunisia. He fell to a sniper's bullet. Protective concentrations of mortar and machine-gun fire, supplied by the Indians on the western approaches, and by New Zealanders along the southern wall of the Castle, finally discouraged and dispersed the paratroopers.

Broad day caught two companies of Essex on the way to Hangman's Hill, crossing the open hillside. From above the battle they watched the attack go in on their comrades below. As they pressed up the slopes to join the Gurkhas they came under heavy fire and sustained serious casualties, reaching their destination in badly mauled condition. It was apparent that they were in no shape to join in the final assault. At this juncture the seriousness of the situation in the Castle area imposed a new ordeal upon them. No sooner had they reached Hangman's Hill than it was decided to withdraw them. Having been marched forward, that evening they were marched back. The enemy was on the alert and beat up the luckless groups as they filtered past his strongpoints. Only a handful regained the shelter of the Castle while others returned to Hangman's Hill. As a cohesive force the battalion had ceased to exist, and it was withdrawn from the fighting. 6th Royal West Kents was borrowed from Seventy-Eighth British Division to take over the Essex commitments.

The frontal assault consequently was postponed until the Kentish men could reach the Gurkhas, but for some reason the filibuster in the rear of Snake's Head Ridge was allowed to proceed. Two columns, one consisting of 3 Sherman and 21 Light tanks and the other of 16 Shermans, together with 7th Brigade's Reconnaissance Squadron, penetrated the low valley which ran down from the north-west. A track was discovered that was tankable, and both columns by-passed Point 569 without difficulty. At first it seemed possible that the feint might be turned into a mortal blow. An agitated enemy message reported to Wehrmacht headquarters that eight tanks had broken through the defences and that an infantry attack from the rear might be anticipated. By 1020 hours the progress of the column was so encouraging that Corps and Divisional commanders agreed that should the tank force bring the Monastery under effective fire, the forces on Hangman's Hill would attack forthwith.

Unfortunately the enemy had over-estimated the threat. The only trail was narrow, the ground on both sides rough and steep. The

THE SECOND ASSAULT FAILS 59

Shermans were obliged to advance in single file. The leading tank struck a mine and brewed up. Enemy gunners found the range. The column commander asked for sappers, and indicated delays. In the hope that smaller tanks would make better progress, the Shermans withdrew, leaving the lighter armour to continue into the enemy positions. Some penetration was effected, but there was not enough weight behind the punch. When a dozen tanks had been knocked out, the expedition was abandoned.

Thus when night fell on March 19th, the battle had reached a stalemate in which the initiative was veering towards the enemy. The utmost efforts of the New Zealanders had failed to clear Cassino Town. (As illustrative of the difficulties of this task, a New Zealand officer was obliged to ask 26th Indian Advanced Dressing Station to withdraw from its cellar shelters while his tanks blasted enemy machine-gun nests on the upper floors of the same building). On Hangman's Hill 1/9 Gurkhas were perched under the walls of the Monastery without the strength to thrust home. Below them a New Zealand force was similarly isolated at Point 202. Further north the much battered Continental Hotel still held out. At the Castle, every effort to dyke the vital corridor had failed, and the enemy now controlled the traffic. Allied armour had intervened and had been frustrated. Neither the Air nor the artillery could bring its weight to bear because the forces were inextricably intermingled; shells and bombs menaced friends as well as foes. The artillery observation officer with the Gurkhas on Hangman's Hill, with a nice sense of humour, recorded in his diary the results of an endeavour to neutralize enemy observation posts on Monastery Hill.

"The smoke nuisance now became acute," he wrote. "Our shelling continued throughout the afternoon with such accuracy that the Gurkha commander's sangar received three direct hits with the shell itself. Attempts by the battery commander, urged by the Gurkha C.O., to shift the target became abusive but fruitless. Relations in all directions assumed an atmosphere of strain. The galling aspect of the whole business was that the smoke so placed screened nothing from nobody."

On March 19th a Corps conference reviewed the battle. It came to the inevitable conclusion that the attack *à l'outrance* must be abandoned in favour of the achievement of a series of objectives. First in priority came the protection and provisioning of the Gurkhas on Hangman's Hill. The Air took over this task, and no further attempts were made to porter supplies overland. There followed a realistic reassessment of the situation around Castle Hill. It was evident that the enemy proposed to protect the Monastery by deploying his utmost strength against the bottleneck, and that this area constituted the key sector. Until the Germans were contained and discouraged from their persistent interference with this corridor, it was futile to carry the battle further.

In pursuance of this decision, it was decided to widen the sallyport by recapture of Point 165, at the lower hairpin bend. In conjunction with this operation 7th Brigade would mount an assault in a new direction, by traversing the reverse or northern slopes of the ridge above the Castle, in order to seize Point 445, where Snake's Head Ridge merges into the main crest. Royal West Kents were given the first of these tasks, and 2/7 Gurkhas of 11th Indian Brigade entrusted with the second operation.

When dark fell on March 20th two companies of the Royal West Kents slipped out of the Castle, leaving the remaining companies as garrison. As the infantry filtered forward towards their start line a heavy explosion, whose origin is still unknown, shook the hillside, inflicting many casualties on the leading company, and preventing its deployment. The survivors were recalled into the shelter of the Castle, and reorganised; by 0330 hours they were ready to set out anew. The enemy unfortunately detected the activity. His spandau teams audaciously crept up the hillside until they covered the Castle gate in a crescent, continuously playing streams of bullets against the entrance. The paratroopers were in sufficient strength to seal up the Castle, and the Royal West Kents were obliged to abandon their attack.

Nor was the attack against Point 445 more successful. A company of 2/7 Gurkhas hammered at this objective for two hours, until rising casualties made it evident that a stronger force must be employed. The infantry attack was then abandoned, and an artillery group raked this area with a heavy shoot for the remainder of the night.

It was characteristic of the intensity and confusion of the fighting that while Royal West Kents and Gurkhas were being repelled by resolute German defenders, other parties of the enemy should move to the attack in the same area. Thrust and counter-thrust occurred within a few hundred yards of each other. Behind Castle Hill, and below the area of the Gurkha attack, companies of 2/7 Gurkhas and of 4/6 Rajputana Rifles beat back an audacious attempt to cut the main supply route from the north. To the west, where perhaps only 500 yards separated Castle Hill from the hairpin bends, another group of German paratroopers infiltrated in an endeavour to link up with the machine-gunners who commanded the Castle gate from the ruined fringes of the town. The boldness and offensive spirit displayed in these repeated efforts to block entry to and exit from the glacis of Monastery Hill, made it evident that defensive measures must be given priority. On the morning of March 21st it was determined by the aid of mines and wire to construct a safe lane between the Castle and the Divisional supply dumps in the upper Rapido Valley. 5th and 7th Brigades were entrusted with this task.

THE SECOND ASSAULT FAILS

From his unequalled observation post on the crest of Monastery Hill, General Heidrich detected the move. Like the Indians and New Zealanders he too had almost reached the limit of his resources. The bitter hurly-burly had depleted his battalions, yet in typical ruthless fashion he decided upon a last bid. He armed his engineers as infantry; at dawn on March 22nd this improvised force plunged downhill in an attempt to carry the Castle by storm. The garrison was alert, and the gunners across the valley were standing to when the rush came. Heavy defensive fire crashed on the slopes above the Castle. The attack disintegrated, leaving the hillside strewn with dead and wounded. Thirty shaken prisoners remained in Indian hands.

Both adversaries were fought out. Fourth Indian Division had lost four thousand men. In Cassino Town the New Zealanders, after stupendous efforts, had reduced the enemy foothold to a narrow wedge; the wedge remained impregnable. It was sadly evident that Castle Hill and every strongpoint were but steps on the road. High above the Monastery towered on its crest, and there the enemy was still secure. No intermediate gain promised to dislodge him. On March 23rd the offensive was abandoned.

The next problem was to get back the Gurkhas from Hangman's Hill. Since the first attempt to overrun them the Germans had intended to ignore this force. However, as day followed day short rations and wintry weather weakened even the tough Nepalese, and as no reinforcements could go forward the companies steadily shrank in strength. Communications presented a tricky problem. The batteries of the battalion's radio sets had run down, and out of fifty replacements dropped by parachute, only four fell within the perimeter. The Germans were closely piqueting the approaches and it was deemed unwise to pass any messages which might be intercepted, interpreted or deciphered. 5th Brigade therefore called upon volunteer officers from each battalion who would commit detailed instructions to memory and would afterwards attempt to reach Hangman's Hill. On the night of March 23/24 Lieutenant Mallinson of the Essex, Captain Norman of the Gurkhas, and Lieutenant Jenkins of the Rajputanas, each with a carrier pigeon, left Castle Hill at half-hourly intervals. Before dawn Lieutenant Mallinson and Captain Norman had reached Hangman's Hill, where they delivered to Colonel Nangle the instructions for withdrawal. (The code word for this operation was "Roche", somewhat to the indignation of the older officers of the battalion, since it was the name of a former commanding officer who had never withdrawn from any position). The signal was radioed at 1220 hours on March 24th; when dark fell that evening the evacuation began. Deceptions and distractions of the enemy were carried out in the form of artillery concentrations on Monastery Hill, a Royal West Kent raid from the Castle, and a series of feint attacks by the New Zealanders in Cassino

THE BATTLEFIELD

JUNCTION RAPIDO AND LIRI VALLEYS

MONASTERY BOMBARDMENT

VESUVIUS BOMBARDMENT

FROM SNAKE'S HEAD

FROM POINT 445

AIR DROPPING—HANGMAN'S HILL

CASSINO SHAMBLES

Town. The enemy cordon on the hillside failed to interrupt the withdrawal. After eight days of ordeal, ten officers and two hundred and forty-seven other ranks came to safety. The same night the New Zealand company on Point 202 was withdrawn.

Military experts will scan the records of this battle for years to come, and doubtless will argue whether any direct attack on Cassino and Monastery Hill could have succeeded. Certainly in the light of what occurred two months later, it must be considered that the operation planned to destroy the enemy in the hard way. To those who were only conversant with the Cassino battle, it appeared from the beginning that the incredible difficulties of a direct assault upon this mountain fastness had been underrated. The Allied High Command, who were in a position to co-ordinate the necessities of all parts of the United Nations fronts, were perhaps aware of considerations which made it essential to persevere with the assault. It is now known that amphibious landings on a major scale had been planned for both coasts of Italy. It is likewise known that the situation in the Anzio bridgehead was desperate. Like Haig's fearful campaign in the Ypres salient in 1917, the tactical failure of Cassino probably will be re-appreciated in the light of its strategical necessity.

Thus after six weeks of almost unequalled strain and privation the ordeal of the fighting men of Fourth Indian Division ended in sad failure. Nor was it only the infantry which bore the burden of this sombre battle. The complete personnel of the Division shared the dangers and disappointments. The gunners who endured fierce shoots in their cramped lines, the porters who crossed and re-crossed the fire-swept slopes of Monastery Hill, the signallers who laid and followed the wires by night and day in an endeavour to keep communications open, the provosts who policed the supply routes for twenty-four hours daily under unremitting bombardment, the sappers and transport services who struggled equally against the obstinate terrain and the malice of the enemy—all these men paid the price in blood. Deeds of gallantry abounded everywhere. During preparations for the second attack, an act of unsurpassed bravery and self-sacrifice brought pride to Fourth Division. A British officer was trapped in a mine-field. Subedar Subramanyan of Madras Sappers and Miners with five other ranks undertook to clear a path to him. One of the sappers trod on a shrapnel mine—a fiendish device which springs from the ground breast high before spraying steel balls in all directions. In the four seconds which elapsed before the mine sprang, Subedar Subramanyan threw himself upon it and absorbed the full force of the burst. His self-sacrifice was recognised by the posthumous award of the George Cross.

During this bitter and difficult battle the work of the Medical Services rose to fresh heights of achievement. Wherever men fell, aid and comfort came to them. It is pleasing to record that during the Cassino fighting the enemy usually respected the Red Cross flag, although on one occasion, for some queer reason, when the Germans had asked for an armistice to pick up their wounded, their snipers refused to observe it. Stretcher parties and First Aid groups moved on their errands of mercy, and although sometimes stopped by enemy sentries and patrols, were usually allowed to proceed.

When the Gurkhas were isolated on Hangman's Hill, two medical orderlies of the Essex Regiment, Lance-Corporal Edmond Hazle, D.C.M., and Lance-Corporal Leonard Piper, remained to take charge of the wounded. For eight days they treated all casualties from the slender resources of a first aid haversack. Major operations and even amputations were performed by Hazle with no other instruments than scissors and pocket-knife. This gallant man, who had won the D.C.M. at El Alamein for rescuing a wounded sepoy, now received the immediate award of a bar to his decoration.

Baz Mir, a dhobi washerman of camp follower category, from whom combatant services were not expected, volunteered to serve as a stretcher bearer when casualties had depleted the field ambulance detachments. He crossed a minefield under heavy fire, and pushed through to Hangman's Hill. Next day he volunteered again, and although intercepted by an enemy post, was allowed to proceed. His award of the Indian Distinguished Service Medal was alike a tribute to his bravery and a portent of the new India to come, in which merit will surmount the barriers of caste.

Naik Mohammed Yusef, I.O.M., I.D.S.M., a Moslem from Rawalpindi, organized the evacuation of wounded along a track from Castle Hill which was systematically swept by artillery and mortar fire. He was afterwards presented to the King Emperor, who complimented him on his bravery. Naik Babu Raju, a Hindu from Madras, gained the Military Medal for tending wounded in the open with utmost contempt for danger. These instances of gallant behaviour by Britons and Indians of diverse creeds are illustrative of the spirit of all ranks of the Indian Medical Services.

When the wounded had been carried, slowly and painfully, down the tracks over the escarpment, they found ambulances waiting beside the Rapido. Many of these ambulances were driven by tall young men of the American Field Service. This remarkable organization some day may publish its own history, but in view of its long association with the Indian forces, it is essential to record the admiration of all ranks for these volunteers. They had first arrived in Syria in 1941—college men predominating, but with a sprinkling of professional men too old for military service, as well as artists and adventurers. In the Western desert they became known to all. Field Ambulance commanders before battles would speculate and entertain high hopes concerning the number of American ambulances which might be allotted to them.

The Americans themselves would scramble for the most dangerous and unpleasant jobs. In their work they exhibited the courage of lions and the tenderness of women. A doctor who daily traversed the evacuation route across the Rapido Valley, a distance of five miles, wrote as follows:—

"The river crossing—Windy Corner—received an unhealthy amount of shelling. Jeeps did not tarry there. Yet in full daylight, an American volunteer halted his ambulance, rescued a wounded man, dressed his wounds, took him to the advance dressing station under continuous fire, and classified it as 'all in the day's work'. Another driver lost his ambulance when a near miss ditched it, but continued on foot and brought in four Indians under a hail of fire. Day and night, and non-stop if necessary, these American boys would carry on. They could always be trusted to get through, no matter how sticky the situation."

Another Indian Army doctor wrote :—

"The unfailing courage, supreme devotion to duty and unquenchable good spirit of these civilians in battle dress, along with their constant thought of the welfare and comfort of the wounded, inspired all with whom they came in contact. Our Medical Services, many thousands of British and Empire wounded, and the people at home who wait for their loved ones, all owe to the American Field Service a debt of gratitude which cannot be measured in words."

(It is interesting to note that a number of these attractive young men, as a result of their contact with Indian forces, abandoned even their documentary neutrality and accepted commissions in Indian regiments. One of them, a man of many adventures, is now adjutant of a Frontier Force Regiment battalion).

Enemy press and radio burst into panegyrics when such famous and doughty opponents as the New Zealanders and Fourth Indian Division admitted failure. Even the Wehrmacht Army Commander, in an order to his troops, allowed colour to creep in. He compared the "orange trees blossoming on the Tyrrhenian Coast" with the "blizzards which rage two thousand metres up on the Cassino heights". He recommended Major-General Baade of Fifteenth Panzer Grenadier Division, and General Heidrich of First Parachute Division, for priority in the Fuehrer's favour.

Among the troops of the United Nations, a gunner officer expressed the characteristic view:—

"There is a fierce chagrin that the two best divisions in the British Army, forming a corps that seemed a perfect combination, should have achieved nothing."

The disappointment of friends, like the vaunts of the enemy, alike had less than fifty days to live.

CHAPTER SEVEN

EIGHTH DIVISION PUNCHES THE HOLE

SEVENTY-EIGHTH BRITISH DIVISION completed the relief of Fourth Indian Division on the hillside above Cassino town on the night of March 27/28th. The battered Indians took the road back to the Adriatic. The winter storms abated, the sun grew in warmth, and a false calm reigned along the Central Italian battle front as spring came out of the south.

Spring was the architect who planned the battle to come. The casual observer, in examining the topography of Cassino, is bound to wonder why Allied High Command chose to storm a wellnigh impregnable mountain when a broad valley on its flank invited advance. Unfortunately the easy ground of the Liri Valley offered a false lure. Under winter conditions tracks and wheels would have churned the greasy clays sodden with rainwater into a morass. The problem of advance along a valley as completely commanded as Monastery Hill commanded the Liri, required that the attack should punch a hole with the utmost expedition, and should by-pass the dominating heights without delay. Winter could promise nothing but obstacles to a programme dependent upon speed of movement. This picture changed when the ground began to dry, when rivers and streams declined to constant flow, and on roads and tracks the mud turned into dust. Then bridges no longer would disappear overnight before a spate of storm water; aircraft would not be grounded on their strips, nor tanks bogged down in their leaguers. The great Allied superiority in weapons then could be utilized to strike a devastating blow.

It has been recorded in an earlier chapter that when winter ended, Fifth Corps of Eighth Army, consisting of two Indian divisions, contained and harassed at least its own number of enemies on the Adriatic front. On the opposite side of Italy, Fifth Army was engaged in two desperate battles—one to hold the Anzio bridgehead and the other to relieve it by an advance from the south. It was apparent that Eighth Army, with five corps available for operations in Central Italy, was in the better position to undertake the new campaign. The beginning of May found four of these corps concentrated in the Cassino area.

The Liri Valley is from four to seven miles in width. It is flanked by parallel mountain ranges bearing into the north-west. Opposite the Monte Cairo-Cassino massif, the forbidding limestone masses of the Arunci range rise into a rocky promontory which gradually falls away towards the Roman plain. The river Gari, as the Rapido is known below Cassino Town, crosses the bottom of this valley. The river Liri flows to the south-east along the foothills of the Arunci. The apex of land enclosed between the confluence of these rivers, six miles south of Cassino, is known as the "Liri Appendix".

From the Appendix the Liri valley extends into the north-west for twenty miles, narrowing gradually between the undulating and well-wooded foothills of the flanking ranges. At Arce, Route 6 turns west, heading for Rome. Route 82 continues to the north through Central Italy. A few miles beyond Arce, at Frosinone, another main road leaves Route 6 and runs northward through the mountains, parallel to Route 82. At the top of the Liri Valley, therefore, there were three main road systems available for advance. This circumstance made it necessary for the enemy to block this corridor at all costs.

The Gustav Line defences south of Cassino Town followed the line of the west bank of the Gari, and after its confluence with the Liri, the line of the Garigliano, as the joint stream is named. A subsidiary switch line, known as the Adolf Hitler defences, was anchored into the Arunci spurs seven miles west of the Gari. It crossed the valley from Pontecorvo to Aquino, climbed the Cassino massif through the villages of Piedemonte and Villa San Lucia, and merged into the Gustav Line at Monte Cairo. These two lines were in fact one defence system, since the whole of the intervening countryside was dotted with strong points. The Forme d'Aquino, a straggling stream of some ten to thirty yards in width, crossed the Liri Valley between the lines. Its marshy approaches and deep cut banks had been heavily fortified. In addition, an anti-tank ditch consisting of a series of craters filled with surface water, had been incorporated in the defence scheme. On both sides of these water barriers extensive mine-fields had been laid, covered by belts of wire twenty feet in depth. The general plan of fortifications consisted of an intricate grid of local strongpoints positioned for mutual support. An outpost zone screened the mine-fields and water barriers, comprising great numbers of semi-mobile dug-in pillboxes, each with a crew of two machine-gunners. Behind these outposts came a belt of reinforced concrete emplacements and weapon pits, linked by tunnels and communication trenches. At the anti-tank nodal points groups of Panther turrets were anchored to concrete bases, with living quarters for the crews underground. The turret guns had all-round traverse and were supported by anti-tank artillery echeloned on the flanks. The Panthers were intended to take the shock, the mobile guns to deal with any attempt to by-pass them.

Infantry was accommodated in deep shelters twenty feet underground, with concrete roofs five feet thick. Such dug-outs were proof against the heaviest bombardment.

Construction of Adolf Hitler defences had begun during the previous winter, when the threat to the Gustav Line became evident. The fortifications, however, had never been completed; although formidable obstacles they lived to some extent on their name. (It is interesting to record that when a major attack became imminent, Berlin immediately re-christened this system the "Dora" Line). On the whole the engineering was not up to German standards. Many emplacements were sunk below crop level so that even the early growth blinded them. There were gaps in the anti-tank ditch. In several other respects the switch line had an "Ersatz" air about it.

A greater weakness lay in the garrison. For some extraordinary reason German High Command maintained sparse forces in this obviously important sector. When Eighth Army prepared to attack, only Fifteenth Panzer Grenadier Division, which had been roughly handled in Fourth Indian Division's assault on Cassino, held the Liri Valley and provided garrisons for the fortifications both of Gustav and Adolf Hitler Lines. On a front of seven miles troops so thin on the ground invited assault in strength and depth, with a view to a sudden brutal rupture of the position. It was this type of attack that Eighth Army had decided to launch when spring came.

Of the four corps available Tenth British Corps was deployed on a wide front north of Cassino with no other function than demonstration and deception. Next came Second Polish Corps, for whom a daring and ambitious operation was contemplated. It may be remembered that in the earlier assault upon Cassino a force of armour under the command of 7th Indian Brigade had exploited a passage through the hills into tankable terrain at the rear of Monastery Hill. Polish divisions were now ordered to crash through this narrow corridor, storm the Monastery from behind, and thereafter to descend into the Liri Valley to effect a junction with Thirteenth British Corps advancing from the line of the Gari. The latter Corps, four divisions strong, would strike the main blow in a frontal smash at the Gustav Line. If a hole was punched on the Gari, a combined thrust by Polish and British Corps was designed to break through the Adolf Hitler system. First Canadian Corps would remain in Army reserve to assist or to exploit, according to the course of the battle.

Thirteenth British Corps held the seven miles between Cassino Town and the Liri Appendix, and planned to attack with Fourth British Division on the right and Eighth Indian Division on the left. Seventy-Eighth British Division would remain in reserve to be used either for an advance along the foothills of the Arunci mountains, or through gaps which might be broken in the Gustav Line. Sixth British Armoured Division likewise was held for the breakthrough and briefed for pursuit when a breach had been established.

On the relief of Eighth Indian Division in the Adriatic sector early in April, 21st Indian Brigade crossed the mountains and took over from 2nd Independent Parachute Brigade in Cassino Town. Ten days later, 17th and 19th Brigades moved to a training area along the Volturno river, twenty miles south of Cassino. Here they met is

Canadian Armoured Brigade, comrades of the Adriatic, and were overjoyed to learn that they would fight together in the battle to come. 17th Brigade was allotted 11th (Ontario) Armoured Regiment, and 19th Brigade 14th (Calgary) Armoured Regiment. Combined training followed in river crossings, the handling of assault craft, bridgement, and co-operation of infantry and armour in battle. At the beginning of May dress rehearsals ensued. Thereafter, 17th Brigade began to filter its units into the sector in which it was to attack. On May 6th, 19th Infantry Brigade came up on the left of 17th Brigade and took over the remainder of the Divisional front. 21st Brigade, having been relieved in Cassino Town, was brought into Divisional reserve. Eighth Indian Division was now ready for the curtain to rise.

During these preparations precautions were taken to lull the enemy and to cloak the stroke which he knew to be imminent. Only a thin screen of Indian troops occupied the forward positions. No movement of men or transport by day was permitted. Air reconnaissance was casual, artillery registration desultory. Tank squadrons ostentatiously lumbered away as if to reinforce the northern front. But each night, under the bright moon, many small parties stole forward to reconnoitre and to adjust details of the plan of battle.

The River Gari separated the adversaries on the entire Divisional front. It was about forty feet in width, six to eight feet in depth, and swiftly flowing. Meadows on both banks were marshy and intersected by numerous rhines and drainage ditches. Beyond the river, on the extreme right stood the tiny hamlet of San Angelo. Near this village the valley bottom was rolling and rugged, with many folds and hillocks. Two prominent knolls, one on each side of San Angelo, and a low escarpment along the secondary road from Cassino Town, constituted the principal relief features. For 3,000 yards the Gari flowed due south, but opposite Panaccioni the stream hooked sharply into the south-east. This bend, which created the neck of the Liri Appendix, caused the left flank sector of the Divisional front to face west instead of north. Here as at San Angelo the valley became rugged and the ground on the left rose sufficiently to afford observation.

It was evident that the heaviest resistance would be encountered on the flanks. General Russell's plan of battle called for three crossings— one on each brigade front and one for good measure and for exploitation. On the right, 17th Brigade would reduce San Angelo and give a firm flank to Fourth British Division. On the left, when 19th Brigade had broken into the enemy's positions one battalion would swing sharply into the south, amputating the Liri Appendix and trapping its defenders. Both flanks secure, the attack would drive frontally up the Liri Valley, with Pignataro, about three miles in advance of the start line, as the immediate objective. The San Angelo-Pignataro-Panaccioni area, when inked in on the map, is the shape of a horseshoe. The seizure of this horseshoe would complete the first phase of the battle.

On May 11th First Royal Fusiliers manned the line of the Gari on both sides of San Angelo. On their left, 1/12 Frontier Force Regiment took over. On 19th Brigade's front, 3/8 Punjabis occupied the centre of the line with 1st Argyll and Sutherland Highlanders as the left flank battalion of the Division. The balmy afternoon faded into fine evening. A waning moon was due to rise at 2300 hours. Among hedges, shrubs, and folds in the ground, the Indian infantry waited. The rising moon gave the signal, and 800 guns shattered the peace of the night. A storm of shell swept the Liri Valley, pounding enemy fortifications and artillery lines. Mortar teams sprang into action, raining their bombs on infantry concentration areas. Indication tracer swept overhead to give prearranged direction. Far on the left machine-guns and mortars of Seventy-Eighth British Division laid down a curtain of high angle fire on the Liri Appendix, to guard the flank of the Indian advance.

As the shoot went down, the meadowland to the east of the Gari suddenly became alive with men. Leading companies moved forward to the river bank. Among them staggered sappers under the weight of assault boats. Mules floundered over the dykes and drainage ditches, laden with machine-guns and ammunition. At 2345 hours the first assault boats were launched, and both brigades struck for the opposite bank. The shoot on the enemy back areas abruptly switched on to a tight barrage advancing from the bank of the Gari at the rate of 100 yards in every six minutes.

On the right of the assault, Royal Fusiliers crossed the river to the north of San Angelo with little difficulty and few casualties. German counter measures, however, had begun, and a slight ground mist was thickened by an enemy smoke screen which drifted down the Liri Valley. The mist and smoke, together with dust and cordite fumes, blended into a pea-soup fog that the Fusiliers' native London could not have bettered. The infantry could scarcely see their hands before their faces. They stumbled forward in single file, each man clinging to the bayonet scabbard of the man in front. With deep-cut muddy ditches to cross it was impossible to keep up with the barrage. In the blind fog it was equally impossible to keep in organized array. The moment that the barrage moved on, the stutter of German machine-guns began. Four hundred enemy field guns and groups of nebelwerfers opened, searching the approaches to the river.

By 0100 hours, the Fusiliers had pushed past San Angelo on the right, to find themselves hemmed in between the defences of the fortified village on one flank and "Platform" knoll on the other. No further advance was possible until these positions had been cleared. A considerable number of men had become detached in the fog, and it was necessary to reorganize. At 0200 hours the British troops dug in about 500 yards forward of the river.

On the left of the Fusiliers, 1/12 Frontier Force Regiment likewise had crossed the Gari without much difficulty. Once again the dense fog and the counter barrage made organization difficult, but by 0200 hours the Indians were deployed in front of "Bank" position, the low escarpment which lay along the lateral road. As they moved forward they stumbled over trip wires which when cut or pulled released additional smoke canisters, thickening the fog and giving German machine-gunners the line on which to lay their weapons. Many men fell dead or wounded. The Frontiersmen doggedly stumbled forward. "A" Company, closely followed by "D" Company, reached a belt of wire lining a mine-field on the approach to "Bank" position. A shower of grenades from outposts greeted them, and automatic weapons slashed the murk in all directions. With an impassable obstacle in front, both companies moved to the right and fought their way on to "Bank" position from the flank. On the left, "C" Company, by similar heroic efforts, reached the lateral road and destroyed the enemy outposts. All types of mechanical communication failed. The battalion commander instructed his officers to report their position by flares. The thick fog snuffed out the lights as soon as fired. Then the primitive device, succeeded—the Mussulman war cry of "Maro nari haidri-ya Ali!" rang above the din of battle and gave the commander pin-points for his positions. The first objectives had been taken.

With reserves standing ready 1/12 Frontier Force Rifles waited for dawn in order to push ahead. The mêlée, however, continued, as sometimes German posts, undetected under the blanket of fog, lay doggo in the midst of the Indians, opening fire from the rear and fighting to the last. Machine-gun fire from San Angelo traversed "Bank" position from time to time. Major Amar Singh, who had led his company in many a gallant action in Italy, was killed. Casualties thinned the ranks. "B" Company of the Frontiersmen was called up from reserve. By making clever use of folds in the ground it closed on the German garrisons of a series of dug-outs before they could emerge. This mopping-up ended immediate resistance, and a firm grip was established on the left flank approaches to San Angelo.

In terms of the original plan, the attack upon the village itself now could go in. 1/5 Gurkhas, however, unlike the other battalions of the Brigade, had encountered trouble in crossing the river. When the riflemen assembled on the far bank, twelve out of sixteen available assault boats had been sunk by shell or mortar fire. Pulling the remaining four boats back and forward along guide lines, the Gurkhas were ferried over in the next five hours. Two companies were despatched to the start line for the assault on San Angelo, while the others waited along the river for the order to advance.

Thus at dawn on May 12th all three battalions of 17th Brigade were across the Gari. Royal Fusiliers were pinned down between two fires, 1/12 Frontier Force Regiment had completed its task in the face of heavy resistance, and the 1/5 Gurkhas were standing by to enter the battle.

We must now pass along the line of attack to the left, and examine the fortunes of the 19th Brigade.

3/8 Punjabis, the right-hand battalion, had been ordered as a first task to secure the line of the lateral road, thereafter striking for Point 63, a pimple of land in the centre of the valley. As they moved up to the Gari, enemy defensive fire crashed on to their launching area, causing many casualties. Undeterred, "A" and "B" Companies embarked and pushed off into the mist. Unfortunately the strength of the current had been under-estimated. On the return trip many of the assault boats were swept downstream and could not be recovered. The Commander of "B" Company, Major Wright, was among those carried away. Other craft were holed or sunk by enemy fire, so that on one company front only one assault boat and two hastily assembled rafts were available to ferry over the remainder of the battalion. The assault boat was fastened to a guide rope, and throughout the night it was hauled backwards and forwards until everyone had crossed. This delay left the Punjabis far behind their artillery programme. When first light broke at 0530 hours, the battalion was deployed on the enemy's side of the river, and committed to attack without benefit of barrage or protection of darkness.

Fortunately the Germans had been too clever. They had used too much smoke. The dense curtain which frustrated the Indians in their first advance now concealed them when in an untenable position. Under cover of this providential cloak the forward companies of the Punjabis deployed for the assault. "A" Company, under Captain Douglas Treman, M.C., felt its way forward until held up by an apron of wire covered by mines. The exploding mines drew heavy and accurate small arms fire; many men fell. Captain Treman himself was severely wounded, but collecting fifteen survivors this dogged officer pushed through a gap in the wire and advanced to the line of the lateral road. Six of his small party had fallen on the way. Captain Treman, weak from loss of blood, ordered his nine men to dig in. Several Germans blundered into the position in the fog and were shot down. When the mist lifted in the forenoon, only three fighting men and their severely wounded leader remained. Out of touch and short of ammunition, this gallant remnant was obliged to surrender.

"D" Company, the other forward company, likewise groped forward through the smoke. Locating their first objective, the Sikhs charged in line abreast. A few yards short of the close, a belt of wire halted them, and four covering machine-guns opened at point-blank range. Major Sujan Singh, who led the charge, fell dead. One platoon, which by the impetus of its rush had penetrated the position, was wiped out to a man. They were afterwards found lying under the muzzles of the machine-guns.

"B" and "C" Companies crossed the river, and came forward to make good the gains. With Major Wright missing, Subedar Sumera Ram took command of "B" Company and Major Gardhari Singh assumed overall command of the assault. The advance was pinned down by a sleet of fire from front and flanks. Movement meant death, until the shining heroism of young Kamal Ram saved the day. This nineteen-year-old sepoy of Karauli State, in action for the first time, crouched near his Company Commander when the machine-guns swept the Punjabis to the ground. A gun firing from the right flank was particularly vexatious. The officer called for a volunteer to deal with it. Kamal Ram crawled through the wire and leapt upon the gun crew singlehanded. He shot the gunner and bayoneted his feeder, swinging about to kill a German officer who sprang at him from a slit trench firing a pistol. With the post silenced he pressed on. Having sniped the gunner of a second nest, he bombed the remainder of the crew into submission. Together with a havilder he attacked a third machine-gun post and dealt with it in a similar fashion. The line was open. The Punjabis moved forward to secure their objective. Later, in a forward reconnaissance, Kamal Ram wiped out a fourth machine-gun nest—an unsurpassed day's work which earned this gallant youngster the Victoria Cross.

On the left of the Divisional attack, the fortunes of Argyll and Sutherland Highlanders were similar to those of Royal Fusiliers on the opposite flank. It will be remembered that high ground in the Liri Appendix commanded this sector in much the same way as the knolls and escarpment on either side of San Angelo commanded the extreme right. These disadvantages of terrain were sufficient to make the difference between success and failure. The Scotsmen moved up to the Gari through a curtain of enemy defensive fire. Many men fell, the casualties including the entire group of forward observation artillerymen.

On the near bank of the river a tragedy occurred. In the January fighting an American division had tried to force the Gari at this point. Its assault had failed. When the Americans withdrew they mined both banks to counter any enemy attempt to follow up. For some days before the Indian attack the reserve battalion of 19th Brigade had been picking up mines, and it was believed that the near bank of the Gari was clean. Unfortunately, as the Scotsmen spread out along the river's edge, a number of men were blown up. This unexpected menace in a launching area disorganized the crossings, threw the advance out of timing, and cost the Argylls the advantage of the barrage.

(Among massed artillery supporting the Eighth Army attack were a number of batteries which had been engaged in the January fighting. Their knowledge of the front led American artillery men to offer odds of ten to one against Eighth Indian Division forcing the Gari. British gunners serving with the Indians are said to have snapped up such offers).

One company and two additional platoons of the Argylls managed to embark in the assault boats. Defensive fire caught them, riddling the boats and killing many. A hastily improvised raft likewise was destroyed. Only a handful of gallant men reached the far side safely and pushed forward through the murk. Belts of wire blocked the way, and machine-guns slashed at them as they sought to evade the obstacles. One company officer was killed and another wounded. A platoon of "D" Company reached and crossed the lateral road, where a few men dug in and maintained a precarious hold on a narrow triangle of waterlogged ground within 200 yards of the main German position. This handful were flank guard to Eighth Army. They alone stood in the way of the constriction of the shallow bridgehead, and an attack upon the Punjabis from the rear.

The din of battle was terrific, but from beyond the left flank of the Argylls a different noise now and then tinkled through the fog. Above the crash and clatter came the faint clank of metal on metal. The Germans heard these sounds, and since they could not see, poured defensive fire into the Liri Appendix, for it seemed certain that a bridge was being built there. As the shoot came down groups of 6th Lancers, who sat solemnly banging bits of angle iron and road rail together, scattered and took refuge. The enemy, who is nothing if not thorough, switched the shoot to the dummy posts and faked emplacements which the cavalrymen had built without undue caution a few days before. Throughout the early hours of the attack, a fair number of enemy guns which might have done damage elsewhere, continued to search an open front, and to splash their shells into empty ground.

The full light of morning saw the battle of the Gari superseded by the battle of the clock. Everywhere except on the extreme left the Indian infantry had made good its footing on the German side of the river. It now became a race to bring up support arms, to reinforce the firing line, and to strike the next blow. The enemy had no river to cross, no bridges to build, so that the race began with the attack carrying a handicap of several hours. This time factor could only be mitigated by exceptional enterprise and exertion. Off the mark on the heels of the infantry, the sappers and supply services hurried into the battle. A correspondent describes the scene.

"Vapours from the river spread over the valley. Before midnight the moon was obscured by smoke and fog. Bofors tracer shell at intervals streaked across the sky, giving direction to the advancing lines of transport; in the mist the shells quickly dimmed and were lost to sight. Tracks to the Gari had been marked by white tape and shaded hurricane lanterns. Long lines of vehicles crept down to the river's edge—

jeeps towing anti-tank guns or carrying collapsible boats, three-ton lorries with bridging sections, ambulances to wait for loads of wounded. Drivers peering blindly forward through the fog drove on the instructions of their mates walking in front."

The Divisional provost companies, supplemented by volunteers from 26 Light A.A. Regiment, controlled the traffic along the narrow, twisting tracks which led to and from the river. Here all men and material came under control of the beach parties, who organized the crossings, launched the assault boats, built rafts and served as ferrymen and stretcher-bearers. Sudden gusts of mortar and artillery fire searched the line of the river, but the work went on without interruption. Moving imperturbably among the beach parties were the bridging sappers, the men who would win or lose this battle of the clock. Even as the infantry took to the water, their labours began. Through the blast and crackle of the barrage came the steady chug of bulldozers as they filled ditches and built up ramps for the launching sites. Behind them, working by feel, engineers fitted the Bailey sections and tightened them into spans. Three bridges, coded as Cardiff, Oxford and Plymouth, were planned. Small arms fire compelled the abandonment of Cardiff bridge on 19th Brigade's front. Oxford bridge grew steadily throughout the night, but when the darkness thinned the Bengal Sappers and Miners needed a few hours more.

Again the German smoke screen served well, protecting the sappers. At 0840 hours, a few minutes before the curtain of fog dispersed, the bridge was completed. Three minutes later the first Canadian tanks rumbled across the Gari, camouflaged with green boughs as though decked for a harvest festival. The roar of the armour was music to the infantry, as the panzers were expected at any moment. Troop after troop of tanks thundered across, and moved forward in search of dead ground to wait for the word to attack.

No crossings were prepared, and no one worked throughout the night on ramps for Plymouth Bridge. At 0930 hours a strange looking object approached the Gari. (Germans captured later in the day asked awe-inspired questions concerning the new British secret weapon). A tank of 14th (Calgary) Armoured Regiment carried a complete Bailey span on its back, which another tank pushed from behind. The leading tank waddled into the river carrying one end of the bridge. In midstream it submerged; the crew climbed out at the last moment, spluttering. The rear tank thrust, and the span slid across the back of the carrier until it reached the far bank. A slight hold-up occurred when the bracket clamping the bridge to the pusher tank refused to disconnect. A Canadian officer blew off the union with a light charge. A new type of bridge, a triumph of mechanical improvisation, was open for its first trial in action.

With the bridging of the Gari on the Indian front the crisis passed.

Fourth British Division had been unable to build bridges before morning and its brigades across the river were without supporting arms. Had Eighth Indian Division not completed its bridges, German armour, held in reserve at a focal point between the British and Polish thrusts, would have had twelve hours of daylight in which to destroy infantry west of the Gari. There is reason to believe that the enemy counted on this advantage, and that the gallantry, skill and speed of the bridge builders upset his plans. Indian Sappers and Miners and Royal Canadian Engineers had collaborated to turn the tide of battle.

The battle, however, was not yet won. On both flanks of the shallow bridgehead the situation was unsatisfactory. Royal Fusiliers were pinned to the drainage ditches north of San Angelo, while on the left only a few sections of Scotsmen, under constant fire and observation, held back the enemy. In the centre Punjabis and Frontier Force Regiment, having secured their immediate objectives, dared not drive deeper into the enemy positions until their flanks were secure. The Canadian armour supporting the infantry found the marshy meadows to be barely tankable, and little dead ground available in which to lie up from artillery observation. Harassing fire swept over the sparse, crowded assembly areas, searching the crossings and their approaches. Plymouth Bridge had subsided under the weight of armour and was unusable for tracks, although light wheel vehicles still crossed. One Bailey bridge therefore served the entire Corps front.

The most pressing need was to clean up San Angelo. This stubborn knuckle of resistance between Royal Fusiliers and Frontier Force Regiment blocked further advance on 17th Brigade's front. The two companies of Gurkhas which had gone forward during the night in search of their start line, lost direction in the fog and brought up among the men of Frontier Force Regiment. It was necessary to sort out, to reorganize and to realign before a fresh attack could be launched.

As soon as visibility was restored, re-deployment began. By afternoon the Gurkhas had mustered in the Frontiersmen's positions to the south of San Angelo, with troops of tanks in close support. At 1700 hours two companies advanced on the village. A blaze of machine-gun fire greeted them. One company swung to flank and cleared a machine-gun nest in a white house, killing twelve and capturing fifteen Germans. The other company swept up a low spur garrisoned by seven machine-gun nests; again the rush won home, and the crews were destroyed. Unfortunately, most of the Canadian tanks were trapped on treacherous footing, bogging down before they could come into action. The Gurkhas therefore dug in on the ground gained, and the assault on San Angelo was postponed until the following day.

As the Gurkha attack was launched from the positions of the Frontier

Force Regiment, that battalion was unable to do more than sit tight and endure the constant harassing fire. On its left, the day fared better for 3/8 Punjabis. It will be recalled that Major Wright, commander of "B" Company, had been washed downstream in his attempt to cross the Gari. He landed well below the Indian front, and spent an exciting night picking his way through the German positions, which with soldierly care he marked down for future attention. Early in the afternoon he encountered a Canadian tank which was reconnoitring ahead of the infantry. Riding outside, Major Wright undertook a tour of his front. He visited a number of pin-pointed positions which the tank shot up thoroughly. In mid-afternoon he rejoined his company with a comprehensive picture in his mind. He asked and obtained permission to attack Point 63 that evening. A most successful little action ensued. Tanks and Frontiersmen raced in and overran the knoll, destroying its defenders. Pushing on the Punjabis stalked another fortified position, surprised the garrison, took 14 prisoners and rescued Captain Treman and his three gallant survivors of "A" Company of Frontier Force Regiment.

Thus at the close of this first day of battle the main assault was yet to be launched on the right of the Division front. In the centre the attack was definitely in the ascendant. Only on the left was the situation still critical. Here it was found necessary to withdraw the handful of Argylls isolated in the midst of the enemy. 6/13 Frontier Force Rifles, the reserve battalion of 19th Brigade, crossed the river to take over, and to proceed with the assault upon Panaccioni at the southern calk of the Horseshoe. The night was spent in making ready for resumption of the attack.

At noon on May 13th Gurkhas and Frontiersmen on the southern fringes of San Angelo were withdrawn to a safe distance. Seven field regiments crashed a vicious shoot on the village. After five minutes of hurricane bombardment, the guns lifted and two companies of Gurkhas dashed in. As the machine-guns opened, the Canadian tanks smashed cannon shells into the nests. Within fifteen minutes the Gurkhas, plying knife and grenade, had established themselves on the fringe of the village. Sixty minutes of deadly fighting followed. No German asked quarter—none was given. By 1300 hours San Angelo was won. In the deep shelters the last fanatical defenders were exterminated. A few groups which fled westward from the village were shot down by tanks which had taken station to intercept any fugitives. This sharp, short battle, which dislodged the keystone of the Gari defences, cost 1/5 Gurkhas 10 officers and 119 men.

The capture of San Angelo immediately reacted upon adjoining opposition. From "Platform" Knoll to the north, which blocked the advance of Royal Fusiliers, the German garrison watched the progress of the attack and the deployment of tanks in the open ground beyond the village. Without further resistance this strong point hung out white flags and surrendered in most un-German fashion.

To the south of San Angelo Frontier Force Regiment was now free to advance up the valley. With right flank secure, General Russell devoted his attention to clearing up the situation on the left. 6/13 Frontier Force Rifles moved towards the high ground barring the way to Panaccioni. Canadian tanks in close attendance found solid footing and terrain suitable for manœuvre. The four companies and their armour skirmished forward in a brilliant set-piece action which paid tribute to the combined training on the Volturno. The Germans had stationed their self-propelled guns and tanks in sunken lanes, hoping to ambush the infantry and to trap its protective armour. The quick-eyed Indians detected and pinpointed these lairs so that the Canadian tanks might work on to the blind side to destroy them. As Jemendar Thakur Singh led his platoon forward, his men spotted four self-propelled guns concealed under the foliage of trees. A burst of tracer gave the tank escorts the clue. They plastered the site with armour-piercing shells as they closed in for the kill. Similarly, when German armoured vehicles sallied out to deal with the Indian skirmishers, the tank men saw them first and smashed them. Their wreckage sign-posted the line of advance. The enemy was unable to frustrate such efficient team work, and Panaccioni fell to Frontier Force Rifles at 1400 hours on the afternoon of May 13th.

Both flanks were now secure and the bridgehead firm. 21st Brigade immediately came forward from reserve to exploit the success by an attack up the Liri Valley on to Pignataro, the final Divisional objective. At 0525 hours on May 14th, 3/15 Punjabis, with Canadian tanks rumbling alongside, passed through Frontier Force Rifles. Two hours later this fine battalion had stormed its immediate objective and was moving into the open. The defence was disorganized and strong-points fell easily. 19th Brigade joined in the advance, with Argyll and Sutherland Highlanders re-crossing the river to swing left and to mop up Liri Appendix. 6/13 Frontier Force Rifles pushed up the valley on the left flank of 21st Brigade. By dusk two brigades had closed up on Pignataro, nearly three miles ahead of the Gari, and the Horseshoe had been cleansed of the enemy. Should Pignataro fall, the Cassino position would be turned from the flank, and the way opened to link up with the Polish Corps in their drive across the Monte Cairo massif.

Eighth Division pressed the pace. 6/13 Frontier Force Rifles with tank support attacked Pignataro at twilight. A lucky circumstance aided in the capture of this strong position. 6/13 Frontier Force Rifles had been on the outskirts of the village throughout the afternoon, and the enemy apparently expected the assault to be preceded by an artillery programme. Towards dusk Argyll and Sutherland High-landers, who had been mopping up at a great pace on the left, were observed advancing towards Pignataro on the opposite side. This movement distracted the defenders who massed their automatic weapons against an attack from the south. As fire opened on the Scotsmen, Major R. R. Eckford's Pathan Company of the Frontiersmen, with a troop of Canadian tanks close behind, dashed at the village.

The assault took the defenders by surprise. The tanks bored in, smashing at the pill boxes with armour-piercing shell at point-blank range. The garrison of Pignataro proved to be students from a school of mountain warfare, who had been collected hastily and entrusted with the defence of this key position. They fought fanatically as the Pathans swarmed in upon them. After the position had been overrun, little groups which had fled in the face of the onslaught returned to dig in and to die in last stands. Prisoners emerged with their hands above their heads, holding grenades which they hurled as their captors went forward to secure them. It was all to no avail. The Dogra Company of the Frontiersmen raced up in support, and by dawn Pignataro was clear of the enemy.

All the principal fortifications of the Gustav Line were now in the rear of the Indians. In four days of fierce fighting, approximately 1,000 Germans had been killed and captured in the San Angelo-Pignataro-Panaccioni Horseshoe. The victory had not been without cost. Approximately one-third of 17th Brigade were casualties, and 19th Brigade's losses were only slightly less. But in comparison with Cassino the Indian troops had smashed the Gustav Line at low cost.

Twenty-four hours after Pignataro fell, the Polish attack was launched from the north of Cassino. After terrific fighting the Poles stormed Snake's Head Ridge and Monastery Hill. Twenty-four hours later they had worked their way down the southern slopes of the buttress and had made contact with Seventy-Eighth British Division on Route 6, to the west of Cassino Town. This completed the destruction of the Gustav positions, and the enemy fell back on the Adolf Hitler Line. Monte Cairo continued as the pivot of the defence system, and the Germans remained in strength at Villa San Lucia and Piedimonte in the mountain spurs above the highway. On the opposite side of the valley, French Expeditionary Corps had attacked along the foothills of the Arunci, and were advancing against the Adolf Hitler positions near the road junction of Pontecorvo.

According to the original plan Eighth Indian Division had completed its task. On May 16th and 17th the Canadian Corps relieved the tired Indians. On May 19th Seventy-Eighth British Division and First Canadian Infantry Division assaulted the Adolf Hitler Line. The attack broke down owing to inadequate artillery support. It was essential to maintain the momentum of the assault, and shortly before midnight on May 19th Eighth Indian Division received instructions to re-enter the battle. Next morning, 21st Brigade moved up Route 6 under the shadow of the broken ridges where the Poles in ferocious fighting sought to smash the hinge of the switch line. The Indians were ordered to provide an infantry screen for Polish tanks which had worked around the flank of Piedimonte in order to assault the village from the south. Simultaneously Polish infantry would be launched in strength against the same position from the north. At 1500 hours on May 20th three companies of Royal West Kents moved forward to storm two strongpoints on the track which led from Route 6 to Piedimonte.

Before turning northward on to the hillsides, the Kentish men had to advance 2,000 yards across open cornfields swept by enemy fire. From the hilltops on the right, and from weapon pits in front, the enemy raked the advance. Royal West Kents went forward by platoons in short rushes, and although suffering considerable casualties, kept admirable cohesion and direction. One company lost both its senior officers; whereupon the subalterns in charge of platoons nominated Company Sergeant-Major Mott as company commander. At last light the Royal West Kents closed on their objective and swept over it, to dig in along a sunken road only 200 yards below the enemy's main battle position on the slopes of Piedimonte Hill. Thirty-three prisoners were captured from the Forty-fourth German Division, which had been rushed into action from a reserve area to the north of Monte Cairo.

In the hills behind Piedimonte a fearful battle raged. First German Parachute Division likewise had been hurried to the scene of the fighting. Toe to toe they met the gallant Poles with the same tenacity and contempt for death that they had shown against the Indians on the glacis of Monastery Hill. They held the conical Piedimonte crest and the ridges behind it in an unshakable grip. When day broke on May 21st they were able to turn their attention to the Royal West Kents, who had all but penetrated the position from the opposite side. Throughout the day the Kentish men were subjected to the heaviest shelling and mortaring that they had ever known. The presence of the Polish tanks convinced the enemy that a major assault from the west was imminent. That night the Poles again smashed at Piedimonte from the north and again failed to make progress. Night after night bitter and deadly fighting continued.

Meanwhile the French Corps on the opposite side of the Liri Valley had broken into Pontecorvo, the left flank anchor position of the Adolf Hitler defences. The battle was now rising to its climax. Day by day the artillery of four corps played on the German lines in the Liri Valley and in the foothills of the Monte Cairo massif. At dawn on May 23rd First Canadian Corps, with 700 guns and two brigades of armour in close support, burst into the German positions. The line cracked and the Canadians poured through. On the same morning the hard-fighting forces in the Anzio bridgehead broke out to link up with

Fifth Army troops advancing from the south. Thirty-six hours later the Poles finally stormed Piedimonte. The enemy feverishly endeavoured to man the line of the Melfa river, five miles higher up the valley; before defences could be organized the Canadians were hacking through. Thirteenth Corps rapidly deployed for the pursuit. As preliminary to launching Sixth British Armoured Division, it was necessary to clear the enemy from his forlorn hope positions along the hilltops above Route 6. On May 25th, 19th Brigade passed through 21st Brigade, and 6/13 Frontier Force Rifles climbed the hillsides to assault Centro Cielo and Madonna di Castro Cielo, a hilltop 2,400 feet above the valley. As the Frontiersmen clambered over the terraces of olive trees, the leading company came under heavy fire from paratroopers dug in as at Cassino, in the lee of boulders and under rocky ledges. New Zealand tanks in support of the Indians laid a smoke screen. The smoke shell fired the grass and flushed the Germans from their coverts. As they ran, the riflemen brought them down. By nightfall the Dogra Company was firmly established on the hilltops, and the Argylls had pushed through to take Cantalupo and Roccasecca against lessening opposition. The enemy was in full retreat, disorganized beyond possibility of immediate recovery. Morale had broken and even the fanatical paratroopers had lost heart. In a chance encounter, five camp followers of 3/8 Punjab Regiment, with only three rifles between them, captured eleven of Hitler's Prides without a shot being fired. A continuous flow of stragglers from dispersed units plodded back to the prisoners' cages.

Thus the travail of Cassino was avenged, and a new chapter opened in the campaign in Italy.

3. CENTRAL ITALY

CHAPTER EIGHT

EIGHTH DIVISION IN PURSUIT

WITH THE LIRI VALLEY OPENED, and Anzio relieved, Fifth Army drove on Rome, while Eighth Army fanned out into Central Italy. The enemy had no alternative to a long retreat. Any defence system covering the capital could be pierced or by-passed. With Rome lost, it was sound strategy to shorten communications and to fall back on terrain where natural obstacles would assist the defenders. The Germans therefore withdrew northwards for two hundred and twenty-five miles. The retreat which began at Roccasecca on May 25th ended on June 18th at Ripa Ridge.

Throughout this period Eighth Indian Division remained in the van of the chase, harrying the enemy with a persistence which bore handsome dividends in the form of casualties inflicted, prisoners taken and equipment captured. The pursuit began auspiciously. On May 27th after the fall of Roccasecca, a mobile force of 6th Lancers, 3/8 Punjabis and New Zealand tanks caught up with the enemy in the gorge of the Melfa Valley, north of Route 6. At a blown bridge the column fell upon a rearguard, killing 25 Germans and taking 14 prisoners. An observer reported:—

"The famed German paratroopers ran pell-mell, scrambling over rocks and diving into shelters as we came upon the scene. Some put up a weak show of resistance, but others surrendered at once. Famished prisoners pocketed their pride and asked for food. They marched back munching biscuits past the huge German cemetery at Roccasecca."

This incursion into the hills took the Indians out of the Liri Valley and off the main axis of advance. This circumstance was turned to advantage when Sixth British Armoured Division, closing on Arce at the top of the valley, was held up. 17th Brigade passed through 19th Brigade, sent one group on a detour to the north as a feint, and attacked the features covering Arce from the east. Royal Fusiliers and 1/5 Gurkhas, supported by New Zealand tanks, stormed Frajoli on the evening of May 27th. Stiff fighting cost the enemy approximately 100 riflemen from One Hundred and Fourteenth Jaeger Division. On the next day, 1/12 Frontier Force Regiment attacked Monte Pavone, a commanding feature which covered the approach to Arce. One and a half companies of German paratroopers stood at bay on the crest of the peak. Subedar Sadhu Singh's Sikhs were pinned down as they tried to close. After tremendous efforts, the New Zea-

8 INDIAN DIV IN PURSUIT

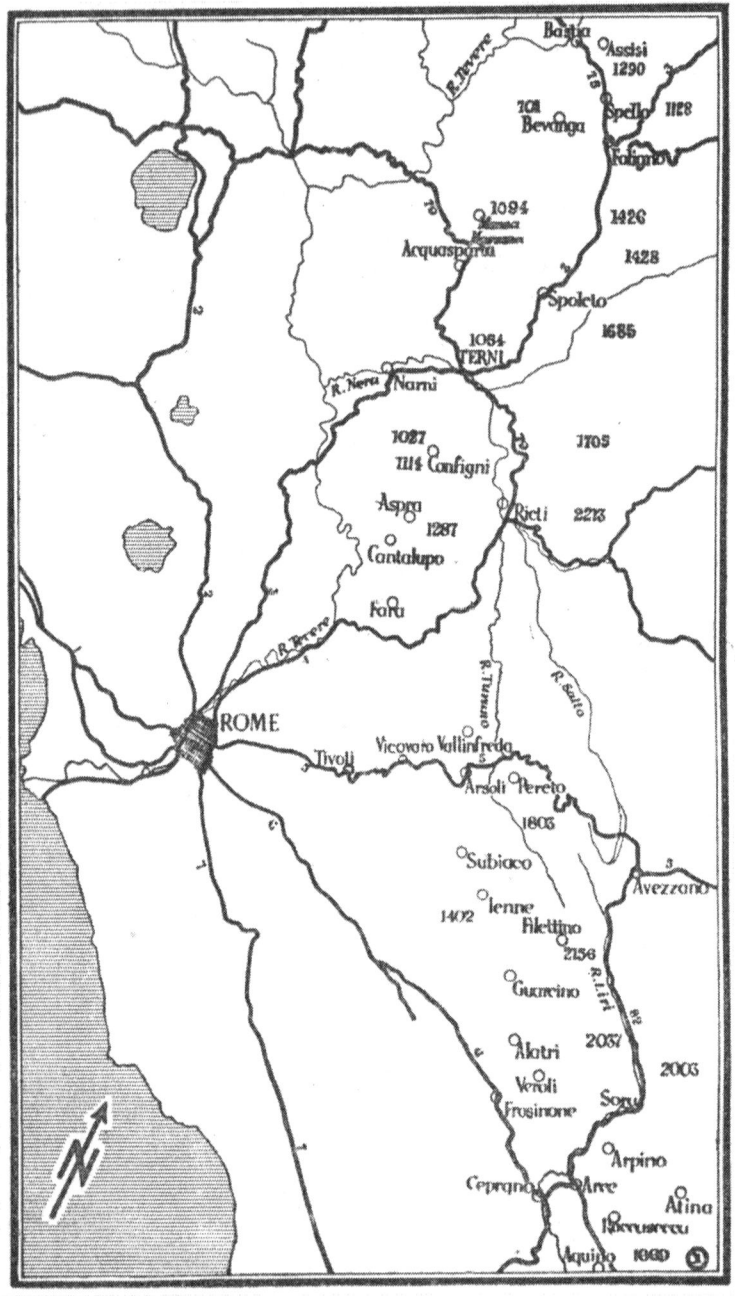

landers worked their tanks three-quarters of the way up the mountainside. They fired at the trees over the enemy positions in order to obtain air bursts whose shrapnel might reach the Germans in their slit trenches. The paratroopers, who were dug in on the reverse slopes, destroyed themselves through over-confidence. Perceiving the Indians to be comparatively few in numbers, they sprang to their feet and charged up the hillside. The Sikhs for an instant were astounded by such foolhardiness; as one man they rose with their war cry of "Sat siri akal!" and leapt to meet their assailants. It was bayonet to bayonet, and the paratroopers were outmatched. They broke and ran. The Sikhs swept forward to seize the enemy positions, capturing a number of prisoners, including a German officer with two bayonet wounds.

Consequent upon this success, 21st Brigade passed through and occupied positions immediately above Arce. Next morning (May 29th) 1/5 Gurkhas and elements of Sixth British Armoured Division entered the town. It was a local fiesta day, celebrated to commemorate a wandering Englishman who had become patron saint of the town in the Middle Ages. The arrival of British troops on such a day was particularly felicitous. The Indian brigades had now reached the gorge of the Liri, where it turns into the north-east towards its source near Avezzano. It was necessary to bridge the river in three places, a delay which enabled the Germans to extricate themselves from the too close attentions of their pursuers. 6/13 Frontier Force Rifles and a squadron of 6th Lancers followed the retreating enemy up Route 82 towards Sora, where enemy anti-tank guns blocked the road. It would have been impossible to dislodge the enemy without casualties had not a Spitfire spotted the holdup, and forced the Germans into cover with series of dummy dives. With the gun crews off guard, the Lancers rushed the position, inflicting 40 casualties.

19th Brigade, also with Lancers and tanks, had struck across country to the left with a view to harassing the flank of one of the main lines of retreat. On approaching Veroli, about ten miles west of the Liri, an enemy rearguard several hundred strong was encountered. 6th Lancers were ambushed losing three armoured cars and their crews. A sharp little action followed, in which intervention by another lone fighter bomber helped greatly. On the morning of June 2nd, Frontier Force Rifles cleared Veroli. The Indians were now veering back towards the axis of advance of the Sixth British Armoured Division. To avoid confusion it was necessary to keep to the right of Via Macerosa, the main north-bound highway. This entailed a certain amount of road making, but did not materially slow up the pursuit. 21st Indian Infantry Brigade, with 18th New Zealand Armoured Regiment attached, became the spearhead of the Division, and moved north on Guarcino through the hills, where the road described a right-angled bend to the west, along the lower haunches of Monte Agnelo. For once the Germans were stupid in their dispositions for defence. Their rearguards had dug in on the slopes of the mountain immediately above the town, in full view of 1/5 Mahrattas across the valley. When the weapons of the Indians were emplaced, no German could move on the hillside without being sniped. Divisional mortar teams had a field day, and plastered the German positions while the infantry cleared Guarcino. Forty shell-shocked members of Fifth Mountain Division surrendered, and as many more were killed, for the loss of one Mahratta.

The capture of German demolition squads at Guarcino revealed no road wrecking to have been accomplished before Subiaco, fifteen miles ahead. On June 5th, in order to facilitate the pursuit, Eighth Indian Division was transferred from Thirteenth to Tenth Corps. This shift ended a happy association with New Zealand armoured regiments. On the infantry's call the Kiwi tank men would go anywhere, and would undertake any task. Neither sheer slopes nor boulders nor deep gullies deterred them; in one fashion or another they barged and squirmed up the mountain sides. If the ground proved impossible, their bulldozers hurried forward to clear the way. When not in action they reconstructed or improved the mountain tracks and roads.

Eighth Division now entered wilder and more mountainous country. Many escaped prisoners of war who had hidden away among the upland farms began to come in. 19th Brigade covered the 15 miles to Subiaco in two days. At the entrance to the town a bridge which crossed a chasm had been blown. The enemy apparently regarded this demolition as a major obstacle, but Frontier Force Rifles, having brought up a mule train, swung into the hills and entered Subiaco from the north, trapping the rearguard. Once again German engineering squads were among the captures, and another fifteen miles of road was discovered to be free of demolitions.

Rome fell, and the pursuit swept on. At Arsoli, the next market town north of Subiaco, Eighth Division wheeled into the west and cleared the countryside as far as Tivoli, a summer resort fifteen miles east of the capital. Sixth British Armoured Division debouched from Rome on the western bank of the Tiber, and worked into the north on the axis of Via Flamina, the main road to Perugia. 17th Brigade, after relieving elements of Fourth British Division on the opposite bank of the Tiber, hurried on. The pace steadily quickened. On June 14th, 6th Lancers and 3/15 Punjabis swept into Terni, an important road junction, rounding up prisoners who had last heard of the Indians at Fara, 25 miles down the road. Divisional sappers had been over-worked during the rapid advance, opening tracks and clearing minefields. Engineers from 25th Army Tank Brigade now arrived to relieve them of the task of bridging the Nera at Terni. No one knows quite how it came about, but an argument between the new arrivals and their supposedly exhausted colleagues led to both parties working side by side throughout the night, with the result that the bridge was completed twelve hours ahead of schedule.

The constant harassing began to tell on the enemy. As the lovely Umbrian countryside unrolled, with its gentle contours and heavy cultivation, the advance screen of reconnaissance cars and light tanks gave the retreating Germans no rest. Persistent encroachment upset the rearguards, who on more than one occasion scattered in disorder, their missions unfulfilled. The enemy demolition sappers in particular slipped up badly. Mines often were obviously and hurriedly sown. Ammunition and supply dumps were unexploded or unburned—a sure sign of demoralization. German back area formations were rounded up while still at work, unaware of the approach of their enemies. A characteristic fat take was the bag of Frontier Force Rifles on June 16th, which included 250 prisoners, a tank, 2 guns, a considerable number of motor vehicles, and a yard of horses complete with saddlery. As the thrustful Indians forced the pace the roads became strewn with an endless litter of abandoned equipment.

The long retreat finally drew to a close. On June 17th, Argyll and Sutherland Highlanders approached Assisi, historic birthplace of St. Francis, its massive monasteries arrayed along the shoulders of the mountain. Machine-gun posts on the outskirts compelled the Scotsmen to deploy and to attack in pouring rain through the vineyards and olive groves which skirted the town. 6th Lancers raced for Bastia, where the main highway crosses the Chiascio river. There they ran into trouble, for the bridge was blown, and anti-tank guns covering the demolition destroyed three armoured cars. On the far bank the enemy stood. 3/8 Punjabis moved up to deal with what appeared to be a tricky obstacle. PIATS were worked forward until they could crash their bombs into the weapon pits on the opposite bank; thereafter, arraying all available tanks and anti-tank guns in a semicircle at point blank range, the German positions were blasted. That night, three companies of Punjabis crossed the river and seized the airfield, while 6th Lancers worked down a lateral road to make contact with Sixth British Armoured Division at Torgiano, on the Tiber. Here again, anti-tank guns gave trouble, and four armoured cars were lost.

Four miles ahead, Perugia, serene and unscarred, stood on a gracious swell above the countryside. Ten miles west of the Umbrian capital the blue bowl of Lake Trasimeno gleamed in a fairy landscape. To the north of the lake the Apennine massif became more substantial, with ruggeder slopes and higher crests. The Tiber Valley narrowed and deepened; steep and wooded slopes stretched upwards to the dominating ridges. The river was fed by a multitude of small and rapid streams, each in its own gashed ravine. Roads were few. Here was natural terrain for defence, ideally suited to the German strategy of selling ground at a high price before withdrawing to lay-back positions where such tactics might be re-enacted.

To the east of Perugia an escarpment marked the beginning of the rough country. A ridge rising to a height of one thousand feet extended for five miles between the Tiber and Chiascio rivers. The villages of Ripa and Civitella stood upon its crest, the former giving the ridge its name. In Civitella a prominent tower afforded observation for miles around.

During the afternoon of June 18th, 1/5 Gurkhas, supported by two troops of North Irish Horse, attacked the escarpment opposite Civitella. German bazooka men lying up in the village cemetery destroyed two of the Irishmen's tanks. At 0400 hours next morning the village was reported as captured and consolidated. After daybreak the Gurkhas attempted to work along the ridge towards Ripa village. As soon as the advance began, heavy shelling and mortaring revealed the presence of substantial enemy forces. German guns knocked out three tanks which reconnoitred too rashly. The enemy shoot on Civitella increased in intensity, and at 1030 hours a counter attack of approximately company strength developed from across the Tiber. The German concentrations had been observed, and the assault broke down under accurate defensive fire. At 1100 hours with Civitella secure, "D" Company of the Gurkhas supported by tanks and artillery, worked in on Ripa village. (An odd sight during this assault was Major Charles, forward observation officer, directing his guns from the top of a stepladder in the firing line, under pelting rain). Well prepared positions blocked all approaches, but as the Gurkhas felt their way around them the rearguards fled precipitately.

Simultaneously Royal Fusiliers advanced against the ridge position above the Chiascio river. At 1530 hours the leading company ran into concentrated machine-gun fire, one thousand yards south-east of its objective. The Company Commander was killed, and all other officers became casualties. Persevering, the Fusiliers worked up on the right of the Gurkhas, took over Ripa village, and reorganized the sector. During this consolidation Major Morland-Hughes, M.B.E., M.C., commanding the Gurkhas, who led his battalion in the bitter Mozzagrogna fighting, was mortally wounded—a great loss to his men and to the Division.

With Ripa ridge secured, 17th Brigade pushed on. 1/12 Frontier Force Regiment worked forward between Civitella and Ripa. A company of the Gurkhas crossed River Grande, a tributary of the Tiber, assailing the high ground on the northern bank. The enemy instantly reacted to this incursion, and the Gurkhas encountered such venomous opposition that they withdrew that evening. Frontier Force Regiment, however, had made good progress, and next day it was decided to re-cross the river. After darkness fell, "B" Company of the Gurkhas once more forded the stream, infiltrated on to the high ground, and established a bridgehead. Again the enemy struck back promptly and vigorously; lorried infantry and motor-cycle machine-gunners charged the intruders. This attack failed to win home, and morning broke on a noisy scene as enemy artillery softened up the Gurkha positions. That afternoon a second enemy counter-attack swept up; the Germans retrieved some ground only to lose it when the reserve company of Gurkhas raced into action. Concurrently, 1/12 Frontier Force Regiment had probed forward until securely ensconced on Belvedere Ridge, a long feature formerly used by the enemy for artillery observation. Attempts to throw back the Frontiersmen were broken up by prompt and accurate curtains of defensive fire.

This series of sharp little actions was proving expensive. Already 17th Brigade had lost half as many men as in the great battle of the Gari. Relief was overdue, for Eighth Indian Division had been fighting steadily with little real rest since the previous November. It was known that Tenth Indian Division was on its way to take over, but General Russell and his men were loath to relinquish the front, as one of his officers put it, "without dotting the Hun one for all the nuisances he had committed". On June 23rd, 3rd King's Own Hussars replaced North Irish Horse as the 17th Brigade's tank regiment, and it was decided to sally once more into the upland ground which had been defended so obstinately. This farewell attack succeeded brilliantly. In a single bound the Hussars carried Piccione, five miles north of Ripa, caught the enemy by surprise and wrought havoc. Two hundred Germans were killed, 50 mules captured, and 11 guns destroyed. Gurkhas, Royal Fusiliers and Royal West Kents followed up to consolidate. Bitter fighting occurred at Columbella, where it was necessary to withdraw the West Kents and to beat up the area with artillery before the ground could be held. The enemy bared his teeth at every attempt to infiltrate, and the situation was still involved when the advance parties from Tenth Indian Division arrived.

After eight and a half months of continuous slogging, Eighth Indian Division was relieved and went out to rest. Seldom has any formation won more laurels in its first campaign.

CHAPTER NINE

TENTH INDIAN DIVISION IN THE TIBER VALLEY

TENTH INDIAN DIVISION took over in a countryside which might have been of its own choosing. Ahead stretched a sea of mountains, with high crests and deep troughs. During the tedious years of waiting in Syria, Cyprus and Palestine, the theme of all Divisional training had been mountain warfare. The men had lived and worked in the mountains. They had thought and dreamed of them. Mountain warfare is flexible and individual, and General Reid had deeply inculcated the basic tactics. The values of high ground and dead ground, of observation points and hidden approaches, of unobtrusive infiltration and deep penetration—a score of such lessons, learned laboriously in training areas, were now to be tested in actual combat.

Corps orders called for Tenth Indian Division to advance along both banks of the Tiber, through the heart of the mountains. The average width of the Tiber Valley above Perugia is somewhat under a mile. The lateral valleys which feed the great Roman river are of no particular length or depth: after entering the foothills they quickly deteriorate into bush-filled gullies impassable to all but the goat-footed.

Two roads, one on each bank, follow the Tiber meanders. At intervals of from ten to twelve miles flourishing market towns have grown up around the sites of old castles and fortifications, usually on a bend or in a loop of the river. On the high ridges and saddlebacks small villages tightly cluster around the churches, whose towers or spires afford observation over miles of countryside. When Tenth Indian Division came into the line at the end of June, the cereal crops had been harvested and the luxuriant fruits for which the valley is famed were still unripe. On the high wooded crests the foresters were cutting and peeling pine, beech, and larch logs, to be slid into the valleys on the first snows.

Tenth Division was deployed with 20th and 25th Brigades east of the river, and 10th Brigade on its western bank. 20th Brigade occupied the right sector of the Divisional front, with 8th Manchesters on the extreme flank, 2/3 Gurkhas in the centre, and 3/5 Mahrattas on Belvedere Ridge. Northwards and eastwards beyond the right flank, 12th Lancers and Skinners' Horse roamed the tracks and hills in a kingdom of their own, covering an open flank which extended over the crests of the Apennines, where the cavalrymen made tenuous contact with the reconnaissance groups of Second Polish Corps on the Adriatic front.

The Divisional tour of duty opened ominously and with rough welcome. On the afternoon of June 28th, troop carriers which had brought up 20th Brigade pulled off the road under Ripa Ridge while waiting for outgoing loads. A vicious concentration shoot, ranged to a yard, crashed down upon them. In a twinkling fourteen vehicles went up in flames. The enemy, well aware that a relief was taking place, raided 8th Manchesters as they took over from 17th Brigade on Monte Pilonico. Costly fighting ensued before the raiders were repelled,

While the Mahrattas were effecting the relief of Frontier Force Regiment, a direct hit on company headquarters killed and wounded a number of officers and men.

On June 29th, 25th Brigade, two battalions strong, relieved 21st Brigade on a line running north and south, its left flank resting on the Tiber at Bosco. On the other side of the river, 10th Indian Brigade augmented by 3/18 Garhwalis assumed responsibility on a wide front to the west of Perugia, its sector reaching more than half-way to Lake Trasimeno. 1st Guards Brigade under Divisional command, filled in the gap between Bosco and Perugia. As soon as the advance began and the line was clear of the Umbrian capital, 10th Brigade spread out and took over the Guards' sector, its four battalions operating on a front of nearly ten miles. To assist in covering such an extensive sector, 3rd Hussars, 12th Lancers, King's Dragoon Guards and troops of Royal Horse Artillery were placed under Divisional command.

Battle tactics called for continuous harassing, linked with unremitting attempts to infiltrate and to penetrate deeply into the defended zone. These probes were intended to compel the enemy to disperse his forces and to weaken his hold upon key positions. Where it was possible, such positions would be by-passed after they had been isolated, to be mopped up at leisure. The tactical plan resembled the making tide, which pokes long intruding fingers into the beach before sweeping in a flood over the islands of higher sand.

The advance began against light opposition, with 20th Brigade safely across the River Grande by the evening of July 1st. Next day, 3/5 Mahrattas carried out the first of a series of characteristic outflanking moves. Self-contained for forty-eight hours, the battalion followed a screen of reconnaissance cars into the north-east until well embodied in enemy territory. The armoured vehicles continued on in the same direction, but the Mahrattas wheeled into the west, and under cover of the foliage of the Ventia ravine, reached and seized Monte Falone without alarm. 2/3 Gurkhas, essaying a similar manœuvre, had less luck, and clashed with outposts on Monte Urbino. On Tiberside, King's Own and 3/1 Punjabis made good progress, clearing a number of villages and brushing aside isolated parties of the enemy, who from the woods and orchards around the hamlets, sniped and bickered with the Indian patrols as they worked forward.

To the west of the Tiber, 10th Brigade joined in the advance on a two-battalion front. They moved across the grain of the ground, and found heavy going. Uphill, downhill, ford a stream, uphill, downhill, ford again. By July 2nd the Brigade was within reach of the first of the German lay-back positions ten miles north of Perugia. Here Monte Corona, a thickly wooded pinnacle, and Monte Acuto, a broad bald sugarloaf, barred the way. The enemy appeared to hold these crests in strength. 4/10 Baluchis and 2/4 Gurkhas swung away on long night marches over unreconnoitred country. Before dawn the Baluchis were on Acuto and the Gurkhas on Corona. After initial surprise, the Germans reacted energetically. A counter attack on the morning of July 3rd threw back the Baluchi company which had occupied the crest of Monte Acuto. A similar attempt against the Gurkhas had less success, but sporadic fighting continued. These objectives promised to give trouble until July 4th, when Thirteenth Corps troops, advancing west of Lake Trasimeno, captured the important road centre of Cortona. This success threatened to trap the enemy on 10th Brigade's front. The fighting on the mountain tops ceased, and the Germans retired hurriedly while an exit remained. Seven miles further north, on the line of the River Nestore, they paused to draw breath and to face their pursuers.

These first miles marked the end of the easy going for Tenth Indian Division. On both sides of the Tiber the ground now favoured the defenders. A regrouping of enemy forces brought the reinforced and rested Three Hundred and Fifth Division into the line on the Indians' front.

25th Brigade, working along the eastern fringe of the Tiber Valley, was first to encounter stiffened resistance. Ten miles beyond their start line, 3/1 Punjabis and King's Own found the little village of Pierantonio a tough nut to crack. An attack on the night of July 2nd cost the British battalion 3 officers and 33 men, of whom 12 were killed. The next day, after a concealed approach march from the west, the position was taken without difficulty. A patrol went forward to reconnoitre Umbertide, a sprawling factory town of yellow-and-grey-walled houses which had grown up around the site of an ancient fortress. This centre likewise was free of the enemy, and 25th Brigade came up in line with the two flank brigades. 3/1 Punjabis immediately pushed on and established contact with the enemy at Montone, five miles to the north, a village standing on a peak above the Tiber Valley. It was an ideal defensive position, as the tracks to the village from south and west climbed open spurs, while on the east the summit was protected by a precipitous hillside. The village and a ridge behind it running into the north, were held by a battalion of One Hundred and Fourteenth Jaeger Division.

On July 6th, 3/1 Punjabis attacked from the south. Throughout the burning heat of the afternoon Sikhs and Mussalman companies battled their way forward across the open countryside. As they surged to gain the shelter of the village, blasts of defensive fire caught them. Colonel Dalton was mortally wounded and his men suffered severely. Fortunately General Reid had not staked everything on the frontal attack. In the dark hours of the previous night 8th Manchesters of 20th Brigade had unobtrusively infiltrated through the hills on the right, and before dawn had tiptoed in upon the German garrison of Carpini, three miles to the east of Montone. Fifteen of the enemy were killed and a number of prisoners taken in a brisk scrimmage in the dark. Following up, King's Own in the next night likewise encircled the Brigade flank in an arduous twelve-mile march over ridges and rivers, and arrived before first light on the crest of Monte Cucco, a mile behind the positions in which the enemy confronted the Punjabis. Without pause King's Own swept down the hillside, into Montone village from the rear. Surprise was complete, and British bayonets were at work before the Germans were awake. The Jaegers in characteristic fashion stuck it obstinately, and several hours of street fighting ensued before Montone was cleared and held. Twenty Germans were killed and sixty-five prisoners taken in return for nineteen British casualties. Lance-Corporal Huntingdon, of Goole, and Private Bradley, of Llanelly, exploited a technique of their own in winkling sullen Boches out of cellars, and the pair brought in twenty-five prisoners.

It would have been unlike the enemy to accept such reverse. A counter-attack was anticipated. To meet such threat 3/5 Mahrattas at midnight on July 7th, passed through Monte Cucco and worked into the north along a bare razor-backed ridge, with precipitous slopes on either side. On this narrow neck of high ground, two platoons bumped into a task force of Germans debouching from their start line on a wooded crest. Pandemonium broke loose as the leading troops clashed. Both German and British gunners, standing by for the signal, intervened with curtains of defensive fire. The British shoot was remarkably accurate, dropping only 300 yards ahead of the Mahrattas. The Indians knew their enemies to be trapped and went in with the steel. Amid battle cries and screams the ridge was cleared, and the Mahrattas pressed on towards Monte Falcione, a bald-headed hilltop. Northumberland Fusilier machine-gunners raked the summit before the rush went in. With the Mahrattas in full cry the assault swept over the crest. Darkness and the noise persuaded a number of Jaegers to remain cowering at the bottom of their slit trenches, easy prey for the mopping-up squads.

At Morlupo a halt was called, and the gains were consolidated. Throughout the following day, the Mahrattas from their lofty perch on the crown of the mountain, scanned the countryside ahead and below, while artillery and mortar shoots searched for enemy strong points. "It was like stirring an ant hill with a stick," wrote an officer. "Every time a ranging shot went over, the target area spewed out Germans who dived into prepared positions." On the following day, two companies of Mahrattas attempted unobtrusively to reach the crest of Monte Marucchino. For a time their progress was undetected, but the watchers at Morlupo saw an Italian who was driving his cows down the forward slopes of the mountains, halt and rush into a large farmhouse. Out poured Germans into their slit trenches, and the fight was on. The Mahrattas emerged from cover and raced up the hillside to encounter murderous machine-gun fire from the thickly wooded crest.

Meanwhile the right flank of the Morlupo position was under counter-assault. A swift enemy rush had pushed back a platoon of Mahrattas from Point 624, one of their forward posts. 2/3 Gurkhas were on their way forward to relieve, and it was decided to restore the situation before they arrived. Without support weapons the intrepid Mahrattas dashed to the attack. As they closed, a machine-gun nest swept them to earth at point-blank range. The company commander and six non-commissioned officers fell dead. Naik Yashwent Ghadge, the only man of his section unhurt, charged on. Throwing a grenade he followed in with tommy-gun blazing. He reached the emplacement out of ammunition, and hurled himself upon the remaining machine-gunners, whom he beat to death with his clubbed tommy-gun. A sniper brought him down with a mortal wound, and he died across the bodies of his enemies. He had saved his company, his dauntless courage winning a posthumous Victoria Cross.

The Mahrattas dug in and waited, but the enemy had had enough and made no further attempt to attack. On the next ridge to the north, a company of the Manchesters had seized a strong-point situated in an ancient castle, which yielded some interesting loot in the form of feminine apparel, cosmetics and wine. Beyond the British flank Skinners' Horse scoured the open countryside as far as the village of Petralunga, at the end of a track on the crest of the High Apennines. In this fastness the partisans and a group of escaped Allied prisoners of war were in control. The enemy was alert, his mountain troops maintaining a cordon in the hills behind the village. The presence of Skinners' Horse led the Germans to close up on all sides, but under cover of a diversionary counter-attack the cavalrymen were able to slip away. For some days clashes continued, as the enemy was in no mood to relinquish his grip upon this mountain position which commanded two of the important lateral roads to the Adriatic coast.

This bickering in the hills was of secondary importance, since advances in the Tiber Valley were bound to lead to enemy withdrawals on the open flank. With the enemy ejected from the Montone lay-back positions, 2/3 Gurkhas despatched strong fighting patrols to explore the massive Monte della Gorgacce buttress, five miles further north. The intervening ridges were higgledy-piggledy, heavily wooded, and with few tracks. Sheltered transport harbours were few and far between. An artillery observation officer, who accompanied one of the Gurkha patrols, was lucky enough to spot forty German vehicles, including tanks, huddled in a valley. It was a gunner's dream target; after a ranging round the Divisional twenty-five rounders, mediums

VILLAGE PATROL

PICKUP VAN

ADVANCE THROUGH THE WHEAT

CARRIERS LEAD THE WAY

ENEMY HOLDS WHITE HOUSE

PIFFERS CLIMB

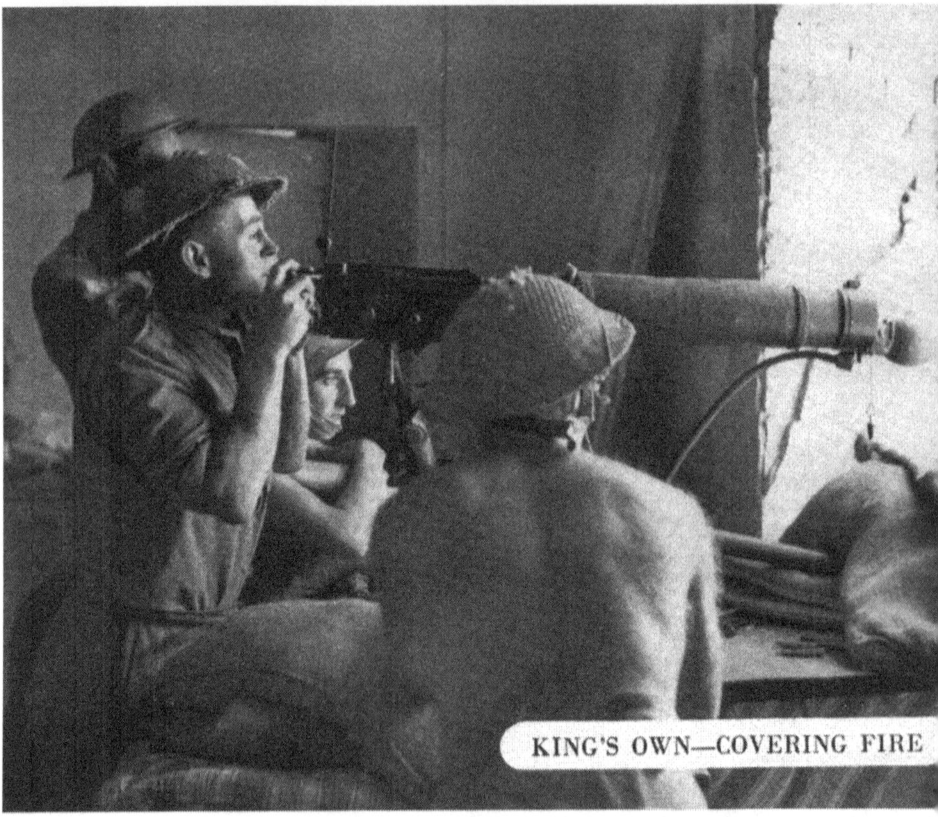

KING'S OWN—COVERING FIRE

ENEMY IN SIGHT

and heavies, plastered the acre with everything fuseable. The result was devastation.

Along the eastern Tiber bank, 25th Brigade matched the aggressive tactics of 20th Brigade in the hills. Two miles west of Montone, Colle di Pazzo, with a fortress-like church, gave 3/1 Punjabis considerable trouble before it succumbed to an assault. Numerous ravines afforded cover for mortars and other high-angle weapons, and the Punjabis advanced through continuous harassing fire. Promano was taken, but the next Tiberside hamlet, San Lucia, was firmly held as part of a continuous position hinging on the bastion of Monte della Gorgacce. 20th Brigade again led in punching the hole. On the night of July 13/14, 2/3 Gurkhas, after a circuitous march, approached the mountain positions from the west. In silence the hillmen began to clamber through the thick scrub. While two companies were winning to the summit by an unorthodox approach, a third company demonstrated from the south along the only track leading to the crest of the mountain. The enemy was completely deceived; when the rush came from an unanticipated direction, resistance broke down. Not for the first time did the maxim that "Sweat saves blood" justify itself. Two nights later, 25th Brigade struck on the river front. King's Own climbed a sheer ravine in the darkness and swept over three company objectives in fine style. Twenty-four hours afterwards, 3/18 Garhwalis, a battalion very much at home in this sort of fighting, filtered through along the boundary between 20th and 25th Brigades, and after a brisk encounter seized the last high ground south of the Soara River.

Three miles beyond the Soara, at Citta di Castello, an important topographical change occurred. The Tiber Valley began to spread out into a basin between the hills. This basin was twenty miles in length and up to five miles in width. Its tankable terrain offered an easier line of advance than the forbidding ridges on either side. Once Citta di Castello, which barred the entrance into this easy ground had fallen, Corps planned to loose armour in the basin. To give the tanks elbow room the axis of advance of Tenth Division veered into the north-west. Conforming to this change in direction, 20th Brigade shifted from the right to the left flank of the Division, crossing the Tiber and coming up on the outside of 10th Brigade. 25th Brigade took over all responsibilities on the eastern bank of the river. The first of these was to break into Citta di Castello. Orders were issued immediately for the crossing of the Soara and the storming of the high ground in front of the town.

A canny bit of deception, in which the Divisional artillery laid down smoke screens on the German positions, while British tanks milled about and simulated attack, led to the disclosure of the enemy's defensive fire plan. Thereafter 25th Brigade knew where not to go. The tanks changed from feint to earnest, and on the night of July 20th two squadrons of 3rd Hussars forded the Soara and rumbled up a V-shaped hill against the German positions. Anti-tank guns knocked out the leading troop, but behind a concentration shoot the armour swept over the crest and ran riot among demoralized defenders. Germans scurried about, as one officer put it, "like fowls in a rainstorm", seeking only to escape. The tanks shot them down as they ran. When King's Own followed up to consolidate, One Hundred and Fourteenth Jaeger Division had lost nine guns and three hundred men, of whom one hundred had been killed. Citta di Castello was undefended, and the thoroughly satisfied Hussars entered next morning.

Directly across the valley from the Montone area so brilliantly cleared by 20th Brigade, the River Nestore emptied into the Tiber, flowing down in a wide bend from the north-west. For the last five miles the Nestore river bottom was broad, flat and open, dominated by high ground to the north. It had been thickly mined, and constituted a continuation of the Montone-Carpini defensive position on the eastern bank of the Tiber. Its capture appeared a difficult proposition, and it lived up to its looks. On July 10th, 2/4 Gurkhas, led by Lieut.-Colonel G. A. Fullerton, D.S.O., with one company of Durham Light Infantry under command, crossed the minefields, and against exceedingly bitter opposition fought up the opposite hillside to the key German position at Trestina. The nodal area of the defence lay around the village church, which was stormed after ferocious hand-to-hand fighting. The remainder of the Durhams, following through in close support, consolidated and exploited the gains.

On July 16th three battalions smashed at the high ground overlooking Citta di Castello from the west. The Durhams stormed Monte Cedrone, taking 38 prisoners, while 2/4 Gurkhas battered their way into Uppiano. 3/10 Baluchis completed the task by seizing Monte Arnato, half-way between the Gurkha and Durham positions.

With both flanks secure, the exploitation of the Tiber Valley began. Skinners' Horse, 3rd Hussars, and Royal Wiltshire Yeomanry spread out and began to work up the widening valley above Citta di Castello. The country was very enclosed, covered with vineyards and fruit trees which reduced visibility to twenty-five yards. From the first, fighting was confused and progress slow. Barging through the vineyards the tanks encountered enemies at touching distances. A German anti-tank gun was knocked out at a range of ten yards. Tank men opened their hatches to hurl grenades at infantry in the ditches. 10th Brigade was in touch with the armour on the left, 2/4 Gurkhas forming the link. The hillmen followed the Hussars into San Fista and San Romano, while the tanks cruised forward in the open ground to the line of the Anghiari-San Sepolcro road, where the Tiber valley again begins to narrow into a gorge. This armour foray paid handsome dividends. Not only did the incursion ease the pressure on the infantry, which advanced in less favourable terrain, but the enterprise showed a profitable balance on general account. For the loss of one tank and six men, the raiders had killed one hundred and wounded three hundred of the enemy, had taken fourteen prisoners, knocked out three anti-tank guns, and destroyed a number of bazookas and machine-gun nests.

When the armour onset ended, the brigades west of the Tiber were busy mopping up in the thickly settled low ground adjacent to the river basin. Progress was slow, as the lie of the land prevented a general assault. Advances by fighting patrols or company groups invited counter-attacks on the same scale. Key positions and lines of approach were ranged to a yard by enemy guns. Intensively mined ground likewise retarded progress. Enemy agents, working in the hours of darkness, sowed Schu-mines in bivouac areas miles behind the forward troops. These devilish inventions were almost impossible to detect either by eye or by instrument. Sepoys prodding with their bayonets for anti-tank mines would be killed or blinded by touching off the delicate trigger of a Schu-mine which responds to a few pounds pressure. One officer, having lifted forty-six Schu-mines, was blinded and lost a leg on the forty-seventh. Lieut.-Colonel A. E. Cocksedge, D.S.O., commanding 3/5 Mahrattas, was another Schu-mine casualty in this area. It is interesting to note that when Colonel Cocksedge was wounded, his artillery liaison officer, Major James, of 68 Field Regiment, immediately assumed command of the infantry, an instance of the intimate co-operation between arms which prevailed throughout this operation.

The clearing of the sac-shaped Tiber basin ended the advance of Tenth Division on both banks of the river. On the night of July 28th, 25th Brigade joined the other two brigades on the west bank. A vigorous push into the north-west began. By July 31st, 25th Brigade were astride the lateral road at Anghiari, where the river enters a ravine in the Apennines. In front loomed the great massif of Alpe di Catenaia, with the abrupt buttress of Monte Montalto as its outpost. On the night of July 31st, after a night march of four miles across precipitous ridges, 3/18 Garhwalis appeared out of nowhere on the crest of this formidable height. Surprise was complete, and the enemy fled. The way had been opened for assault on the towering summits to the north.

A major operation now loomed, different in type to the flexible guerilla-like warfare which had characterized Tenth Division's advance from Perugia. During this month of constant fighting, in which the three brigades had advanced for more than forty miles over most difficult terrain, the technique of attack had steadily intensified. The operation had constituted invaluable training for the greater battles to come. The experience gained in deep reconnaissance, night marches, sudden assaults, and the varying tactics of surprise, gave unmistakable cues for success for the future. General Reid, ever quick-minded, hammered home the lessons learned. He had a penchant for slogans, rightly believing that a significant phrase can mean more than a tome. As Tenth Division prepared for the critical work ahead, the instruction "Always lean forward" became its watchword. Interpreted, this slogan demanded deeper penetration, more intimate exploration of the enemy's rear, speedier infiltration. The assault must be stepped up.

Alpe di Catenaia consisted of an agglomeration of ridges and peaks rising to 4,000 feet, eight miles to the north-west of the Divisional positions along the Sovara River. Like the great mass of Prato Magno to the west of Arezzo, and the Alpe della Luna to the east of the Tiber, this solid block could not be by-passed by way of either of the river valleys. These inhospitable trackless heights must be stormed before sufficient forces could be deployed to meet the enemy in his main positions around Florence. Nor was infiltration feasible amid this tangle of ravines, peaks and ridges. The massif could only be taken by frontal assault.

Three Hundred and Fifth German Infantry Division held Alpe di Catenaia with all three regiments in the forward positions. In addition, elements of Fifteenth Panzer Grenadier Division and One Hundred and Fourteenth Jaeger Division were available as reserves. A survey of the terrain made it apparent that at most a brigade group could be maintained on the crest of the mountains, so that the assault must go in against heavy odds. A jeep track would be pushed through as rapidly as possible, but the construction even of the roughest road up the precipitous hillsides promised to take too long to influence the course of the battle.

20th Brigade, which had been resting for a week, was selected to lead the assault. At 2100 hours on August 3rd, 3/5 Mahrattas followed by 2/3 Gurkhas and 8th Manchesters, crossed the Sovara and began to work up the slopes. Machine-gun nests opened fire, but false crests and deep wooded ravines gave the Mahrattas cover as they clambered up the hillsides. The battalions were organized on a mule and manpack basis and the assault troops were heavily laden. To maintain reasonable speed of movement required tremendous physical effort. The loose shale surfaces gave uncertain footing, and the heavy undergrowth compelled constant detours. Fortunately the enemy had concentrated the bulk of his troops on the higher ridges, and the slopes were too steep to be effectively curtained by defensive fire. The Mahrattas plodded on, and two and a half hours after crossing the river, reached their start line at Point 941. High above loomed the defended positions, where Point 1201 stood at the northern tip of a ridge running into the main system. At 0200 the assault went in with the bayonet. After grim and bitter fighting the Mahrattas surged over the crest and destroyed the garrison of Point 1201. Without pause "B" Company moved off in the darkness, feeling for Monte Filetto, the first of the pinnacles which crowned the main ridge. Once again a swift rush broke into the enemy positions. Daylight revealed the Mahrattas to be firmly established on the southern buttresses of Alpe di Catenaia.

To march four miles, climb three thousand feet and storm two strong positions, made a great night's work. Dawn brought no rest. During the forenoon the Mahrattas began to infiltrate along the high saddleback towards the summit of Monte Altuccia. When evening fell two companies had secured this wooded peak. Leaving "D" Company in garrison, "C" Company pushed on across the connecting ridge towards Monte Castello, the highest crest of all, standing four thousand six hundred feet above the valley. 2/3 Gurkhas moved up in close support while King's Own supplied garrisons for Points 941 and 1201, covering the right flank of the advanced positions. For a loss of one hundred men a foothold had been gained in the heart of the German defences.

It is difficult to understand why the enemy, with a full division available, launched no counter-attack during the first twenty-four hours of the new battle. It is possible that the Mahrattas' audacious enterprise caught the Germans unaware. Moreover, enemy communications, stemming from a lateral road between the Arno and Tiber valleys, were little more than goat paths along a bleak and precipitous mountainside. Furthermore, mist and rain cloaked the high crests and pinnacles, limiting accurate observation. In lieu of counter-attack, therefore, enemy artillery groups for hour after hour plastered the approaches to the ridges. King's Own reported six hundred shells as their portion of a single day's hate. The Gurkhas counted one thousand shells during the hours of daylight, with no man killed and only a few wounded. The shoot searched the rear areas and ignored the summits of the ridges—an indication that the enemy was unaware of the exact situation and was groping for targets.

Meanwhile the sappers and road construction units had moved forward, and were hard at work on a track to the mountain top battlefield. The troops mustered for this task included three companies of Indian Sappers and Miners, a Canadian drilling section, two Italian pioneer companies and a number of specialized mechanical units. From roadhead south of the Sovara the gangs cleared a way into the river bottom, a drop of four hundred feet. Beyond the crossing, the track followed old footpaths along the steep hillside, winding in and out of gullies, marching up the bed of mountain streams and ever climbing, until six miles beyond the Sovara it reached the battle positions three thousand seven hundred feet above the valley. Giant boulders, crumbling surfaces, rocky ledges, patches of scrub and heavy forest, alike succumbed to the caterpillars, picks and shovels and high explosive of the urgent sappers. Neither enemy shell fire nor direct attack impeded the progress. (Divisional anti-tank gunners, who supplied covering parties to the construction units, beat off an enemy raiding party which had penetrated as far as truckhead, and took seven prisoners.) The teamwork and pertinacity of the engineers triumphed over every obstacle and the bare log of accomplishment does less than justice to a superb achievement.

Mule track . .	5 miles built by two platoons in 18 hours.
Jeep track . .	6 miles of high quality track for jeeps and trailers completed by four platoons and two Italian pioneer companies in 66 hours.
Tank track . .	5 miles completed by three platoons in 36 hours.

With the forward company of Mahrattas on the slopes of Monte Castello, 2/3 Gurkhas concentrated at Monte Filetto and prepared to pass through for assault on the highest ground of all. The mopping up of the heavily wooded ridges delayed the next phase of the operation, but by the evening of August 5th the hillmen had taken over, had passed through, and had established themselves firmly on the summit of Monte Castello. One company thereupon moved downhill into the north-west towards Regina, a bare eroded bluff where the main ridge curved into the east. The lie of the ground can best be visualized by thinking of the Gurkhas' favourite weapon, with Altuccia and Castello forming the handle, and Regina nestling in the crook of the blade. A narrow neck of falling ground joined Regina to Castello on one side and Regina to the eastering main ridge on the other. A deep ravine separated the crests between the extremities of the arc. Cliff faces protected the Regina position on the north and west. The ridge was held by two battalions of the Fifteenth Panzer Grenadier Division.

The first exploratory advance of the Gurkhas encountered intense resistance, and the assault was not pushed home. On the following evening, two additional companies moved up to stiffen the attack. One company, with battalion headquarters and attached machine-gunners from Northumberland Fusiliers, remained in garrison on Monte Castello. As the Gurkhas advanced to their start line, a leading section overran an enemy outpost, taking prisoners. The frightened Germans gave accurate details of the Regina defences. In view of the strength revealed it was decided to set back the attack for a few hours, pending more detailed reconnaissance of the enemy positions.

Never was a more opportune and fortunate decision. While the Gurkhas on the saddleback adjoining Regina were waiting for additional information, elements of two fresh enemy battalions crossed the deep ravine eight hundred yards behind the forward companies and after a short bombardment dashed for the crest of Monte Castello. The machine-gunners on the right flank were overrun. Had the enemy been able to seize this dominating height, the Gurkhas would have been cut off and the success of the main operation jeopardized. Quickly appraising the situation, Colonel Somerville contacted his forward companies by wireless, bade them face about, deploy and hurry back, to fall upon the rear of the attacking force. The manœuvre was executed as planned. The Gurkhas retraced their steps, and moving silently through the night, encircled and trapped the Germans. Day broke on a fearful scene. The hillmen went berserk, hunting to the death, springing in with the stroke from behind trees, from out of the undergrowth. Screams rang through the woods as Germans fled until brought down; others knelt in the open glades with arms upraised imploring mercy. Few escaped, and for years to come foresters cutting the summer growth will find in the bracken and bramble coverts skeletons which bear mute witness to swift and fearful retribution.

That evening two companies of Mahrattas came forward to take over the assault on Regina feature from the Gurkhas. Stubborn fighting ensued with swift counter-attacks upon the heels of every Indian gain. Ammunition ran low, and the final Mahratta attack went in with the bare steel. Beaten off the crest, the enemy infiltrated back along the slopes on either side. The Mahrattas withdrew; as the Germans followed up, curtain fire crashed down on all approaches to Regina. The enemy went to ground, and no further attempts made to interfere with the retirement.

With the Castello position secure, a breathing space ensued for 20th Brigade while the flank brigades worked up along the slopes of the mountain. This operation was still in progress when Tenth Corps was obliged to relinquish a division to the imminent offensive on the Adriatic front. Thereupon Tenth Indian Division spread out over double frontage, a circumstance which led to the interruption of the Alpe di Catenaia advance. To aid in covering the extended sector, 4/11 Sikhs, 1/4 Essex and Lovat Scouts were taken under command. On August 9th Tenth Division began to sideslip into the new positions. By August 14th, when realignment was completed, the Divisional units were dispersed over fifteen miles between the Tiber and Monte Grillo, to the west of the Arno. 12th Lancers and half of Lovat Scouts patrolled the top of the Tiber basin. 25th Brigade, with 4/11 Sikhs, held the high ground astride the Sovara river. 20th Brigade remained on the Alpe di Catenaia crests. Central Force consisting of King's Own, Royal Garhwalis, and part of Skinners' Horse, guarded the western slopes of the same massif. 10th Brigade, with the remainder of Skinners' Horse and Lovat Scouts, assumed responsibility for the left flank of the Division amid the high outcrops and spurs of the Prato Magno.

With such an extensive front, it was impossible to commit the Indians to a major assault, and battle tactics reverted to the type of exploitation so successfully employed in the advance up the Tiber Valley. General Reid gave his men a new slogan "Step up. Keep stepping up," he said. In other words, wherever patrols penetrated, the support groups must be at their heels. A patrol would find an opening. A platoon would occupy the position unobtrusively. Next night a company would consolidate the ground. The battalion would then move in, and the patrols would set forth on a fresh venture.

The dispersal of forces did not in any degree dissipate the offensive spirit of Tenth Indian Division. Instead, everyone welcomed the return to flexible operations. Over the wide front the German garrisons nowhere were safe. On the extreme right of the Division a patrol of 8th Manchesters, consisting of one officer and four men, in broad daylight penetrated an enemy minefield covering Monte Doglio, disarmed two perfunctory sentries and took twenty-six sun-bathers prisoner. (Two days later the German officer commanding the detachment walked over to surrender, complete with batman. He deserted rather than face court-martial for negligence.) Subedar Alam Singh Chaudri of 3/18 Garhwalis with four men emulated Gideon's tactics in thick undergrowth, speeding around a German post and blazing from all directions to create an impression of superior numbers. Fifteen Germans emerged waving handkerchiefs. The Nazi corporal in command, when he twigged the ruse, threw his forage cap on the ground and jumped on it in disgust. Three days after the Manchesters' exploit at Monte Doglio, Royal Wiltshire Yeomanry and Royal Horse Artillery raided the same positions in strength. The tanks ran riot, killing 60 and wounding 200, for a loss of 1 officer and 4 men.

This thrustfulness on the Tiber was re-enacted on the opposite flank, where 10th Brigade with Durhams and Gurkhas leading, pushed deeper and deeper into the fastnesses of Prato Magno. In the broken country, Wheeler Force, consisting of Skinners' Horse and part of Lovat Scouts, operated over a wide front, probing and harassing the scattered enemy outposts. On August 22nd, Lovat Scouts picked up a prisoner who revealed the enemy's signal for a general withdrawal. Next evening three Italian partisans passed through the lines, located the headquarters of 115th German Reconnaissance Regiment, and from near at hand fired the proper flares. From hill to hill detached units repeated the signal. Within fifteen minutes demolitions and dump explosions began. Next day Prato Magno was clear of the enemy.

In the centre, on Alpe di Catenaia, 20th Brigade had gone into reserve, leaving 25th Brigade in charge of the Divisional front between the Arno and the Tiber. For a fortnight after the massacre on the approaches to Regina the enemy held grimly to this feature, until progress on the flanks weakened his hold. On the night of August 19th, 3/1 Punjabis stalked Regina from the rear, and secured the crest against negligible opposition. Two nights later, 3/18 Garhwalis cleared Monte Foresto further down the slopes. (Lieutenant G. R. Grogan, M.C., in the course of this latter operation, attacked a house single-handed and captured 29 prisoners.) The enemy withdrawal was now in full swing. From Tiberside for 15 miles westward, the Indians probed, infiltrated, mopped up and pushed on. At Rassina, five miles south of Bibbiena, the Arno runs through a narrow gorge. Hills on both sides rise sheerly to 1,500 feet above the valley. The road is accommodated in a ledge cut in the cliff side. Any attempt to force this gap would have resulted in demolitions which would have blocked the highway indefinitely, so 10th Brigade swung into the hills, brushed aside opposition, by-passed the bottleneck, and hurried on. On August 27th, King's Dragoon Guards found the right flank to be open, with the Germans retreating into the mountains to the north-east. On the same day a patrol of 25th Brigade reached Bibbiena, the last important centre on the Arno below Florence. Among those liberated was Professor Fanny Copeland, O.B.E., a Scotswoman who had lived for twenty years in Yugo-Slavia. Her joy at liberation was concealed behind the pawky comment that she had expected to hear the pibroch and to see kilts on the leading troops.

By the end of August the eviction of the enemy from the upper Arno and Tiber valleys was all but complete. The Germans were withdrawing into the shelter of their latest and greatest defensive barrier on the wall of the High Apeninnes. During the months of retreat their engineers had toiled earnestly at the construction of a fortified zone along the crests of the mountains which stood in middle air a few miles to the north. The Gothic Line, as the new system was named, began on the Adriatic plain among the rolling ridges anchored to the buttress of the tiny city republic of San Marino. Thereafter, marching across high saddlebacks and steep-sided valleys, the defences followed the southern glacis of the highest watershed in Italy.

The Gothic Line had been highly publicized by the enemy. The Germans had dropped and fired over pamphlets touchingly entreating the Allies to avoid the carnage attendant upon assault upon such mighty fortifications. To Tenth Indian Division, however, the new positions meant no more than higher mountains and more numerous enemies, which in turn meant that additional effort that good soldiers conserve for emergency. As the Indian brigades closed upon the Gothic Line outposts, the prevalent attitude of the sepoys was one of curiosity and eagerness. It was left to 1/2 Punjabis, which had returned to the Division on August 26th as a component of 25th Brigade, to put the matter to the test.

On September 2nd this fine battalion approached Monte del Verna, a position of great strength on the outskirts of the fortified zone. The operation began in characteristic impromptu fashion. A patrol of platoon strength reconnoitring the village of Montellone, suddenly fixed bayonets and charged at the dead run. The German garrison, caught off guard, was overwhelmed, twenty being killed and sixteen captured. From this satisfactory takeoff the Punjabis moved to the east along the lateral road against La Verna. On September 5th the assault went in. Desperate fighting followed. The Punjabis cleared Monte Faggiolo with the bayonet. The enemy smashed back, only to break his teeth on a granite defence. Five counter-attacks were repulsed in the course of the day, and it took five hours of mopping up to destroy the diehard squads who fought to the death around La Verna.

With this important feature in the bag and the Punjabis still full of fight, the attack turned into the east and struck for the high ground under the shoulders of Monte Castelsavino. Pouring rain beat on the faces of the indomitable sepoys as the assault was launched on a two-company front. The Indians had outrun their artillery and surged unsupported to the battle. Fighting of unbridled bitterness followed as they broke through the defences. By the end of the day the German garrison was destroyed, sixty-five dead being picked up along the ridge. Exhausted and chilled to the bone, the triumphant Punjabis handed over to King's Own, who pushed on through heavy mist and rain to storm the summit of Castelsavino.

On 20th Brigade's front, across the Arno to the west, the advance likewise pressed remorselessly. On September 1st, Manchesters and Mahrattas were in contact with Gothic Line outposts at Poggio, Baralla and Gressa. Skinners' Horse brought up a seventy-five millimetre gun and pumped an introductory shell at the Line. In front of Gressa the Mahrattas engaged in a wild hurly-burly with enemy raiders who left eleven dead and two prisoners in a futile attempt to snatch identifications. By the middle of September Tenth Indian Division was closed up against the main German positions on its entire front. From Bulciano on the right to Morciano on the left the mountains were studded with strong-points in which the enemy stood in strength. Nevertheless, the reconnoitring craft of the Indians enabled small detachments to penetrate this fortified zone. Moving by night and lying up by day these stealthy patrols spied out the land and brought back valuable information. To test German intentions the Manchesters staged a mock attack near Morciano which revealed the pattern of the enemy's defensive fire plan. A series of similar devices enabled the Indians to ink in the picture of what confronted them. The more they learned the surer they felt that they had the foe's measure. All ranks looked forward to a major operation with the greatest confidence.

Tenth Division, however, was not destined to fight in the mountains it knew so well. At the beginning of September Eighth Army had opened a massive offensive on the Adriatic front. In the last ten days of that month the Indians were relieved and at once moved to join in the great new battle. Wheeler Force, which consisted of Skinners' Horse, the Manchesters and Nabha Akal Infantry (a fine State Forces unit lately arrived from Middle East) remained behind to open up

Route 71 between Bibbiena and Florence. For the next month this detached column mopped up and harried rearguards in such fashion as to earn encomiums from the Army Commander. At the conclusion of this task the Manchesters, reduced to skeleton strength by casualties and repatriation of long service men, left the Division. The other units rejoined their respective formations on the Adriatic front.

Before following Tenth Indian Division into the Adriatic battle, it is necessary to record the fortunes of others during the advance through Central Italy.

CHAPTER TEN

FOURTH INDIAN DIVISION IN THE ARNO VALLEY

IT WILL BE REMEMBERED that after relief on the Adriatic coast on June 13th, Fourth Indian Division shifted to Campobasso training area. Within a fortnight 7th Brigade was again on the move, trekking northwards through Central Italy. 5th Brigade followed, and during the first week of July the Umbrian villagers heard a good deal of Hindustani as the newcomers exchanged greetings with the rear echelons of Tenth Indian Division. By July 7th, 7th Brigade was concentrated south of Umbertide, and next day Fourth Indian Division took over responsibilities west of the Tiber.

(10th Brigade of Tenth Indian Division at this juncture passed under command of Fourth Indian Division. In the Italian campaign Indian formations so seldom operated together that it has been considered best to retain divisional identities on those occasions when they fought beside each other. The present chapter therefore will deal only with the operations of 5th, 7th and 11th Brigades. 10th Brigade's participation has been recounted in the previous chapter.)

7th Brigade deployed with two battalions forward, 1/2 Gurkhas took over on Monte Bastiola with 2/11 Sikhs on their left, and Royal Sussex in reserve. To the west of 7th Brigade, Sack Force, an independent and flexible formation which included Argyll and Sutherland Highlanders from 8th Indian Division, linked up with the 2nd New Zealand Division astride Route 71 to the north of Lake Trasimeno.

A glance at the map revealed a disheartening circumstance on Fourth Division's front. There were no north-south roads between the valleys of the Arno and the Tiber, a distance of twenty-two miles. Three lateral roads, however, did cross the front, which meant that the enemy had ample facilities for reinforcing any threatened sector of his defences.

In the twenty miles intervening between Fourth Division's start line and the block of mountains which stoppered the bottleneck between Arezzo and the Tiber basin, nine rivers criss-crossed the line of advance. Fortunately in midsummer none of these streams constituted a major obstacle. Moreover, the terrain tended to become easier towards the west; the valleys more gentle, the ridges less precipitous. The countryside was well wooded, with cultivated patches in the glades and along the valleys. In the fields the harvested corn still stood in stook and on the high isolated peaks strongly-built sixteenth and seventeenth-century *palazzi*—half castle and half squire's manor—each girt about with clusters of cottages, dominated the countryside. These dwellings were so solidly built that each represented a potential strong-point in which the Germans might lie up during the day and from which they sallied to man their defences at nightfall.

In a war of automatic weapons an advance through a wooded countryside with few tracks and little visibility constituted a hazardous enterprise. The first necessity was to locate the enemy, the second to by-pass his fixed positions, and the final task was to mop him up. The routine of infiltration varied with local conditions, but the usual method was to send reconnaissance patrols of not more than three or four men to explore the terrain ahead. Within close supporting distance a fighting patrol approximately one platoon in strength, lay in wait. Within equally easy reach of the fighting patrol a force of one or two companies, with machine-gunners, mortar teams and an artillery observation officer remained on call. The screen of reconnaissance patrols would infiltrate between the enemy posts, or in some instances would bump into them. A pinpointed picture of German dispositions would emerge, from which objectives would be allocated. These objectives were key sectors which when seized would force the enemy to withdraw from his other positions.

This type of warfare suited Indian troops. It retained something of the bushwhacking technique of the endless little squabbles of the North-West Frontier. The deep patrols brought out military qualities inherent in the blood of men whose ancestors have been soldiers for a thousand years. Keen sight, silent movement, quick decision and abounding courage were the counters to win in this sort of game, and these abilities Indian troops have always possessed in full.

On the morning of July 9th, both forward battalions of 7th Brigade, with tanks of Warwickshire Yeomanry in close support, closed up on Monte Alvieri overlooking the river Nestore. 1/2 Gurkhas were first to draw blood. Near Ghironzo a reconnaissance squad silently closed on a German bathing party. An Italian woman gave the alarm as the Gurkhas raced in with the knife. Six Germans were cut down as the nudists bolted in all directions. With little or no opposition the advance continued for two days on a front of four miles. On the afternoon of July 11th the Gurkhas crossed Toppo Ridge, and explored the valley of the River Aggia. Their covering tanks bogged down in the soft gravel of the stream, but the infantry pushed forward to Monte San Maria Tiberina, a ridge which commands the road along the western bank of the Tiber. After a brisk scrimmage the enemy withdrew, but that night a strong force attempted to regain the position. Although well ahead of support weapons, the Gurkhas stood firm and threw back the enemy. Next morning the Sikhs worked forward two miles to the west of the Gurkhas' position and after brisk fighting stormed Monte Pagliaiola. In this action Sepoy Kartar Singh cleared his company position single-handed, destroying three machine-gun posts before falling severely wounded. Still further to the west, on the same afternoon another company of Sikhs seized Monte Favalto, the highest ground on the front. This summit, nearly eight miles west of Monte San Maria Tiberina, gave source to streams flowing north, south and east. The crest commanded Palazzo di Pero in the loop of the lateral road which joins Arezzo and San Sepolcro. This highway skirts the southern flanks of the great buttress of Alpe di Poti and the juxtaposition of first-class communications and mountain fastness indicated a strong defensive position. Before launching the next assault it was felt necessary to reinforce the fighting line. Royal Sussex and 1/9 Gurkhas came forward. The Sussex moved through 1/2 Gurkhas to attack the village of San Maria di Tiberina, while 1/9 Gurkhas crossed Monte Favalto on the opposite flank to exploit towards Civatella, half-way to Palazzo di Pero on the lateral road. The remainder of 5th Brigade (1/4th Essex and 3/10 Baluchis) moved up in close support of the right of the Divisional front, where the heaviest resistance was anticipated.

San Maria di Tiberina was a delightful walled village of the picture-book variety, standing on an isolated pinnacle high above the ridge of the same name. To north and south there was an abrupt drop to the river valley. The approaches from east and west were along an exposed and unusually narrow ridge. A road climbed the southern face of the hill in a series of sharp and complicated bends. The village *palazzo* had walls of such thickness that shell-fire made little impression upon it, and the surrounding houses clustered so tightly that the streets were safe against everything but high angle bombs. On the afternoon of July 12th, Divisional guns and Corps artillery laid down a heavy shoot, wreathing San Maria di Tiberina in smoke to protect the advance of the infantry. By 2200 hours Royal Sussex were within a mile of the village and deployed for the assault. The defence, however, had only been demonstration, and at dawn the Sussex occupied the pinnacle against slight rearguard opposition. A platoon was immediately sent along the ridge to seize Monte Cedrone, two miles to the north-east.

This high ground commanded Citta di Castello and the entrance to the Tiber basin. The Durhams and Baluchis of 10th Brigade at the same time closed up on this position from the south. Although the Sussex reached the crest, the position was deemed insecure, and before dawn on July 14th the platoon was withdrawn. Next morning, 4/10 Baluchis of 10th Brigade battled strenuously to regain Monte Cedrone, but without success. The sister battalion of Baluchis from 5th Brigade thereupon came forward to mount an attack from the south-west. The assault went in at 0200 hours on July 15th. Heavy and accurate defensive fire caught the Indians beyond their start line. The mule trains stampeded in the darkness, dragging and hurling unhappy drivers in all directions. The Baluchis were recalled, Monte Cedrone remaining in the grip of the enemy.

The task of neutralizing this strong position now fell upon 1st Durhams of 10th Brigade, who had been mopping up in the broken ground between San Maria di Tiberina ridge and the river. Here the north countrymen had been waging Red Indian warfare against an opposing Jaeger battalion in "The Arena", a tree-girt stadium-shaped depression between two ridges held by the opposing forces. Irregular outcrops of rock, thick foliage and deceptive folds in the ground made "The Arena" a death-trap for the unwary. The Durhams proved excellent stalkers; patrols seldom came back empty-handed, yet only once were casualties sustained. Forward positions were so close that individual enemies became well known. A tall German officer emerged daily on the slopes of the opposite ridge to examine the British positions. With bullets pelting around him he sauntered about. He bore a charmed life, and like the legendary Mad Major of the Great War and the Man on the Grey Horse in Eritrea, his fate is unknown.

On the night of July 15/16, 10th Brigade attacked between Monte Cedrone and the Tiber. 4/10 Baluchis and 2/4 Gurkhas broke through the Uppiano positions. After a two-hour concentration from two hundred guns the Durhams smashed at Monte Cedrone. By good fortune the attack coincided with a relief and the position was seized without difficulty. Before dawn the Germans had rallied, but the impetus of a bayonet charge broke their first attempt at counter-attack. Four similar assaults failed to shake the grip of the Gurkhas and Baluchis on the positions along the river. Thereafter the enemy gave up the fight.

On the left of the Divisional front, 1/9 Gurkhas held Monte Civatella, while the Sikhs remained on Monte Favolto. The Essex came into the line between Royal Sussex and the Gurkhas, and preparations began for the next advance. Communications now became an urgent problem; it was necessary to devise a route on which supplies and support weapons might be brought forward. The construction even of a jeep track across the broken and precipitous ground to the north of the Aggio River presented exceptional difficulty, yet a way had to be found to reach the lateral road between Arezzo and the Tiber valley. A line which disdained obstacles was drawn on a map. The route chosen crossed a boulder-strewn valley, traversed deep clefts, climbed cliffs and burrowed through heavy forests. The first survey estimated ten days as the minimum period for construction. There were not ten days to spare.

By the morning of July 14th a cross-section of the United Nations had assembled in this wild spot. Detachments of Central India Horse provided covering parties in the woods on the crests of the ridges. Italian labour companies plied pick and shovel. British sappers drove bulldozers. Canadian engineers supplied explosive squads which dealt with boulders and rocky outcrops. Bombay and Madras Sappers and Miners laid the road. For twenty-eight hours they blasted rocks, rooted out stumps, notched the hillside, reared retaining walls and eased out the hairpin bends. On the next afternoon (June 15th) the first wheels went through, followed by tanks. Before the track was open Major Patterson of Central India Horse, accompanied by a sapper officer, manhandled a jeep to within two miles of Palazzo di Pero, and completed the journey on a collapsible parachutist motor-cycle. They arrived in time to greet a New Zealand armoured car patrol which had entered from the west. Enemy infantry were still dug in within three hundred yards of the town. Thus by high audacity and gruelling toil "Jacob's Ladder" came into being. The story of its building was bruited abroad throughout two armies, and when His Majesty the King visited Italy he asked to be driven over it.

With the Arezzo-San Sepolcro road under control, the stage was set for a direct assault on the Alpe de Poti massif. 7th Brigade began to draw together from its scattered front in order to concentrate on this objective. Central India Horse, which had rejoined the Division on July 14th, relieved 2/11 Sikhs along Jacob's Ladder. During an early reconnaissance a C.I.H. patrol was trapped on a mine-field. Sowar Ditto Ram, a young soldier of only two years' service, had his leg blown off. Hearing calls for aid, he pulled himself painfully across the mine-field and applied bandages to a wounded comrade before losing consciousness. He died a few minutes later. Lieut. St. J. G. Young, the patrol leader also crawled across the deadly ground, digging up mines with his hands. One he failed to detect; it mangled his right leg. He dragged himself on, dressed a wounded man, sent a messenger back for aid, and ordered his men not to move until help came. Five hours later, when sappers and stretcher-bearers arrived, Lieut. Young was still conscious, but he died before reaching hospital. The posthumous award of George Crosses to these young soldiers for identical acts of selfless gallantry linked them in a blood brotherhood transcending rank and race.

On approaching Alpe di Poti the grain of the ground worsened. Higher crests, vertical-sided gorges and heavily wooded trackless valley taxed the supply services to the utmost. No carriers save men and mules could negotiate such terrain. Concerning the hard-working and indomitable mule transport companies, an observer wrote:—

"Mules were in great demand in these hills. They performed wonders and earned the undying gratitude of the fighting troops whom they served. Daily they carried food, water and ammunition along paths exposed to incessant shell and mortar fire. One Sikh mule unit attached to a British battalion established a proud record. No mule was ever left unattended or allowed to break away from a supply column under fire. The Sikhs' tendency to treat their mules like potential Derby winners led one officer to estimate casualties to be higher among the drivers than among the mules. When fire was directed on them the Sikhs would bring their animals' heads together and would stand in front of them. One Sikh muleteer sheltered his mules in the corner of two walls while eighteen shells exploded around him."

On July 17th, 11th Brigade arrived from Southern Italy, Fourth Division was complete once more and able to concentrate its attention on the formidable objective ahead. On the night of July 17 2/11 Sikhs and 1/2 Gurkhas crossed the lateral highway, and began to climb the slopes of Alpe di Poti. By 0300 hours the Gurkhas had reached the crest, having encountered no resistance. The Sikhs on the left had run into heavy mortar fire, and it was not until noon on the 18th that the intervention of Royal Wiltshire Yeomanry opened the way. With great skill the tanks followed the infantry on to the mountain top, where the composite force reorganized and pushed on. By dawn on July 20th, the Gurkhas were in the midst of the German defences, holding a scimitar-shaped ridge of great tactical importance. Not content with the night's gains, at noon the sturdy hillmen threw in an attack and seized Point 755, one thousand yards to the north-east of their main position. The enemy behaved like a bad-tempered child, fairly screaming his rage. In the next six hours no less than ten counter-attacks surged against Point 755. Thick scrub and belts of tall firs allowed the Germans to approach the Gurkha positions unseen. Fortunately the Divisional artillery had the ground ranged to a yard. On a shout over the radio from the forward observation officer, a curtain of defensive fire dropped in a twinkling. Attack after attack was smashed, and concurrently the Gurkhas extended their gains. A company assault afterwards described by the corps commander as "brilliantly successful," enabled Major the Hon. L. C. F. Shore and his men to storm a further objective. Unfortunately this splendid officer, whose family had been connected with Second Gurkhas for well over a hundred years, fell in the moment of victory.

Arezzo had fallen to the New Zealanders, who now turned into the west for their drive on Florence. To cover the gap, 11th Brigade came into the line with 2/7 Gurkhas on the east of the Arezzo-Florence highway, and 2nd Camerons on the other side of the road. The Scotsmen found happy hunting. One of their officers wrote :—

"During the first two weeks, we had only four or five casualties: against which we inflicted thirty on the enemy and took twenty-eight prisoners. These were weeks of gay swashbuckling bravado, almost piratical insolence, and daring individual effort. There was no real front, although roughly it could be taken as the line of the Arno, which with its steep wooded banks and its little villages nestling among the trees provided an ideal playground for grim games of hide-and-seek. A German sauntering into the village of Casteluccioni in search of 'vino' suddenly drops dead in the road. Two Germans hanging out their washing at a house in Balze are brought down by Corporal Cameron before they can regain the safety of their building. A German sergeant, taking a Sunday afternoon nap in a house which he considered well behind his own lines, is spirited away by some Jocks without disturbing the Sabbath's harmony."

2/7 Gurkhas in lower positions across the road were less carefree. Their area was subject to concentration shoots of surprising accuracy, A search of San Polo, a nearby village, unearthed an Italian colonel. whose wireless set had been used to pinpoint targets.

As darkness deepened on July 23rd, 3/12 Frontier Force Regiment, until now in 11th Brigade reserve, moved forward to attack Campriano, on the crest of a ridge two and a half miles east of the road to Florence. Tanks of the Warwickshire Yeomanry accompanied the three assault companies. An observer describes the weird effect of the afterglow of the setting sun reflected on the white smoke screen, intermingled with columns of brown dust from the German counter-barrage. Night closed in with signal lights soaring to denote positions gained or calls for aid. The Frontiersmen had disappeared into the cauldron of battle; hour by hour the artillery thundered on. At dawn the Indians held both flank objectives but had been unable to prise the centre from the grip of the enemy. Casualties had been heavy, and "A" and "B" Companies of Frontiersmen had been merged. Heavy counter-attacks swept against the Indians, to be thrown back again and again. Towards evening the enemy intensified his efforts and the forward companies were obliged to withdraw to the south of the ridge.

On the same day His Majesty the King rode up Jacob's Ladder in a jeep. At the top of the pass he met the men of Fourth Indian Division for the second time. (He had first visited them at Tripoli in June, 1943.) From an observation post His Majesty watched a concentration shoot fired in support of the hard battling Frontier Force Regiment.

That night 5th Brigade sallied into the hills across 7th Brigade's front, climbed steep slopes, pushed their way through tangled undergrowth, and appeared out of nowhere among the German forward positions. 1/9 Gurkhas swept over Monte Castiglione with the kukri; the enemy fled precipitately. 3/10 Baluchis on the left seized and held high ground against persistent counter-attacks. In the next night 1/4 Essex passed through the Baluchis and after a number of scrimmages, reached Gello on the extreme right of the Divisional front. (Strictly speaking the Home County men were off the map, having sallied into Tenth Division's territory.) This quick advance to the east squeezed a number of enemy formations in a narrow salient between the two Indian divisions, and cleared the intervening sector without further fighting.

It was in Gello that the ghost music was heard. The sentimental Boche, carolling his *lieder*, has guided his assailants on more than one dark night. But never before had thin instrumental strains come down the wind, to rise, to die, to pause and begin again, and ever to draw nearer. Along a steep mountain pathway the Essex stood to arms. A German corporal came ambling up the trail playing his mouth organ. He was sure the English would not shoot him if they heard music. He was a soldier of eleven years' service who had fought in Norway, in France and at El Alamein. His company commander was an idiot. He preferred to desert rather than to serve under such a fool.

On the opposite flank, 11th Brigade was busily tidying up. After withdrawal from Campriano two companies of Frontier Force Regiment had dug in on the approaches to the ridge. They next gave attention to a monastery a half mile further west, on a pinnacle a few hundred feet higher than Campriano. This hospice was employed by the enemy as an observation post from which to direct fire on to all parts of the Brigade front. After nightfall on July 27th a company of Frontiersmen crossed the valley and chased enemy artillerymen from the chapel tower. As if expecting ejection, the chancel was found to be abundantly booby-trapped.

Throughout this district the Germans had made war in the most detestable Nazi fashion. At Talla on Prato Magno three Allied prisoners of war had been hanged. Near Arezzo, after three partisans had been shot, their bodies were bombed into senseless mutilation. In a nearby village an Indian Army observer saw the body of a girl who had been violated, murdered and mutilated. When an Essex patrol shot up the enemy garrison in Guilano, the Germans burned the village, even though it cost them their billets. These incidents revealed the atavistic Hun to be loosed. Months of unremitting defeat had cracked the veneer. In point of fact the German divisions in front of the Indians were fought out. Fifth Mountain Division and Three Hundred and Fifth Division had been reinforced over and over again by the "cannabalizing" process. One Hundred and Fourteenth Division was two-thirds under strength, and Forty-Fourth Division was estimated to muster no more than eight hundred rifles.

As has been recorded in the previous chapter, the lie of the Tiber basin diverted the axes of advance of the two Indian divisions into the north-west. With six brigades to find fronts Fourth Indian Division wheeled west, and began to probe the ridge systems of Prato Magno. A detached formation, LINDFORCE, was formed to operate on the open flank. Central India Horse and King's Dragoon Guards, together with tanks and self-propelled guns explored the mountains above the valleys of the western branch of the Arno. The front proper lay about ten miles south of Bibbiena, a small town where the main north-south highway divides. One road paralleled the Arno into Florence, and the other, bearing to the north-east, crossed the mountains into the Adriatic plain. Bibbiena was thus a natural jump-off position for assault upon the Gothic Line, whose defences followed the crests of the High Apennines.

The plan for the next advance made speed its watchword, in order that any penetration might be utilized to outflank and encircle nodal points and key centres of resistance. 5th Brigade and two battalions of 11th Brigade were ordered to attack east of the Arno, along the western flanks of Alpe di Catenaia, in support of Tenth Division's thrust over the summits of those mountains. After clearing the immediate front, both brigades would cross the Arno, and press northwards along the western bank. 7th Brigade would deploy at Castiglioni at the toe of Prato Magno, with orders to drive into the heart of that fastness.

At 2130 hours on August 3rd, "Operation Vandal" was launched. On 5th Brigade's front four companies of 1/9 Gurkhas, in touch with Tenth Indian Division on their right, swept along the broken lower slopes of Alpe di Catenaia. In sharp and bloody fighting a number of enemy posts were destroyed. 1/4th Essex closed up, and by the following evening reached high ground well on the way to the Brigade's objectives.

The start line for 11th Brigade lay south of Subbiano, on both sides of the Arno. After an approach march by moonlight 2nd Camerons attacked at dawn on August 4th, driving in a north-westerly direction. Monte Terrato and Bibbiano fell and "A" Company pushed through to Poggio del Grillo. Monte Ferrato and Poggio del Grillo were situated on the eastern arm of a barren "V"-shaped ridge which stands above the western bank of the Arno. Grillo claimed strategic importance by its control of a secondary road which crossed Prato Magno to the north-east, over which supplies reached the enemy garrisons in the mountains.

The Germans reacted venomously to the Camerons' stroke. Two companies of Fifteenth Panzer Grenadier Division, with a platoon of assault engineers, threw in a fierce counter-attack. For three hours fighting continued until the Camerons were hemmed in a small area around the house used as Company headquarters. Calls to surrender were ignored. Assault engineers reached the house, blowing in the door with pole charges. From room to room Scotsmen and Germans fought to the death. Amid the wreckage of the orderly room, with fifteen dead and dying on the floor, Major Underwood, the last man on his feet, was pulled down. As he was led away another platoon of Camerons came dashing to the rescue. The company commander escaped—the sole survivor of three officers and sixty men of the Grillo garrison.

That evening, under the glare of the full moon, "C" Company undertook to avenge the disaster. With magnificent dash the Camerons surged to the attack. Armoured cars from Central India Horse followed in close support; when the track narrowed, and the vehicles were held up, the cavalrymen dismounted their machine-guns, evaded an enemy ambush, and rushed to the assault beside the Scotsmen. Throughout the night a battle royal raged. Towards morning it became apparent that Grillo was held in too great strength for a company attack to succeed. Next morning 2/7 Gurkhas took over the task of reducing this key position, and swept to all objectives without great difficulty. Five counter-attacks disputed consolidation, but each in turn broke down under accurate defensive fire.

On the left flank of 11th Brigade, 1/2 Gurkhas and 2/11 Sikhs worked forward for six miles against patchy opposition. Still further to the west, Lovat Scouts and Skinners' Horse harried the ridges, destroying outpost detachments or driving them deeper into the mountains.

The battle had opened auspiciously. Despite stubborn stands in key positions, the speed and weight of the Indian thrust had disrupted the enemy defences. It seemed the hour to rally all strength for a staggering smash. But far back at Allied Headquarters the planning staff had sifted the intelligence, and had built up a new picture. As a result Field-Marshal Alexander decided to open his assault upon the Gothic Line on the opposite slopes of the Apennines. At the end of August formations began to regroup for this operation and the call came to Fourth Indian Division. Operation "Vandal" was handed over to Tenth Indian Division, which spread out across the Corps front. For the information of enemy agents 1/4 Essex remained with Tenth Division with instructions to display Fourth Division flashes as ostentatiously as possible. The remainder of the Division removed identifications both from bodies and from vehicles, and trekked back to Lake Trasimeno, to refit and to train for the ordeals to come.

CHAPTER ELEVEN

EIGHTH DIVISION CLEARS FLORENCE

EARLY IN JULY global strategy reacted on Eighth Indian Division. "D" day was an accomplished fact; the Normandy bridgeheads had been stormed and held. A landing in the south of France was scheduled to follow. French Expeditionary Corps, holding the right flank of Fifth Army, was selected to take part in this operation. Eighth Army thereupon was asked to extend its responsibilities and to cover the former French front. Divisions at rest were called forward. On July 21st the narrow picturesque streets of Siena were crammed with Indians as they moved up to deploy under Thirteenth Corps at Poggibonsi, a road junction fifteen miles to the north-west.

Thirteenth Corps held a front of something over thirty miles, between the mountain mass of the Prato Magno and the river Elsa, a tributary of the Arno twenty miles west of Florence. In earlier chapters the difficulties encountered by Fourth and Tenth Indian Divisions in their progress across the eastern expanses of Prato Magno have been recorded. These difficulties were shared to the full by Fourth British Division and Sixth British Armoured Division, which had been fighting their way northwards through the western elements of the massif. But still further to the west, where the Prato Magno began to flatten out, the going had been easier, in undulating and highly cultivated countryside. The new plan of battle called for intensification of the offensive in this more favourable terrain, where Sixth South African Armoured Division and Second New Zealand Division were briefed to lead the drive for Florence and the Arno crossings. The role of Eighth Indian Division, on the left of this thrust, was to keep pace with the progress of the main attack in the centre, and to exploit South African and New Zealand gains as opportunity offered.

General Russell planned his advance on a two brigade front. 21st Brigade on the right would push up Route 2 for the first few miles, and thereafter would wheel into the north-west, heading for the mouth of the Pesa river, which flows into the Arno thirteen miles west of Florence. Seven miles to the left, 19th Brigade would maintain a parallel course, following the highway along the easy valley of the River Elsa, which reaches the Arno below Empoli. Both assault Brigades would be supported by old friends in 12th and 14th Canadian Armoured Regiments.

On July 23rd the move began. 3/5 Mahrattas led 21st Brigade, and at 0900 hours chased German rearguards from the village of Barberino. Beyond the turn-off into the north-west the road and its verges were found to be heavily mined, with delayed action mines in the culverts; the old and beautiful plane trees which lined the highway had been notched for charges which fortunately had not been laid. Mahratta pioneers cleared away at top speed to let the infantry through. On the left brigade sector Royal West Kents advanced untroubled. Except for occasional pot shots little resistance was encountered in the first two days.

On July 25th 3/15 Punjabis and 3/5 Mahrattas closed up on Montespertoli, where infantry posts in a cliffside interrupted the advance. Batteries of mortars hidden in the town began to play with remarkable accuracy on the nearby hamlet of San Pietro, where a company of Mahrattas was stationed. During this shoot church bells began to clang and the Mahratta captain, an observant man, detected an interesting phenomenon. When the bells clanged once, the next flight of bombs lit in the centre of the village; on two strokes, a salvo fell behind the church; whereas three peals induced the missiles to drop on a dried watercourse. A search, even a sentry in the belfry, failed to solve the mystery, but when all the civilians in the village had been locked in a single crypt, the signals ceased. Neither the enemy agent nor his ingenious method of ringing the church bells was ever discovered.

19th Brigade columns, forming the left prong of the advance, worked up the Elsa valley for eight miles against spotty resistance. 3/8 Punjabis were missing on this tour of duty, for news had come through that the King-Emperor would arrive within a few days to pin the Victoria Cross on Sepoy Kemal Ram. Such an occasion demanded great "bandobast", and the most urgent need was to find Kemal Ram, who had been wounded in the scrimmage at Bastiola two months before, and was now somewhere on lines of communication. The signallers succumbed to the prevailing excitement and dispatched messages in all directions enquiring for Colonel Ram. It was not until the evening before the presentation that the sepoy was found and flown to his battalion. The subedar-major spent a busy evening teaching the young hero how to roll his short puttees and how to comport himself on ceremonial parade, for like most of the fighting men in this war Kemal Ram was unversed in the rituals. Nevertheless, he and his battalion made a brave show next day, and it was heart-warming to see British, Canadian and New Zealand comrades crowding to congratulate him and to honour the outstanding courage which makes all brave men kin.

That same evening (July 26th) the New Zealanders on the right lashed at the enemy. Next morning the front of 21st Brigade was open. By nightfall Royal West Kents were within two and a half miles of the Arno. On 19th Brigade's front likewise the enemy broke contact, and here the pursuit swept forward to reach the Arno east of Empoli on the evening of July 29th. On the extreme right, when nearing the river the Mahrattas turned south-east on a non-military mission—to secure the castle of the Chesterfield Sitwells at Montegufoni. Here the priceless art treasures of the Florentine galleries were stored, including Botticelli's "Primavera" and other of the world's most famous paintings. German detachments were dug in within a mile of the castle, and Tiger tanks roamed the neighbourhood. The Mahrattas introduced a modern note amidst the mediæval decor. A suit of damascened armour was topped by a shrapnel helmet, and a Bren gun detected in a stand of pikes and harbequeses.

The surge of the New Zealanders had carried them into the hilly suburbs of Florence to the south of the river. Here the Kiwis met fierce resistance. In order to relieve the pressure Eighth Indian Division was ordered to change direction, and to move into the north-east, crossing the Pesa river and closing up on the western outskirts of the city. Speed was the essential of this thrust to flank. On August 1st both leading Indian brigades brushed aside light opposition and occupied commanding ground within nine miles of Florence. When the sun rose next morning the Indians caught their first glimpses of the symmetrical wooded ridges and glittering spires of one of the most beautiful cities in the world.

Both brigades approached the Arno on the reach where it loops through the heavily populated countryside to the south-west of the city. Aided by excellent observation the enemy now showed his teeth. Intermittent mortaring and shelling searched the lateral roads and assembly areas along the south bank of the river. At one time it was considered that the Germans were in sufficient strength to necessitate a set piece attack. Engineers from Second U.S. Corps began to reconnoitre the river on the Indian front in search of crossings. Fortunately the heavy blows of the New Zealanders and South Africans in the centre took such toll that resistance south of the river became sporadic and finally ceased altogether.

Ordinarily Eighth Indian Division would not have shared in the capture of Florence, but on July 6th, as a result of regrouping, 17th Brigade moved eastwards to relieve a brigade of First Canadian Division, which in turn had relieved a South African brigade. The Indian force was really a brigade group since with the infantry went the Mahratta Machine Gun Battalion, the Mahratta Anti-Tank Regiment, 6th Lancers and 11th Canadian Armoured Regiment. Fourth German Parachute Division, tough veterans of Crete, Leros and Anzio, held the line of the Mugnone Canal, which encircles the northern confines of the city. Self-propelled guns and tanks covered all approaches to the Canal, while along the waterfront Fascist snipers lurked in attics and on the rooftops. All the beautiful Arno bridges had been destroyed except the world famous Ponte Vecchio, which had been blocked by extensive demolitions at either end. Within the

German perimeter the Florentines lived in fear; civilians found on the streets after dark were shot out of hand.

17th Brigade established contact with the enemy with Royal Fusiliers on the right, Gurkhas in the centre and Frontier Force Regiment on the left. Enemy mortar and artillery fire augmented the sniper nuisance. As the Army Commander had issued orders that nothing beyond small arms fire should be directed across the river, for some days a one-sided duel continued. Appreciating their advantage, the paratroopers grew belligerent and began to despatch raiding parties across the Arno. On several occasions Frontier Force Regiment received unwelcome attentions. On August 10th something like a small battle broke out in Columbaro. After a heavy bombardment paratroopers and Fascist irregulars isolated a platoon of Frontiersmen. Fierce close-quarter fighting followed, with Canadian tanks lumbering to the rescue in the nick of time. On the next night, a savage shoot again crashed down on the Indian front. The Gurkhas counted four hundred shells falling within a few acres. When no infantry attack developed, it was realized that the paratroopers were expending local dumps preparatory to withdrawal. At dawn a Gurkha reconnaissance patrol forded the Arno, and penetrated to the centre of the city. By one of those happy circumstances common in British forces, Eighth Division was able to supply a patrol leader who had spent many months in Florence, and who knew every street corner.

Of this entry an observer wrote :—

"The Gurkhas advanced warily, scanning the windows and roofs for snipers, treading carefully where mines were suspected. They darted from corner to corner: ahead was heard the clatter of machine-guns. Italian partisans turned up, warning of booby traps, and bewailing the damage to their famous city. The Florentines began to appear at windows, cheering the Gurkhas. People thronged into the street, picking their way between miles of rubble, to queue up for water, or to gaze angrily at the destruction."

The northern sections of the city were in dire need, having been without food, water, gas and electricity for five days. General Russell, finding his commitments in Florence to be increasing, ordered 21st Brigade to reinforce the garrison, with instructions to restore law and order and thereafter to contact the enemy on the outskirts of the city. At midday on August 13th Royal West Kents occupied the centre of the city. The magnificent cathedral was found to be undamaged. Divisional engineers speedily opened a ford which allowed supplies to come in from the south. Food for the civilian population arrived, and with pressing needs satisfied all three battalions of 21st Brigade commenced house to house searches in order to clear away the last vestiges of the enemy occupation.

During the next few days a number of Germans and even German tanks bobbed up from unsuspected hideouts. Sharp sudden scuffles occurred. In a disturbance outside the Palazzo Riccardi, eight Italian carabinieri were killed. On the Piazza Vasari a party of Germans backed by two tanks emerged from cover, sallied among the Mahratta billets and shot up a number of houses. The Royal West Kents in turn dispersed a foolhardy group of paratroopers who appeared on one of the main streets looking for trouble. Bit by bit the great city was brought under control, the last enemies extirpated and the public services restored. On August 16th, 21st Brigade was relieved in Florence by a British infantry brigade and moved back to rest, with the consciousness of a job well done.

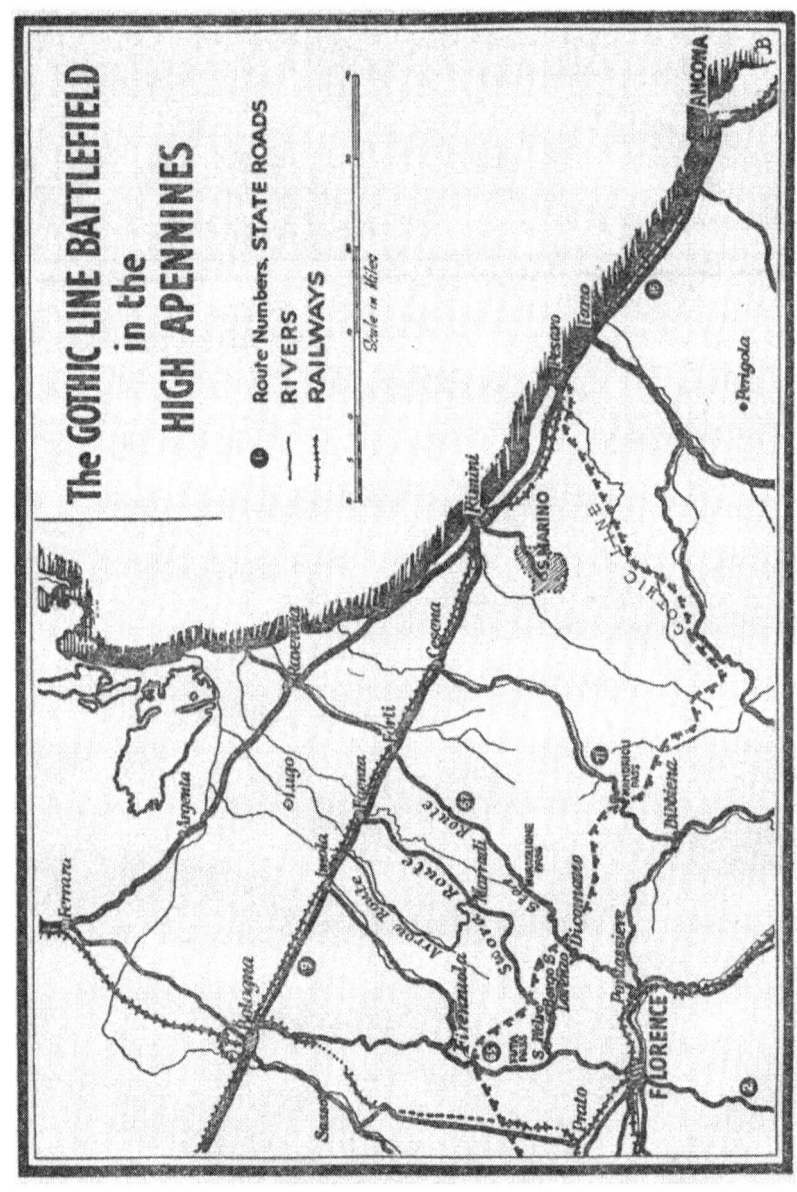

4. THE GOTHIC LINE

CHAPTER TWELVE

THE ENEMY AT BAY

BY THE END OF AUGUST, 1944, not only the German High Command but the enemy rank and file knew that the war could not be won. Month after month of unremitting defeat, with the strongest positions torn from their grasp, the stoutest counter-attacks flung back, with stop-gap successes fewer and fewer, brought home to the Nazi cannon-fodder the certainty that they were battling in a lost cause. The system of keeping reliable troops in battle until exhausted, in order that substantial reserves might be available in lay-back positions, was a passable short-term but bad long-term policy, and when the adversaries drew up for a decisive battle on the slopes of the Apennines, the morale of the opposing forces boded ill for the defenders. Each day the wireless brought exhilarating news to the men of the United Nations from the Western European, Russian, Burmese and Southern Pacific fronts, and correspondingly depressing tidings to the enemy. The Allied Commanders, unlike the Wehrmacht leaders, had nursed their formations, interspersing operational tours with rest and training periods. They had been chary of expending lives to-day when bombs and shells might save them to-morrow. As a result the men of the British Commonwealth closed up on the Gothic Line in no mood of desperation, but rather with exuberant confidence in their ability to put paid to any foes who might be persuaded to stand and fight it out.

From time to time this narrative has recorded the surrender or desertion of Germans who crossed the lines to escape punishment or because of dislike for their commanders, or simply in order to save their skins. These incidents were typical of the war weariness and lack of offensive spirit which now characterized many enemy formations. A hard core of disciplined and even fanatical soldiery remained in the Wehrmacht, but around this residuum an ever increasing number of Germans were softening up. Nor was this deterioration restricted to the raggle-taggle, the slovenly weaklings found in every army, who are the first to break. Disillusion had permeated even among the officer cadres, and particularly among the junior officers who bore the stresses of battle. Many diaries and letters, as well as the evidence of recently liberated Italians, revealed the same hectic pursuit of pleasure and the same sardonic attitude towards superiors which characterized British subalterns after the bloodbath of the Third Battle of Ypres in the Great War. In Florence and other occupied cities, life was very gay. German officers attended parties night after night, to return home in the small hours and to sleep until noon. (Before General Heidrich, last noticed at Cassino, shifted from his villa at Reggello, he gave a monster party. The time of assembly had been faithfully reported to the Desert Air Force, whose bombers arrived at the reception hour to give house and grounds a thorough pasting.)

Indeed, the picture of the German occupation in Central Italy was quite un-Prussian, and nowhere more so than in the case of the 278th Berlin-Brandenburg Infantry Division, now entrusted with the unenviable task of holding up the Indians. Its commander, Major-General Harry Hoppe, who in person resembled the caricature of Colonel Blimp, was an eccentric and irascible man. He welcomed a new draft peculiarly. "You have come here to die," he said, "and to be quick about it." But he eased the rigours of training with instructions that "three times in each week, men will rest for one and a half hours after lunch". His men sang ironically, "Do you know the Hoppe step— one pace forward, then two back?" He fostered morale by broadcasting clichés: "They Shall Not Pass" and "Better Death than Captivity". (When the Poles crashed through his front at Ancona, one thousand of his men disagreed with him).

The Italian partisan movement had begun to contribute to the deterioration of German morale. The Forces of Italian Liberation no longer marched to battle as before Orsogna, with bands playing and flags flying. Better armed, better organized, and with the best imaginable terrain in which to operate, they were a constant drain and a danger to enemy detachments in the high mountains and sparsely settled areas. (General Hoppe was obliged to describe Easter, 1944, as a "sombre festival", for on Good Friday partisans blew up a considerable number of his young men at a cinema performance). Death lurked for unwary Germans in the shadow of the woods, in dark alleys, on lonely roads. An even more serious aspect of the Italian revolt emerged during the construction of the Gothic Line. These fortifications had been planned at the time of the Allied invasion of Italy. Until the breakthrough at Cassino the work had proceeded slowly and spasmodically. Thereafter the Todt organization hurriedly conscripted many thousands of Italians and rushed the defences to completion. The German press gangs netted many partisans who supplemented the natural lethargy of forced labour with clever and effective sabotage. A poor quality of cement was supplied from Italian mills. Emplacements were built with blind traverses; pill-boxes unaccountably did not command all approaches. When battle was joined on the Gothic Line many of the gaps in the defences and "soft spots" exploited by Eighth Army owed their origin to bold and dangerous intervention by the patriot forces.

Thus neither the Gothic Line nor the men who manned it lived up to the traditions of German military genius—a fortunate circumstance for the United Nations, since few stronger natural positions exist than the wall of mountains which stands sentinel above the valley of the Po and the plains of northern Italy. From the Gulf of Genoa to the Adriatic is one hundred and thirty miles; for more than a hundred of these miles the barrier of the High Apennines is unbroken. The Gothic Line followed the southern slopes of the transverse range from the Carrara massif on the west coast, over the Alpe Apuane, along the broken crests of Tuscany until beyond Florence, where the cross range fuses into the great central spine of the Kingdom. Thereafter the fortifications marched along the basic mountain core into the massive promontory of peaks and ridges which abutted to within a few miles of the Adriatic Coast. The eastern bulwarks of the defence system were anchored into the easy beaches to the south of Rimini.

Both Eighth and Fifth Armies were briefed for the assault upon this great mountain barrier. The main drive on Fifth Army's front was directly across the grain of the ground—into the north-east, on the shortest route to the Emilian plain. But concurrently the right hand corps of this Army would attack almost due east from Florence, in a diverging drive feeling across the highest mountains of all towards the eastern Po crossings. Eighth Army would concentrate in great strength on a narrow front on the Adriatic foreshore, for advance along the eastern foothills of the Apennines. This thrust would bear into the north-west, and if successful would converge on the axis of advance of the right-hand corps of Fifth Army in the Forli-Faenza area. In grand dimension therefore the Allied attack would be a straight left plus a left hook, with a ponderous right swing reaching for the left hook's mark.

Eighth Army's responsibilities extended over a front of forty miles, but the lie of the ground restricted the fighting area to approximately one-third of that distance. On the Adriatic Coast Second Polish Corps held the line. Ten miles inland First Canadian Corps took over. Beyond the Canadians, Fifth British Corps was arrayed, with First British Armoured Division, Fourth, Forty-Sixth, and Fifty-Sixth British Infantry Divisions, and Fourth Indian Division on the western flank of Eighth Army. On the left of the Indians a wide gap extended over the watershed of the Apennines as far as the Tiber Valley. A composite force of 27th Lancers, 12th Lancers and the Household Cavalry Regiment patrolled this hole in the line. At the Tiber Thirteenth British Corps, the right-hand corps of Fifth Army, took over.

All Indian Divisions were destined to fight in the new battle. As "D" Day drew near, Fourth Indian Division moved up from Lake Trasimeno. Tenth Indian Division, under Tenth British Corps, waited for the call among the mountains between the Arno and the Tiber. Eighth Indian Division, having cleared Florence, had moved eastwards to join Thirteenth Corps in the left hook across the Apennines. In addition, a new Indian formation was closing up for the fray. It had been found necessary to alter Western Desert establishment and the proportional strength of men and machines in armoured divisions. In Italy fewer tanks and more infantry were needed. Thirty-first Indian Armoured Division, which had long rusticated in Paiforce and Middle East, had yielded up 43rd Indian Infantry Brigade to serve as lorried troops. (Although so described they saw little enough of their lorries in the campaign to come.) Under Brigadier A. R. Barker, O.B.E., M.C., 2/6th, 2/8th and 2/10th Gurkha Rifles landed at Taranto at the beginning of August, and staged forward to join First British Armoured Division. With them came their gunners, 23rd Field Regiment. Throughout its Italian service this brigade remained an independent unit, destined to serve many masters.

The narrative must now revert to the records of individual Indian formations.

CHAPTER THIRTEEN

FOURTH DIVISION OPENS THE BATTLE

AFTER WITHDRAWAL from the mountain fighting above the Arno valley, Fourth Indian Division paused briefly in the playground countryside around Lake Trasimeno. Events were on the march, and four days after concentration in the rest area, the Division began to move towards a new battlefield.

Their line of march crossed the High Apennines by way of Gubbio, fifteen miles east of Umbertide, where the Division had mustered early in July for the advance between the Arno and Tiber valleys. Gubbio was thirty-five miles south of the left flank of Eighth Army as marshalled for assault upon the Gothic Line. It was hoped to deny the enemy knowledge that a formation of divisional strength was moving up on what was more or less an open front, so Fourth Division's advance was organized behind an elaborate veil of secrecy. Units provided by Corpo Italiano Liberazione screened the advance, and the Indian units masqueraded in various ingenious guises. Experience, however, had disillusioned British commanders with the adequacy of any security measures in a countryside lately occupied by the enemy, and it was determined to supplement secrecy by speed of movement. Fourth Division was ordered to push through to its battle positions and to go over to the attack immediately, without waiting for zero hour on the remainder of Eighth Army's front. It was hoped that an extempore assault on an exposed flank might accomplish initial penetration which would distract the enemy from the main blow mounted against him elsewhere.

(As a matter of record, the enemy knew everything needful about the forces arrayed against him. German generals daily advised their commanders concerning the progress of Eighth Army's preparations, and combatant officers in turn gave their men approximate dates exhorting them to meet the shock manfully. A battalion commander of a Jaeger Division was able to supply his subalterns with intimate details of Allied formations as regularly as they arrived on the front).

At Fossato, eight miles north of Gubbio, Fourth Indian Division deployed. 7th Brigade moved off astride Route 3, while 5th Brigade worked across country. The highway offered no great advantage since many stretches had been demolished beyond repair. On the first day 1/9 Gurkhas, riding in jeeps and 3/10 Baluchis slogging on foot, each advanced sixteen miles as the crow flies, and probably twice that distance by actual measurement. No opposition was encountered on 5th Brigade's front, but 2/11 Sikhs, leading 7th Brigade with an escort from 6th Royal Tank Regiment, were obliged to fight for a river crossing only ten miles beyond their start line. Next day both brigades crossed the Matauro river and closed up on Urbino, an important road junction perched on a peak thirteen hundred feet high. Twenty thousand inhabitants turned out to jam the narrow streets, to cheer and embrace the dusty sweating jawans as they moved through. Contact was established with Durhams and Leicesters of Forty-Sixth British Division on the right. Ahead lay the easy ground of the Foglia valley, and beyond the river, the high ridges which concealed the outworks of the Gothic Line.

The Foglia valley had been sown with mines, extensively wired and honeycombed with entrenchments. Yet in the high mountains on the left the defences were rather better than incomplete. British and Canadian patrols brought back reports of dominating positions unoccupied, outposts empty, dumps of uncoiled wire, unlaid mines— a general air of unreadiness. It appeared that the Indians had arrived before the enemy expected them, and that a speedy thrust might affect the situation. On August 29th 3/10 Baluchis reconnoitred the crossings of the Foglia, and found them uncovered. That night the Baluchis and 4/11th Sikhs, an original Fourth Division battalion which had returned to the fold when the Essex were left behind in the Arno valley, crossed the river, climbed the ridge and seized Monte della Croce, a hamlet overlooking the valley. To the astonishment of everyone, Indian troops had penetrated the defence zone without firing a shot. The silence was uncanny; Major Sardar Ali commanding a company of Baluchis reported on arrival that there was not even the smell of enemies. It was afterwards learned that responsibility for this flank position was shared by three German formations and that this circumstance created a muddle.

The grand assault was now only twenty-four hours away. When light broke on August 30th, Fourth Divisional commanders surveyed their positions with a view to exploiting their good fortune to the full. The Foglia curved into the south, on an arc of five miles. Snugly following the northern bank, a ridge one thousand feet high stood above the river. Monte della Croce lay in the lap of the curve, while a mile to the north Monte Calvo commanded the bend in the river both to the east and to the west. From this village a ribbon of road wound precariously along the crest of the spur for three miles to Tavoleto, situated on a higher east-west ridge. Beyond Tavoleto this main ridge climbed steadily for four miles into the west to its summit at Monte San Giovanni, a razor-backed feature standing above the valley of the Conca.

That night fifteen miles between the Indians and the Adriatic burst into flame. A thunderous bombardment heralded the assault. By dawn Forty-Sixth British Division on the right had broken into strongly fortified and desperately defended positions to a depth of two thousand yards. At 1115 hours Fourth Divisional artillery concentrated on Monte Calvo while fighter bombers swooped with cannon fire against enemy strongpoints. 5th Brigade passed to the attack with all three battalions committed. 3/10 Baluchis followed by tanks pushed down the crest of the spur in a frontal assault on Monte Calvo, 4/11 Sikhs and 1/9 Gurkhas worked forward along the eastern slopes. From folds in the ground and hideouts enemy riflemen and machine-gunners opened fire. A number of British tanks brewed up on mines. On the flanks the advance made rapid headway, and the Gurkhas speedily swung into the north, with a view to intercepting any defenders who tried to scuttle at the last moment. In face of this threat the Germans withdrew to Tavoleto. Sikhs and Baluchis mopped up Monte Calvo, taking forty prisoners.

Leaving the Baluchis in garrison, Sikhs and Gurkhas pressed on to exploit the gains. 2/7 Gurkhas of 11th Brigade closed up to thicken the fighting line, and the three battalions battled forward for a mile towards Tavoleto. On the right the onslaught continued in full fury; a battalion of Hampshires from Forty-Sixth Division swarmed over Monte Gridolfo, almost beside the Indians, killing sixty and taking a hundred prisoners. The enemy stood at bay along the entire front, and began to strike back. As darkness fell on September 1st, harassing fire searched Monte Calvo spur and the approaches to Tavoleto. At midnight a sharp counter-attack surged against 1/9 Gurkhas, apparently to gain time or in hope of dislocating the offensive. Some ground was lost, but at dawn the advance was renewed as planned. Enemy reinforcements had arrived; mobile guns, mortars and small arms interposed a hail of steel in the path of the attack. After some progress the assaulting troops were pinned down a thousand yards short of Tavoleto.

Meanwhile 7th Brigade had deployed on the left of the Monte

Calvo position. The brigade objective was the commanding height of Monte San Giovanni above the Conca valley. The way was barred by the village of Auditore, on the northern slopes of the Foglia, and by Poggio San Giovanni, a hamlet a mile and a half east of Tavoleto. The miscellany of tasks incumbent upon 7th Brigade as the flanking formation of Eighth Army, limited the rifle strength available for the assault. On the morning of September 2nd, a platoon of 1/2 Gurkhas crossed the Foglia and closed up on Auditore. Wiring, pill-boxes and dugout entrances were identified, but silence reigned and the village appeared to be deserted. The Gurkha jemadar smelled a trap. Stationing his platoon in front of the village, he wormed his way with a section in the rear. A German incautiously stepped from a house into the arms of the patrol. Before he died he gave the alarm, and the village erupted like a hornet's nest. The jemadar's caution had sprung the trap ahead of the quarry. Without delay this intelligent officer scurried back to his platoon, disposed his men in dead ground, and remained throughout the day directing and correcting the artillery shoot which played on the village. That night 1/2 Gurkhas stormed Auditore with little loss, owing much to the foresight and military acumen of a junior officer.

Throughout September 3rd the sappers toiled in the Foglia valley, raising mines, building approaches and smoothing crossings. Mule trains were soon across, followed later in the day by wheeled convoys. That night 1/2 Gurkhas with 2/11 Sikhs on their right, struck for the high knife-edged crest of San Giovanni. Bitter fighting followed, against a determined enemy in well-constructed defences. The battle continued throughout the next day, with the Indians infiltrating for small gains.

On the night of September 3rd, an unusual sequence of events led to the storming of Tavoleto by troops uncommitted to the assault. 4/11th Sikhs and 2nd Camerons had assembled on their start line for attack on the village. To distract the enemy the artillery laid down a deception shoot on an alternative approach. The Germans, believing this barrage to herald an infantry advance, dashed downhill against 2/7 Gurkhas, in the hope of upsetting the attack. This move had been foreseen, and waiting gunners instantly replied with defensive fire which threw the assault parties into confusion. As the baffled raiders retreated uphill, a spur of the moment decision impelled Lieut. Smith of "C" Company of the Gurkhas to lead his men silently after them. Sikhs and Camerons were waiting for the signal, when the night was shattered by a bedlam of shots, shouts and screams from the village ahead. "What is happening in Tavoleto," reported a Camerons officer, "is nobody's business." At dawn only dead Germans and gibbering prisoners remained in Tavoleto and less than thirty men of "C" Company were standing.

(The log of the artillery for this night's work affords a characteristic illustration of the intricacy, speed and flexibility achieved by Divisional gunners in fire programmes. For this action Fourth Indian Division had borrowed two field regiments from Fifty-Sixth London Division. The fire plan called for a deception shoot off the infantry objective, a concentration shoot on Tavoleto, protective fire in case the deception shoot achieved its object, and a straight barrage programme for the Sikhs' and Camerons' attack. When the Gurkhas took unpremeditated action, it was necessary to cancel these schedules and to improvise new shoots. Yet throughout the night the guns answered every call, thanks to intrepid forward observation officers who kept the batteries informed from minute to minute of the course of the action.)

While the Gurkhas plied knife and bomb in Tavoleto, 7th Brigade had renewed the assault on San Giovanni. 2/11 Sikhs found Poggio San Giovanni to have been evacuated; according to the villagers the enemy carried away fifty wounded. In the first light a spotter plane wheeled down with information as to enemy dispositions on the crest of the main ridge. 1/2 Gurkhas then knew where to go, and began to clamber up the slopes. By 1545 hours that afternoon the agile hillmen had reached the summit, two thousand feet above the valley, and were working into the north along the narrow crest. Fifty enemy dead were scattered in their wake.

In four days' fighting Fourth Indian Division had penetrated the enemy's main defensive zone to a depth of several miles. On the right British divisions had been even more successful, and had advanced sufficiently for the battle line to pivot on the Indians' positions, and to face into the north-west. The Germans, however, had recovered from the confusion of the opening days of the assault, and were clinging tenaciously to their strongholds. By September 5th, 7th and 11th Brigades were facing the Pian di Castello ridge beyond the Ventano river, a negligible tributary of the Conca. At this juncture the weather broke, and pelting rains heralded the coming of autumn. The watercourses of innumerable small streams ceased to be beds of gravel; turbid torrents spread across the valley bottom, filling rhines and ditches and dredging the soggy pastures with sluices and canals. Under the flail of floodwater the river banks began to crumble. The fields turned into bogs, and the hillside tracks into mud slides. The malice of the weather, however, failed to dampen the spirits of the Indian troops. An observer records that he watched drenched German prisoners marching to the rear, exhausted and miserable. Their sepoy escort had thrown his head back to catch the rain in his face, and he sang blithely as he marched his captives along.

On the night of September 5/6th, 11th Brigade launched its attack on Pian di Castello, with 3/12 Frontier Force Regiment on the right and the Camerons on the opposite flank. The ridge was a faithful reproduction of the standard type of Adriatic obstacle. The enemy had an uninterrupted view of the slopes down which attacking troops must move to the river. Along the line of the river mortar fire crashed in a continuous curtain. Anti-tank and anti-personnel mines were strewn in cunning patterns on both banks. On the slopes above the river, scattered farmhouses and cemeteries had been transformed into strongpoints.

Under the handicaps of rain and mud, the new advance became a slow and expensive slogging match. At dawn the enemy threw in a counter-attack which the Frontiersmen smashed. During the day, tanks of the 6th Royal Tank Regiment negotiated the floods and moved up in close support. Their intervention turned the tide of battle, and 11th Brigade consolidated its objectives. On the morning of September 6th, Royal Sussex of 7th Brigade moved against a hamlet on the southern end of Pian di Castello. Once again the battle hung in the balance until British armour had skidded and slithered through the valley bottom and had churned up the greasy slopes to support the infantry in the rush which won home. That night 5th Brigade took over the offensive. 1/9 Gurkhas passed through Frontier Force Regiment while 4/11 Sikhs moved to the attack through Cameron Highlanders. At the end of a stiff night's fighting, in which a self-propelled gun across the valley wrought havoc among the tanks supporting the Gurkhas, the Indians were firmly ensconced on the crest of the ridge to the north-west of Castel Nuovo.

Dawn broke on a foul day, with the wind howling and sleet pelting a battlefield ankle deep in mud. The enemy was in such straits that the inevitable counter-attack was delayed for twenty-four hours. At 0445 hours on September 7th a heavy thrust reached the Gurkha positions. A wild free-for-all ensued as the hillmen, exulting in the opportunity, sprang at their foes. A Gurkha machine-gunner, who had exhausted his ammunition, finished his first adversary with the barrel of his weapon, grappled with the next and gave him quietus by jumping on him on the ground. A similar attack struck at the Royal Sussex; whereupon a platoon commander armed with grenades dashed ahead of his men to meet the Germans and drove them back in disorder. Beaten everywhere, the Germans sullenly withdrew to their next layback positions.

This toe-to-toe slogging, with its interminable succession of attacks, consolidations, and counter-attacks repulsed, characterized much of the Italian campaign. In compiling the narrative it is right and proper that the infantry should occupy the centre of the picture. Yet other arms should never be crowded from view. On many occasions air, artillery or armour took over the battle, to win or retrieve the day. The adventures of 6th Royal Tank Regiment in close support of the

Indians in the Pian di Castello fighting deserve to be chronicled as typical of the manner in which support arms shared the rigours of the battlefield, and helped to enforce the decision upon the enemy.

After midnight on September 8th, "B" Squadron of 6th Royal Tank Regiment moved off to come up in close support of the Royal Sussex at Cemetery Hill, one thousand yards to the north-west of Pian di Castello village. As it took the trail, the leading tank blew up on a mine, blocking the narrow lane. The next tank in line, in extricating itself, shed a track. The remainder cut across country to their rendezvous and arrived only twenty minutes late. The infantry were later still, and the armour entered the attack without a protective screen. A well-sited German gun blew up the leading tank, but the following troop manœuvred into position and destroyed the gun. Still advancing, this troop spotted fifty Germans racing for cover into a house a few hundred yards ahead. A dozen rapid rounds blew the house to pieces. Only a handful of survivors, frantically waving white rags, emerged.

The forward Observation Officer with the tanks walked across a cornfield to inspect the ruins. Twenty yards from the house he heard a faint noise coming out of the ground. Carefully moving aside the corn stooks he discovered the muzzle of a Spandau protruding from a weapon-pit. A tank lurched forward, and three Germans, including an officer climbed out to surrender, literally shaking with fright. Armed with a captured Luger pistol and covered by the tank, the artillery officer began to investigate other stooks. He unearthed twenty Germans, five with bazookas which they had not attempted to use, even at point-blank range.

The Chaplain of the Royal Sussex rushed up to pull the wounded from a blazing tank. Out of nowhere, twenty Germans appeared, without arms, clamouring to be taken prisoner. Having cleared Cemetery Hill, "C" Company of the Sussex in carriers and escorted by two troops of tanks, followed the barrage up the ridge towards the next high ground. In the darkness and without warning the leading troop lurched over a thirty foot precipice. The first Sherman executed a faultless forward somersault, landed on its tracks and continued imperturbably. The next three tumbled in such fashion as to disable themselves. The remaining three slid cautiously down the declivity and continued on their way.

The Sussex mopped up the high ground, and consolidation began. Carrier tanks brought up mortar teams to engage the forward slopes of the hill, since the angle of descent was too steep for the gunners to search it. In line with the infantry the remaining tanks took over the battle. Five times a German force of battalion strength emerged from cover and charged for Cemetery Hill. Browning guns from the tanks sprayed the front until white hot. The infantry could hear the agonized screams of the Germans as the tank fire caught them in the open. After five attempts the enemy threw in his hand. According to the record the Royal Sussex had won another position, but the infantry themselves were the first to pay unstinted tribute to the essential and indefatigable support of 6th Royal Tank Regiment.

Four miles to the north of the Indian positions on Pian di Castello, the battle rose to climatic intensity around the enemy bastion of Gemmano. This ridge, rising to thirteen hundred feet above the valley, extended for nearly three miles across the front of Fifty-sixth British Division. The Londoners had launched their first attack upon this ground on September 5th. After four days of bitter fighting in which positions changed hands again and again, Forty-sixth Division took over the assault. When the new battle was planned, Fourth Indian Division was asked to co-operate by an advance on Gemmano from the west. On the night of September 11/12th 5th and 7th Brigades lined up on the Ventano. The Sikh battalion of each brigade led the way. Forcing the river in the face of intense opposition, 4/11 Sikhs were thrown back by savage panzer attacks before they could consolidate. On 7th Brigade's front 2/11 Sikhs struck for Onferno, a small hamlet to the west of Castelnuovo. Once again the defenders held on stubbornly, and the leading Sikh companies were compelled to dig in on the face of a spur with the enemy holding the crest above them. Tanks from 6th Royal Tank Regiment came up into the firing line, smashing at the enemy strongpoints, and holding off the counter-attack. Throughout the day and night and into the next day, the bitter struggle continued. Only a thin line of Sikhs remained, yet they disdained to yield ground. Towards evening on September 13th an enemy observation post which had been directing the harassing fire was discovered in the rear of the Sikhs' position and destroyed. With unabated frenzy the Germans sought to break the assault, counter-attacking continually until a final effort pushed the gallant remnants of 2/11 Sikhs from the spur. On this same day 3/10 Baluchis joined in the fray, but encountered such intense fire that only limited gains could be made across the steep wet slopes, churned by incessant shell-fire into slippery mud runs.

Forty-sixth Division on the right had no greater luck; on the British front September 13th was marked by bitter fighting in which ground changed hands again and again. By evening the British divisions had attacked Gemmano eleven times, each time to be thwarted by a desperate defence. The Corps Commander thereupon decided to commit Fourth Indian Division exclusively against this formidable obstacle. 11th Brigade took over the left sector of Forty-Sixth Division's front. At 0300 hours on September 15th, the artillery struck with crushing effect. Behind a shoot of devastating intensity the twelfth assault, led by 2nd Camerons, won home. With comparatively few casualties Gemmano was stormed and consolidated. Part of the credit for the reduction of this exceedingly difficult obstacle undoubtedly belongs to the Scotsmen, whose dashing attack pierced the defences, and part likewise goes to the British battalions that smashed at Gemmano again and again until the enemy's will to resist weakened. But the chief honour remains with the gunners, whose performance on this occasion may be cited in detail as a superb example of modern artillery technique.

Two hundred and sixty guns played on the German positions around Gemmano, in addition to machine-gun groups briefed for continuous high angle fire. The artillery included Bofors 40 mm. guns, 3·7 howitzers, 75 mm. guns and twenty-five pounders, 3·7 heavy anti-aircraft guns, 4·5 and 5·5 howitzers, 155 mm. guns and 7·2 howitzers. The softening up began in the early afternoon when the heavy guns pumped shells at regular intervals into the German strongholds. Ninety minutes before the Camerons' attack, all guns were turned on the tiny intermediate objective of Zolana. Two thousand shells were cast on a few acres in the next thirty minutes. Forty minutes before zero hour Bofors guns began to lay deception lines of tracer to the west of where the attack would go in. Steadily the high angle machine-gun groups sprayed areas which the enemy support troops must traverse. Five minutes before zero hour all available artillery concentrated in a series of crash shoots on the four principal targets. As the hour ticked, the field guns switched to a straight barrage programme, while the mediums and heavies went over to counter-battery and counter-mortar shoots. Only far-sighted planning, accurate registration and thorough organization made such intensive support possible on such a crowded front. (On first sight of the fire plan the officers commanding the adjoining British troops were very unhappy, fearing complications. Yet this intricate enterprise was conducted without incident or misadventure.)

Gemmano was a scene of desolation. Mangled trees, grass bleached by the blast of shells, houses gaping or reduced to rubble, and German dead everywhere, marked the scene of some of the toughest fighting of the Italian campaign. It has been reported that the enemy lost over nine hundred killed on the few acres of high ground surrounding the village.

The capture of this dominating feature was immediately reflected in marked gains elsewhere. Forth-sixth Division advanced rapidly and forced the Conca. 11th Brigade occupied Monte San Colombo, picking up forty prisoners from Fifth Mountain Division after a sharp encounter. The Germans, however, continued to cling like limpets to Altavelio on the left of the battlefield. Here on September 15th a small action revealed a classic appreciation of tactical values upon the part of a non-commissioned officer. Havildar Kul Bahadur of 1/2 Gurkhas was in charge of a patrol of platoon strength sent to probe the front.

Within three hundred yards of a group of farmhouses he crawled forward with two men for closer inspection. The houses were found to hold Germans. Distributing his sections to cover all exits, the havildar with two riflemen silently moved to the attack. Surprise was complete, twelve out of twenty-two Germans being killed without loss to the Gurkhas. Continuing to Altavelio, the Havildar Kul Bahadur explored in the same fashion, discovering a self-propelled gun and its crew in the village square. While mopping up this party a group of Germans on the outskirts of Altavelio attacked the covering section, while a still stronger enemy force worked around to cut the Gurkhas' line of withdrawal. Detecting the move the havildar immediately sent half his platoon to block the encirclement while the remainder broke off the fight and retired. Throughout this brisk skirmish everyone behaved as on manœuvres, and no staff officer could have improved on Havildar Kul Bahadur's handling of the situation. Divisional pickup vans, knowing only one platoon of Gurkhas to be in action, were astounded when excited intercepts revealed that a German reserve battalion, nine miles away, had been ordered to force march to the relief of the Altavelio garrison.

The progress of the British divisions in the centre of the Eighth Army attack enabled Fourth Indian Division to widen the battlefield by a move into the west. Forty-Sixth Division had occupied Montescudo, and the seizure of this important road junction permitted 5th Brigade to pass through and to strike for San Marino, the Gibraltar-shaped buttress with a skyline like a Disney drawing, which stood high above the countryside seven miles to the west. During the night of September 17/18th, 3/10 Baluchis reached the frontier of San Marino State on the Merano River. Along the boundary, white crosses had been cut in the chalky soil to proclaim the neutrality of the oldest republic in the world. (Its independence is alleged to date from A.D. 300.) San Marino town is built along the western slopes of the mountainside. The only road winds up from the Adriatic to encircle the northern haunches of the buttress before climbing in a series of switchbacks into the town. The peacetime population of 14,000 was now swollen to 120,000 by refugees from the coastal areas. Nine days before Eighth Army's attack opened, Marshal Kesselring had demanded the use of state territory and had occupied the mountain crest.

Forward companies of the Baluchis crossed the Merano at dusk and established a bridgehead north and south of Faetano. 1/9 Gurkhas passed through and struck for two commanding knolls above the river. Bitter fighting ensued, and it was only after five hours' stubborn battling that the first of these knolls, Point 343, was captured. Although dawn was near the gallant Gurkhas pushed on to bid for the second hummock, Point 366. The enemy was strongly entrenched and the hillmen encountered vicious opposition. From a leading platoon

Rifleman Sher Bahadur Thapa and his section commander charged an enemy post, killing the machine-gunner and putting the rest of the detachment to flight. The Germans struck back at once and the section commander fell badly wounded. Sher Bahadur Thapa thereupon dashed lone-handed to the attack, gained the crest of the knoll and brought his machine-gun into play against the main body of the counter-attack. He silenced a number of machine-guns and shot down several Germans who disputed his point of vantage. For two hours in the open he held up the enemy. The crossings on the Merano had been delayed, and the ammunition mules were late, so it was felt necessary to break off the action. As the forward elements withdrew, Sher Bahadur Thapa covered their retirement, blocking enemy advance to the crest of the knoll until his ammunition ran out. He then dashed forward and rescued two wounded comrades who lay on the reverse slopes in full view of the enemy. He remained the great-hearted commander of a one-man army until he died under a hail of bullets, to join the gallant company which has not lived to know of the supreme honour of a posthumous Victoria Cross.

As dawn broke the Germans struck at the Gurkhas on Point 343, which stands above a ravine with precipitous clay cliffsides. Clinging like flies to a wall, the Gurkhas refused to be dislodged. Their precarious predicament led to a multiple "clear-all-lines" to corps artillery. Within ten minutes four hundred guns had intervened with an impenetrable curtain of defensive fire. The Germans scattered. With the high ground lost, they gave up the fight in Faetano. 4/11 Sikhs moving wide around the right flank, swept up to Valdragona without halt.

5th Brigade now lay under the shadow of San Marino, with its cliffsides crowned by spires and towers. At noon on September 19th, the Camerons had mopped up Valdragona, and had sent forward strong fighting patrols to deal with any enemies who might be lurking under the shelter of the cliffs. After nightfall the Scotsmen pushed on, closing upon three sides of the San Marino buttress. In the intense darkness, sharp hand-to-hand fighting ensued as patrols clashed. Lieut. Ellis of "D" Company killed six Germans and captured six more, without loss to his party. Behind these patrols the remainder of the battalion began to work around the hillsides into the west, where the road mounted into the town. Machine-guns at the foot of the switchback held up the advance until tanks came forward to deal with them. By the evening of the next day San Marino was isolated, and all but in Camerons' hands. This commanding position, which with proper defences might have proved another Cassino, was won at the low cost of four killed and thirty-four wounded. Twenty dead Germans and fifty-four bedraggled and miserable prisoners were picked along the mountainsides. Next morning the Divisional Commander, General Holworthy, accompanied by Brigadier Saunders Jacobs of 5th Brigade, drove into San Marino in their jeeps.

"I was taken to the Governor's Palace," wrote General Holworthy, "where I was met by the San Marino Military Guard and escorted into the sanctum sanctorum. The Captain Regent was seated beside a large table. He wore a tail coat, butterfly collar, pepper and salt trousers, and elastic-sided boots. I was in shorts, khaki shirt, battle-dress blouse, and coat duffle. With the aid of an 'American-speaking' local girl, we discussed matters. I told him that refugees had to be kept off the roads until military movement was finished. We wanted local labour to mend road blows. We had come to kick out the Boche and not to take over the Republic.

"We then adjourned through the Council Chamber to a dining-room, where I signed my name in the Golden Book. We had some wine. I was asked to state what I desired. I said I wanted headquarters for myself and one for Brigade, and some stamps. I was allotted a villa and was told that all the stamps of the Republic were at my disposal. I could have anything I wanted. The Captain Regent expressed his gratitude to the Allies for their restraint in not bombarding the town. We then shook hands warmly and I went back to see how the battle was going."

The battle was still moving into the west. The remainder of 11th Brigade and 3/12 Frontier Force Regiment had seized Monte Cerreto, a height above the Marecchia River, three miles beyond San Marino. Next day the Frontiersmen and 2/7 Gurkhas reconnoitred for crossings. While examining the position, General Holworthy and Brigadier de Fonblanque, the Corps Artillery Commander, drew an accurate enemy shoot which forced the party into the roadside ditches and seriously wounded Brigadier de Fonblanque.

It was decided to seize high ground across the Marecchia that same night. The objective was a shaggy ridge, fourteen hundred feet high, standing in a loop of the river. This feature was more than a mile in length. Its crest rose in a series of knolls, each of which bore a hamlet: Montebelle at the southern end and Scortica at the northern end were of military importance. At 2300 hours 2/7 Gurkhas and 3/12 Frontier Force Regiment crossed the river and pushed up the hill. The Gurkhas struck for the northern, the Frontiersmen for the southern extremity of the ridge. The advance began in silence and ominous silence it proved. Both battalions were ambushed by units of One Hundred and Fourteenth Division, which was encountered in its most aggressive and belligerent mood. Throughout the night the Jaeger riflemen swarmed to counter-attack after counter-attack, striking at the companies which had penetrated their defences. Ammunition began to run short yet the Gurkhas and Frontiersmen stuck it; as each rush swept in upon them, they gave as good as they got. By dawn one hundred and thirty Gurkhas were down, but their comrades were still pushing forward. 2nd Camerons, with tanks close behind surged across the river and thickened the fighting line. During the forenoon Frontier Force Regiment smashed through as far as Montebello; from counter-attack the enemy reverted to desperate defence. By noon 11th Brigade's positions on the ridge were secure.

7th Brigade now moved up on 11th Brigade's right flank and linked up with Forty-Sixth Division. During the night of September 24/25 the Royal Sussex occupied Trebbio, on the enemy's side of the Marecchia. Next morning the South Countrymen pushed on until they stood above the valley of the insignificant stream which bears the famous name of Rubicon. Twenty-four hours later they endeavoured to cross only to find both Trebola on the near bank, and Reggiano on the far bank, to be strongly held. Large scale reinforcements including a new division from Ravenna had arrived, and the enemy was set for a fresh stand. Yet the obstinacy of the Germans was a less obstacle than the inclemency of the weather. It was next to impossible to keep roads and tracks open. Mud and slides blocked diversions, hastily repaired demolitions were undermined, stormwater scoured away the footing in the fords. Hour-long traffic jams held up food, water, ammunition, and ambulances. In connection with the evacuation of wounded, old friends of American Field Service reappeared in a graphic letter from a Medical Officer.

"Here as elsewhere," he writes, "the exploits of the American drivers have become the talk of the Division. McKinley, so well known and beloved from Tunisian days, has reappeared and is in the thick of it. Attached to the Sussex Regimental Aid Post he has driven every type of transport except a tank in his efforts to get the wounded across the flooded Rubicon. When he could not get his ambulance forward he deserted it for a jeep or a DUKW. At one stage when evacuation was impossible, he established his own First Aid Post under the noses of the enemy. We felt uneasy that day and we thought we might have lost him, but he soon appeared with his six badly wounded men to inform us that thereafter his Dodge would get through."

"Then there was Jack, with his rows of last-war ribbons, leading any convoy and getting every vehicle through when it seemed impossible to do so. I fell asleep one night with little hope of seeing my unit for twenty-four hours, and then not all of it. I was awakened at 0130 hours by a voice enquiring, 'Where do I put them, Doc? They are all outside.' Jack confessed that he had to ditch a few Brigade vehicles to clear the road, but he didn't appear to be worried. That night I damn nearly kissed him."

At 0100 hours on October 1st, 7th Brigade resumed the attack. Royal Sussex and 1/2 Gurkhas, both of whom had been badly knocked about, were left to contain the enemy garrisons in Reggiano, while

2nd Camerons and 2nd Royal Sikhs pushed forward. The attack was supported by a shoot by Corps artillery, which fired 22,000 shells in under three hours. The Camerons were speedily on their objectives and "D" Company had shooting gallery practice when fifty Germans rabbited across their front in search of safety. 2/11 Sikhs ran on a mine-field, but by morning they likewise had taken their objective with forty-eight prisoners. The weather worsened; after a night's rain the ground mist reduced visibility to a few yards. In an endeavour to push home the attack a Sikh company was ambushed near San Martino and pinned down by automatic weapon fire. An enemy force with self-propelled guns in the van raced out of the mist and overran the Indians. Only a handful escaped to join up with the Camerons, whose company strength by this time averaged less than thirty rifles.

Tempestuous gales, pouring rain, bitter cold, rivers in flood and crumbling roads had done more to halt the offensive than the tenacity of the enemy. It was now thirty-five days since Fourth Indian Division had moved out of Fossato, and thirty-one days since its commital to continuous battle. During this period the Indians had advanced over sixty miles, the last twenty-five miles through a defensive zone heavily massed by first line troops with a great weight of artillery and armour in support. Mile by mile the wearers of the Red Eagles had smashed, probed, and infiltrated through the strongest defences. Many of the battalions famous in Africa had disappeared, but the new units maintained the indomitable spirit of their predecessors.

"I don't believe the old crowd was better," wrote an officer. "They couldn't be."

The Division moved to rest in Umbria in anticipation of rejoining Eighth Army for the final overthrow of the enemy in Italy. At Lake Trasimeno, as at Sidi Barrani, as at Keren, as at Enfidaville, dramatic news arrived. Greece was about to be liberated, and Fourth Indian Division would proceed to that theatre at once.

CHAPTER FOURTEEN

THE GURKHA LORRIED BRIGADE JOINS THE FRAY

WHEN MEN OF 43RD INDIAN INFANTRY BRIGADE came forward for their first ordeal by battle, they found themselves in a countryside of fields and vineyards, with the late fruit still on the vines. It was rolling land, so that they saw little except the gentle slopes of the ridges before and behind; but likewise in the north-west they saw a tall mountain on the horizon, which bore three castles on its crest, and which commanded the countryside for many miles around. On all sides of San Marino the ground fell away in ridges broad and narrow, with watercourses between them. These ridges were slashed by deep eroded ravines, whose streams fed rivers which twisted and turned, now north, now south, now directly east, on their way to the Adriatic. There was no constant grain to the ground, and the high crests tended to be higgledy-piggledy in direction. The rounded contours of the ridges along the Adriatic gave fruitful soil, so that greenery and farmhouses showed everywhere. The countryside was crazy-patched by farm boundaries, each with its hedgerow and ditching, and sometimes with sunken lanes. Arcady to the pastoral, it was a countryside stiff with menaces for the soldier.

During the month which the Gurkha Lorried Brigade had spent in moving forward, the officers and men had found full comrades in the officers and men of First British Armoured Division. The British troops consisted of Second Armoured Brigade, and 18th Lorried Infantry Brigade. The armoured regiments were the Queen's Bays, Ninth Lancers and Tenth Hussars. The riflemen took a proprietarial pride in their armoured escorts, and the tankmen in turn admired the good humour, discipline and soldierly bearing of the Gurkhas.

On September 5th, after a fortnight near Ancona, First Armoured Division moved into the line on the left of the Canadian Corps, taking over from elements of Forty-Sixth and Fifty-Sixth British Divisions, who were committing more and more of their strength to the stern struggle on the approaches to the Conca. The plan of battle called for the storming of the Passano-Coriano Ridge. The unblooded Gurkhas, with 18th Lorried Infantry, would strike for the left flank of the ridge, and would exploit northwards towards Coriano, which was the most westerly objective of the Canadian Corps. Further to the west, Fifty-Sixth and Forty-Sixth Divisions would join in assaults upon Croce and Gemmano.

From the flat beaches at Riccione to Gemmano is slightly over seven miles. Five divisions were to move into battle on this narrow front. The deployment of the enemy was equally dense. In the coastal sector First Parachute Division, One Hundred and Sixty-Second Turcoman Division, and Twenty-Ninth Panzer Division confronted the Canadians. Twenty-Sixth Panzer and Ninety-Eighth Infantry Divisions were opposed to First British Armoured Division. Further to the left, Two Hundred and Seventy-ninth Infantry Division, Fifth Mountain Division, Seventy-First Infantry Division and One Hundred and Fourteenth Jaeger Division were arrayed against two British and one Indian Divisions. On the Gurkhas' front, Twenty-Sixth Panzer Division, which had held its ground in Eighth Army's opening attack, was strongly supported by artillery, and confident that it would break the teeth of any assault.

On the evening of September 12th, the assault battalions moved silently towards the line of the Fosse del Valle, a small tributary of the Conca which it was necessary to cross before a start line could be established. The night was dark, warm and dry. The low skyline of the ridge ahead indicated the objective. Along its crest, the glow of smouldering fires identified the villages: during the day bombers had plastered key points with incendiaries which would act as a guide for the advance. The Gurkhas themselves had left nothing to chance. Air photographs had been intensively studied, and the riflemen had been told the number of hedgerows they must count before they closed with the enemy.

As 2300 hours five hundred and four guns crashed into action. Passano Ridge disappeared in the dust and smoke of the torrent of shell cast upon it. The Gurkhas, arrayed on their start line, began to trudge forward. But the Germans likewise were standing to their guns, and immediately laid a counter-barrage on the line of the Fosse del Valle. Star shell illuminated the slopes with chandelier flares. Enemy outposts inside the barrage—close to the start line—gave trouble, and a flanking machine-gun nest was knocked out just in time. The Gurkhas marched steadily up the hillside. On the crest of the ridge spandau teams which had survived the bombardment sprang from their bolt holes and spat fire down the slopes. Out of the night the little hillmen swarmed to close quarters, for the hand-to-hand fighting in which they have no peers. One Gurkha officer killed six Germans, another five, in clearing farmhouses. Three German tanks were pounced upon, and their crews slaughtered. Half an hour after midnight, 2/8 Gurkhas had taken all objectives with twenty-seven prisoners. 2/10 Gurkhas were slowed up by tenacious resistance, and it was an hour later before they reported success. They had taken sixty-seven prisoners. Casualties in both battalions had been light.

When dawn broke the Brigade had made excellent progress in consolidation. Their officers, peering through the smoke from the crest of the ridge, were less concerned with what lay ahead than what had happened behind. The enemy barrage still fell in curtain fire along the Fosse del Valle, and there were no signs of urgently needed support weapons for the defence of this tankable terrain. Would bridges be thrown across in time for British armour to come up, or would the panzers arrive first?

Of this battle, as of nearly every battle in Italy, the story is really of two battles—the storming of the high ground by the infantry, and the equally grim fight against time by the sappers and armour to construct crossings and to get support weapons forward before the enemy could throw his reserves at the newly won positions. It is perhaps as well that the anxious officers on Passano Ridge could not see the grim destruction on the tracks leading to the Fosse del Valle. Smashed and blazing vehicles cluttered the approaches, and supplied fresh targets in the long lines of blocked transport. One "Ark" Bridge had been knocked out by a direct hit, and the other had gone astray. Other crossings were disorganized by serious casualties among the sappers. Tanks and self-propelled guns, striving to penetrate the barrage, had been disabled and overturned. Queen's Bays and troops of anti-tank gunners, chafing at the delay, disentangled themselves and swung away on a long detour. After a search they found a crossing of their own. At dawn the armour came sweeping up the ridge, led by Honey tanks carrying much needed ammunition. The forenoon was nearly spent before the counter-attack developed. It struck at "D" Company of 2/10 Gurkhas, who blasted the first waves of enemy infantry into the ground. The panzers sheered off when they found artillery waiting for them. Thereafter hour by hour, the tanks, self-propelled guns, and the deadly 17-pounder anti-tank guns thickened around Pesano, until counter-attack counted as suicide.

The ridge had been won, and Eighth Army had elbow room to continue the battle. Far away in Whitehall the soldier's eye of the Prime Minister had followed the course of the fighting. His congratulations on "this brilliant feat of arms" was a proud tribute to the first engagement of Gurkha Lorried Brigade.

From their weapon pits and strong points around Passano the Gurkhas looked northward into the valley of the Marano with Ripabianca Ridge between them and the river, and the higher Mulazzano ridge dominating the further bank. On September 14th, 18th Lorried Infantry Brigade with 2nd Armoured Brigade in support, pushed obliquely across the Gurkhas' front, and after bitter fighting cleared Ripabianca of the enemy. On the next day 43rd Brigade took up the running. Desert Air Force spent the afternoon hammering Mulazzano Ridge. By 1700 hours, 2/6 and 2/8 Gurkhas were deployed on the eastern bank of the Marano. A terrific artillery shoot crashed down on the high ground across the river. The Gurkhas leapt into the stream, clambered up the far bank, and surged into the smoke. The early hour of the attack had taken the enemy by surprise and had forestalled the arrival of reinforcements which at that moment were moving up the reverse slopes of Mulazzano Ridge. The artillery wrought fearful havoc among these columns. A complete mortar company was found afterwards, slaughtered to a man as they hurried along a sunken lane to battle positions. German dead were strewn everywhere—in the ditches, under the vines, in the broken farmhouses. More than fifty machine-guns were picked up on the Brigade front. One hundred and twenty-five prisoners were taken, together with all the equipment of the battalion which held Mulazzano—half-track vehicles, telephones, wireless sets, mortars, and certain interesting documents which should not have been allowed so far forward. 2/6 Gurkhas had very few casualties, and the 2/8 battalion on the left lost under fifty men in all.

Once again, from the crest of Mulazzano, a river and a ridge confronted the victorious Gurkhas. This time the ridge lay five miles away across a wide watercourse, and it was less a ridge than a hump in the plain upon which the fortress of Sanarcangelo stood, with its walled town closely clustered about it. Between the Gurkhas on the high ground and the Marecchia river lay a low valley through which a metalled road led up to San Marino. Beyond this road three miles of broken land intervened. Then came the watercourse of the Maricchia, one thousand yards wide, with a number of small streams feeling their way through the gravel. Behind the river Sanarcangelo sat on its knoll, with the main highway from Rimini to Bologna skirting its southern walls. Beyond the highway, the plains of Northern Italy opened in a cape of low fruitful farmlands.

While the Gurkhas consolidated at Mulazzano, the two flanking divisions—Fourth British Division from the east and Fifty-Sixth London Division from the west—launched converging attacks over the difficult ground on the Gurkhas' front. The enemy fought grimly, with great strength in anti-tank and self-propelled guns. 2nd Armoured Brigade went forward to punch a hole on to the plains. It was a black day; Queen's Bays alone lost thirty tanks along the Marecchia valley. When the armour assault failed 43rd Brigade was ordered forward to reconnoitre the crossings and to join in the battle.

Contradictory information concerning the situation on the flanks raised doubts in Brigadier Barker's mind. On the Brigade front itself the position remained confused. The enemy was standing at bay, and it seemed obvious that careful reconnaissance, plus a substantial artillery programme, would be necessary to eject him. Intelligence reports, however, insisted that only scattered rearguards held Sanarcangelo and its adjoining ridges, and that a quick attack would significantly affect the battle. At 1915 hours on September 22nd, 43rd Brigade was ordered to establish a bridgehead over the Marecchia that night. Without reconnaissance or even detailed maps, battalion orders were completed half an hour before midnight. Thirty minutes later 2/8 Gurkhas moved in single file through 2/6 Gurkhas front, heading on a compass bearing for the line of the river. 2/10 Gurkhas set out immediately afterwards, and came up on the left. After an hour's march through rain and mist, the Gurkhas reached the Marecchia and organized for the assault.

At 0300 hours both battalions crossed the river without opposition and began to close upon Sanarcangelo. A thousand yards beyond the river, on the line of a railway embankment, the leading companies of 2/8 Gurkhas were greeted with intense machine-gun fire from close at hand. The hillmen slipped through and around this opposition, struggled forward and seized Point 88 on Sanarcangelo Ridge. Battle flared up on all sides as the flanking British divisions went over to the assault. With dawn it became apparent that the intelligence summaries had painted a too rosy picture. The British line of attack was by no means up to Sanarcangelo Ridge, and the Gurkha thrust had created a narrow and dangerous salient in a strongly fortified position. Sanarcangelo itself was held in force, with self-propelled guns sited well forward to sweep its approaches. The Gurkhas on Point 88 were almost completely surrounded by German machine-gun nests. The wireless sets of the artillery Observation Officers had succumbed, and the only support came from three detached aircraft which appeared out of nowhere, and as long as their petrol lasted attacked with audacity and success the self-propelled guns which were harassing the Gurkhas. The reinforcing companies lost heavily from shell fire on their way forward. The enemy threw in a counter-attack supported by tanks which forced the leading companies back to the railway embankment.

2/10 Gurkhas had no greater fortune. "D" Company was half-way up the hill when machine-gun fire opened from a series of nests along the crest. A large manor house was the centre of resistance, and this strongpoint only fell after two attacks. The enemy struck back with a company of infantry and seven tanks. Without anti-tank guns or PIATS, the Gurkhas were obliged to withdraw to the line of the embankment occupied by the survivors of 2/8 battalion. It was characteristic of the melee that while withdrawing 2/10 Gurkhas should have encountered panzers roving freely in the rear of their former positions; that on arrival on the line of the railway embankment they should find one of their companies engaged in hand-to-hand fighting with an enemy force which had struck from the flank; that battalion headquarters should have been attacked by a platoon of the enemy which had bobbed up out of the dark. Everything indicated that the enemy was so sure of his flanks that he could devote the full weight of his battle reserves to the ejection of the gallant few who had penetrated his defences.

Brigadier Barker was not prepared to accept defeat. On September 23rd 2/6 Gurkhas came forward to thicken the fighting line. After a number of attempts tanks managed to make their way across the Marecchia, and the artillery moved up to bring Sanarcangelo Ridge within range. In spite of heavy casualties the hillmen were full of fight, and that evening all three battalions of the Lorried Brigade drew together and surged forward. Tanks of 10th Hussars rolled among them as they struck with a momentum that would not be denied. The ridge was won and 2/6 Gurkhas broke into Sanarcangelo town. The castle garrison was mopped up, and partisans led by the local barber flocked to join the victors. Morning revealed that the Boche had taken his beating and had dropped back across the Rubicon,

BALUCHI TOMMYGUNNER

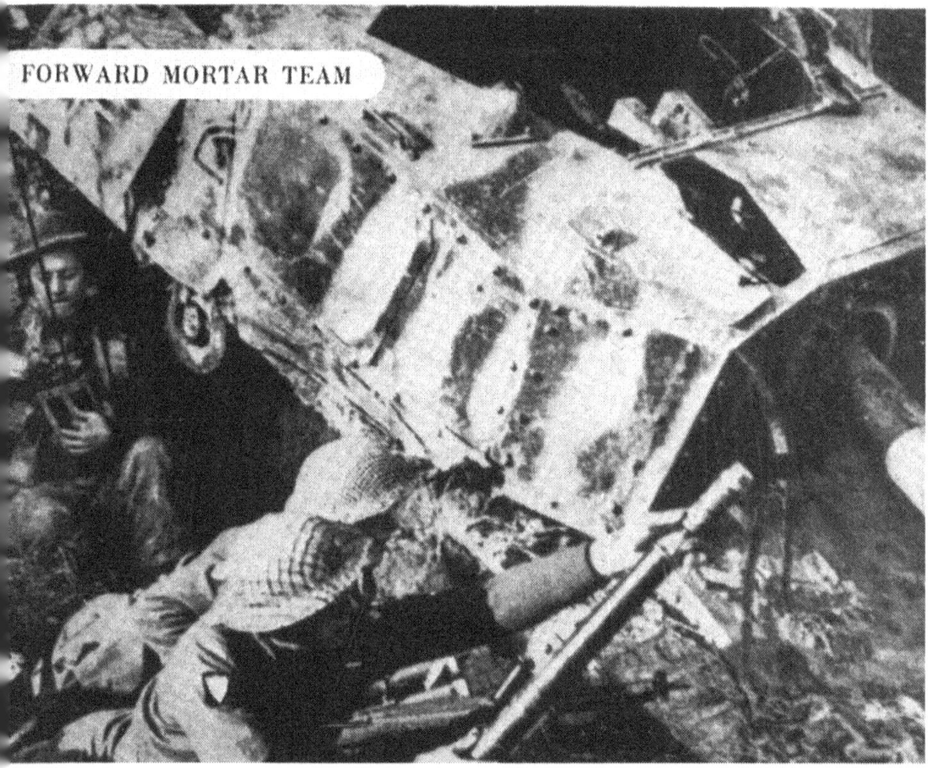

FORWARD MORTAR TEAM

TAVOLETO BURNS

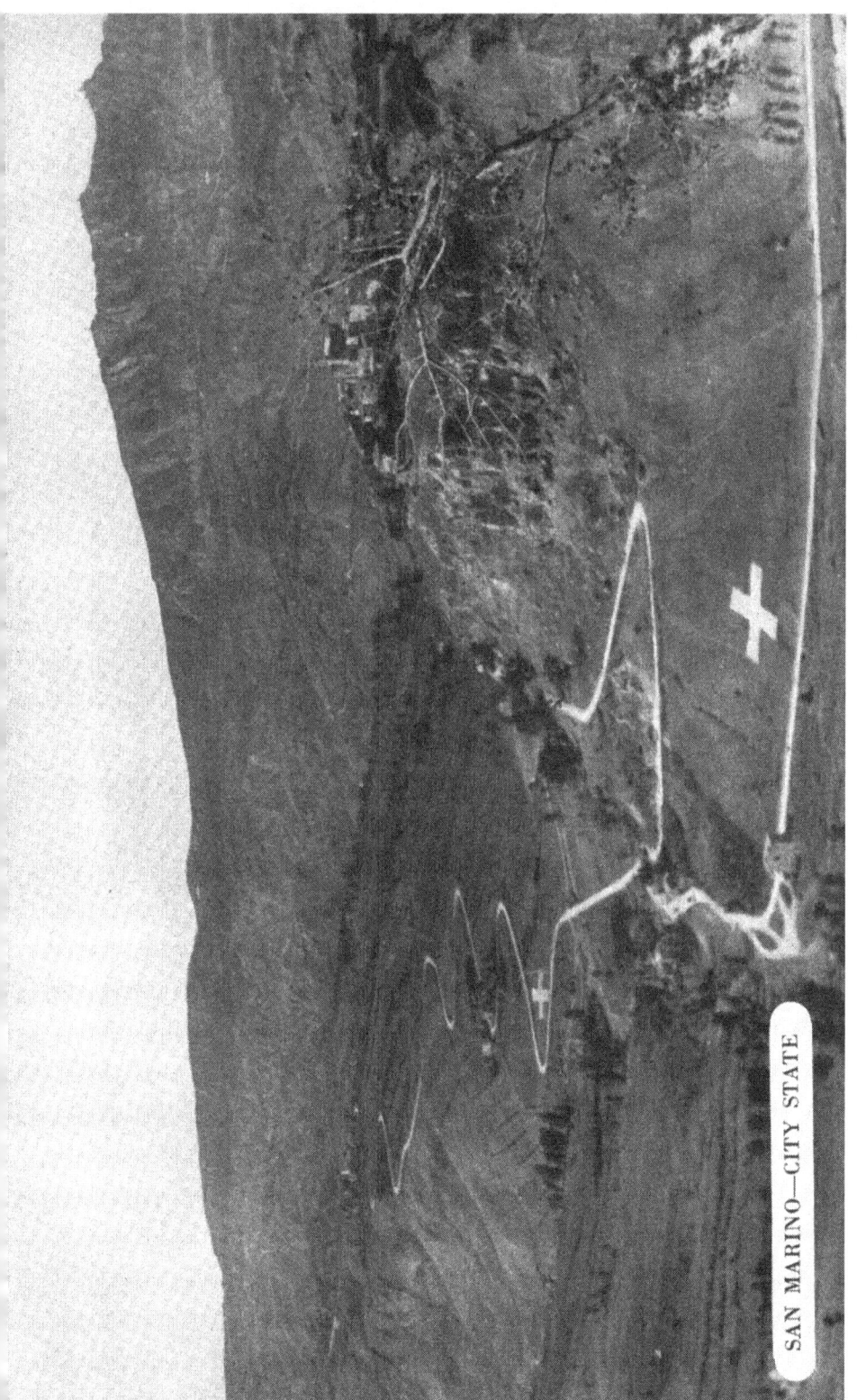

SAN MARINO—CITY STATE

FOR SUPRE

1. SEPOY KAMAL RAM, v.c.
3/8 Punjab Regiment, Liri River
May 12th, 1944.

2. RIFLEMAN
SHER BAHADUR THAPA,
v.c., 1/9 Gurkha Rifles, Faetano,
Gothic Line. Sept. 18th, 1944.
POSTHUMOUS

3. NAIK
YASHWENT GHADGE, v.c.
3/5 Mahratta Light Infantry,
Morlupo . . July 9th, 1944
POSTHUMOUS

ME VALOUR

4. RIFLEMAN
THAMAN GURUNG, v.c.
1/5 Royal Gurkha Rifles, Monte
Bartolo . November 11th, 1944
POSTHUMOUS

5. SEPOY
NAMDEO JADHEO, v.c.
1/5 Mahratta Light Infantry,
Senio Crossing. April 9th, 1945.

6. SEPOY ALI HAIDAR, v.c.
6/13 Frontier Force Rifles, Senio
Crossing . April 9th, 1945.

SIXTH LANCERS MOP UP

THEIR HAUL

MAHRATTAS AT MONTE VERUCA

the next water barrier to the north. 18th Lorried Infantry Brigade and a brigade of Fifty-Sixth London Division passed through the Gurkhas, who came out to rest after eleven days of continuous fighting, in which when under fire for the first time they had borne themselves like veterans.

The battle had caused sad losses, of which not the least was the end of a much prized association with First British Armoured Division. To the Gurkhas the White Rhino flash remained a warm and living memory, for the Englishmen who wore it had been mentors, sponsors and great comrades from the time of the Brigade's arrival in Italy. On October 1st, 43rd Brigade came under command of Fifty-Sixth London Division on the line of the Fiumicino, a stream which wanders down from the Apennine spurs on the left of Sanarcangelo. The cold autumnal rains were now continuous, the crossings of the Maricchia still insecure, and the forward roads impassable for large-scale troop movements. Plans for forcing the Fiumicino were postponed from day to day owing to the vagaries of stormwater.

The emphasis of Eighth Army's attack tended to shift westwards, on to higher ground and firmer footing. Tenth Indian Division had arrived from Central Italy, and now came forward to relieve Fourth Indian Division. On October 7th the Gurkha Lorried Brigade passed under command of the newcomers and moved eight miles to the east to occupy a less water-logged sector.

CHAPTER FIFTEEN

TENTH INDIAN DIVISION ON THE GOTHIC LINE

NINE DAYS AFTER HANDING OVER on the Arno-Tiber Front, Tenth Indian Division moved forward through torrential rains, over mud-soup roads, to the relief of Fourth Indian Division on the line of the Rubicon. For a week wellnigh impassable tracks hampered troop movements and delayed the take-over. The men waited under the inclement elements with no more shelter than bivouac sheets provided. The effect of the weather on offensive operations is often emphasized in this narrative; it should be remembered that what hampers wheels and tracks can affect bodies as well. Only the highest discipline and assurance can sustain morale during comfortless days and nights in which nothing happens. It says much for Indian troops that during such periods they remained in good heart and in good health.

On October 3rd, 25th Indian Brigade took over from 7th Indian

Brigade at Borghi, on the edge of the Rubicon Valley. 20th Brigade relieved 11th Brigade on the Montebello Ridge just north of the Marecchia. The Divisional front therefore ran north and south, with a sag in the centre. At its nearest point the Indian troops were little more than ten miles from the sea. Their mission was to thrust into the west in order to widen Eighth Army's battlefield. The countryside lacked the substance of the Tiber landscape. The hills were little more than bare, sharp ridges, slashed by precipitous ravines. The area was heavily populated; everywhere solidly built villages and farmsteads provided the enemy with ready-made pill-boxes and strongpoints. The village church with its observation tower and the high, thick walls of the village cemetery, supplied the nodal points of such defences. As Allied artillery and aircraft were loath to attack consecrated ground, the Germans established their headquarters in sanctuary and enjoyed a measure of immunity during the early stages of any battle.

Once in the line, Tenth Indian Division lost no time in getting down to business. On the night after taking over, King's Own clashed with a German patrol near Borghi, killing two scouts dressed in civilian clothes. The bodies identified One Hundred and Fourteenth Jaeger Division, old opponents from the Tiber basin, as on this front. Within forty-eight hours of arrival, a two-brigade assault went in. 20th Brigade struck from the Montebello positions for Sogliano, five miles to the west on the Rubicon. Starting four hours later, 25th Brigade also drove down the line of the Rubicon to clear San Martino. These attacks were destined to converge but not to meet, as the capture of either point would be sufficient to squeeze out resistance east of the Rubicon.

On the right of the Divisional front, King's Own, using artificial moonlight, went over to the attack at 0300 hours on the morning of October 5th. Skirting San Martino they swung left-handed and advanced from the south. Against fierce opposition the leading company burst into the village. Out of the darkness a heavy counter-attack surged. The British troops were thrown back, losing fifty men. A company in close support refused to give ground, and throughout the day counter-attack after counter-attack broke down. That evening a troop of North Irish Horse tanks arrived, and King's Own smashed at San Martino again. By 2100 hours the village was in their grip. Before daylight 1st Durhams from 10th Brigade arrived up to strengthen the battle line.

On the left, 2/3 Gurkhas with tanks of North Irish Horse in support, led the thrust on Sogliano. After easy initial gains, stubborn fighting ensued at a cross-roads which offered the only breakaway route for the defenders. The Gurkhas stormed this position, and leaving a Mahratta company in garrison turned into the south, along the approaches to Sogliano. On arrival at the village the hillmen found themselves forestalled by fighting patrols of 1/2 Punjabis, their left flank neighbours, who on being held up on the approaches to Strigara, turned north and established themselves in Sogliano, afterwards exploiting into the north-west along a road which descends seven hundred feet with seventeen hairpin bends in less than a mile. This quick thrust served a notable end by seizing intact two important bridges across the Fiumicino River.

Early in the morning of October 6th, in thick fog and pouring rain, 1/2 Punjabis attacked Strigara anew. The abominable weather contributed its meed to the tenacious resistance of the garrison. The attack was suspended during daylight, but resumed immediately after dark, when the Punjabis were reinforced by two companies of 4/10 Baluchis. The Indians would not be denied, and after ninety minutes' fighting Strigara was captured.

Thus in two days Tenth Indian Division had cleared the line of the Rubicon on a front of approximately five miles. The axis of advance now turned into the north-west towards Monte Farneto, where a triangle of precipitous and difficult terrain confronted the assault brigades. Its apex was at Cesena, eight miles to the north. It was bounded to the north-west by Route 9 from Rimini to Casena. To the east the valley of the Savio divided these bad lands from the equally rugged foothills of the Apennines. These blunt upland capes thrust into the path of Eighth Army; until they were secured substantial forces could not find elbow room for battle, nor fan out on to the northern plains. These ten square miles of broken ground were held in strength and a major battle loomed.

Facing the left of the Indian front, two high bare hills stood sentinel. On the right Monte Farneto, sixteen hundred feet high, was protected by a maze of deep-cut watercourses, impassable to vehicles and in wet weather next to unscalable by men. More than two thousand yards to the west of Farneto stood Montecodruzzo. This abrupt buttress rose thirteen hundred feet above the plain, with steep and trackless slopes. Its crest marked the beginning of a long ridge arching into the north, which gradually fell away into hillocks towards Cesena. Along the summit of this ridge the hamlets of Montecodruzzo, Monte Del Erta, Monteguzzo and Monte Chicco possessed the natural defences of precipitous slopes, deep ravines on either side, and difficult approaches along a razor-backed crest. Behind Monte Farneto a similar system of ridges worked into the north in higgledy-piggledy fashion by way of Monte Spaccato, Monte Leone, and Monte Reale. Standing a few hundred feet above the flourishing town of Cesena, Aquarola represented the northern extremity of these features.

Tenth Indian Division was now confronted with its sternest test. The flexible tactics which had won ground at low cost in the Arno and Tiber valleys were no longer of avail. Two German divisions, strong and full of fight, held these ridge systems. Only a frontal assault could dislodge them, and that assault must go in against every obstacle that the terrain, the weather and the enemy could impose.

It was a mountaineers' battlefield, and at this juncture Tenth Division had the good fortune to inherit 43rd Gurkha Lorried Brigade. This acquisition allowed General Reid to commit a strong force to the attack. On the night of October 6th, 20th Brigade opened the offensive. At 2000 hours, 2/3 Gurkhas and 3/5 Mahrattas trudged off on a long night march into the north. In the early hours they closed up on Monte Farneto. The pelting rain and the impenetrable night served well, for the enemy apparently had decided that hostilities were impossible in such weather. His forward positions were unmanned, and the two battalions swept over their objectives with little loss. At dawn the chug and roar of tanks announced the arrival of North Irish Horse, only an hour behind the infantry—a magnificent performance for tracked vehicles over such terrain.

The enemy was dumbfounded and disorganized. It was only at noon that the routine counter-attack mustered in the north. By this time the Divisional artillery had ranged; when an enemy force of battalion strength struck at Monte Farneto, it was thrown back. As a second counter-attack developed, the Air weighed in with fighter-bomber attacks. That evening Northumberland Fusilier machine-gunners backed the infantry in smashing a third assault. All night and all next day counter-attacks of varying strength proved equally fruitless. A forward section of Mahrattas was destroyed in the mortar barrage which preceded one rush. Another section under Lance Naik Keshav Shinde disappeared in the melee as their enemies swept over them, but they emerged battling to clear their post with bomb and bayonet. An enemy order picked up on the battlefield instructed the Germans that they must regain Monte Farneto or perish in the attempt.

On the evening of October 7th, 25th and 10th Brigades went into action against a ridge taking off from Monte Farneto into the north. Within seventy-five minutes of leaving their start lines 3/18 Garhwalis beat down opposition and swept over Monte Gattona and San Lorenzo. Thirty-eight killed and fourteen prisoners were the trophies of this sharp encounter, which cost the Garhwalis less than a dozen casualties. To the south-west of the Garhwalis, 3/1 Punjabis ran into almost impassable ground, with deep nullah-like watercourses and gradients too steep to be searched by gun fire. A church on the left flank had been strongly fortified. Attempts to reach it failed. A similar situation confronted 2/4 Gurkhas of 10th Brigade, who attacked between the Punjabis and Monte Farneto. They had been directed on San Paolo, situated on a road junction to the left flank rear of Roncofreddo, one of the bastions of the enemy defences. The Gurkhas closed on the village to encounter another Mozzagrogna. House by house the hamlet was cleared, but as the battling hillmen fought forward fresh enemies sprang up behind them. As usual the cemetery and the church became the chief centres of resistance; among the tombstones ferocious fighting ensued. Dawn brought no cessation, for in the last hours of darkness the Germans managed to infiltrate reinforcements into the northern fringe of San Paolo. Throughout the day fighting flared up again and again. In the end the series of quick deadly clashes proved too much for the enemy, who withdrew the remnants of his garrison during the next night.

10th Brigade had despatched 4/10 Baluchis to seize ground on the approaches to Montecodruzzo. In an advance along slopes slashed by innumerable ravines, the Baluchis encountered heavy going. Whereupon 43rd Brigade, was ordered to concentrate on this flank, and to devote itself to the assault on the western ridge system.

On the right of the Divisional battlefield 3/1 Punjabis, thwarted in their first assault, succeeded brilliantly on the night of October 9/10th. In an attack on Roncofreddo, they swept through the town in dashing style. Unfortunately Lieut.-Colonel Clifford was killed next day, the second commander of this battalion to fall in Italy.

No rest was vouchsafed the enemy. When, after fanatical resistance, he relinquished San Paolo, the Durhams of 10th Brigade passed through at once to attack Monte Spaccato, on the next ridge to the north. As at Monte Farneto the miserable weather was turned to good account. During a period of ground mist the Durhams, who were no mean woodsmen, found a number of gaps in the enemy's defences and filtered through. When the sun broke out, the Germans, going about their morning chores, found "C" Company of the North Countrymen embedded in their midst. Fierce hand-to-hand fighting followed. All company officers became casualties, but the Durhams clung to their positions. Two bodies could not occupy one space so the enemy, throwing in a counter-attack as a screen for his purpose, fell back to a reserve line of defence.

By the evening of October 10th Tenth Indian Division was master of the forelands of the peninsula of high ground which blocked the way to the plains. Only on the extreme left, where 4/10 Baluchis had encountered tough going, did the enemy hold ground below the main crests. 43rd Brigade now entered the battle. On the night of October 11th, although neither tracks nor wheels nor animals could negotiate the greasy rain-soaked slopes of Montecodruzzo, three companies of the 2/6 Gurkhas made their way up the hillsides. One company walked into an outpost of the Twentieth German Air Force Division. The sentries slept. Three were killed and six captured without alarm. At first light the hillmen stood on the crest of Montecodruzzo, having seized the hamlet and the large square church. It is difficult to understand how the enemy, at a time when he was rising to frenzy in his attempts to regain Monte Farneto, should have allowed its companion ridge system to have been virtually unguarded. Indeed of the two features Montecodruzzo was of greater importance, as it ran at right angles to the crests against which the other brigades of Tenth Division were launched, and so constituted a flank menace to successive enemy defence positions. Yet for the two days 2/6 Gurkhas continued to consolidate and to prepare for the next phase with little interference from the enemy.

On the afternoon of October 12th, after a long and arduous march, 2/10 Gurkhas arrived at Montecodruzzo. Two companies immediately pushed forward towards Monte Del Erta. Once again Germans on outpost were found asleep, and fifteen prisoners taken. Tenacious resistance from enemy-held houses slowed down the progress along the narrow ridge, but after bitter fighting, in which elements of two German divisions were identified in successive counter-attacks, the Gurkhas established themselves in the Monte Del Erta. From Montecodruzzo, 2/6 battalion moved up to leap-frog their comrades and to push through to Monte Chicco, the last high knoll and dominating position, which stood above the river Savio where the triangle of high ground approached its apex.

On account of the importance of the Chicco position, it had been decided to synchronize its assault with a similar attack on the parallel ridge system to the east, where Monte del Vacche occupied a similar knoll at the northern extremity of the high ground. To expedite this operation, Durham Light Infantry lost no time in exploiting their success at Monte Spaccato. On October 12th a daylight patrol worked across the Soara Valley, on to the forward slopes of the rising ground to the north. "A" company followed up, and after a sharp fight, in which twenty-three prisoners were taken, established a firm grip upon the crest of the ridge. Simultaneously, on the left, 2/4 Gurkhas moved against Monte Bora, situated on a subsidiary spur of the main saddleback. When the leading company was held up, Major Scott brought forward a second company to attack from flank. His men were caught in the open by enemy tanks which raked them with high explosive and machine-guns. Major Scott was wounded but remained with his men. At dawn next morning both Gurkha companies dashed at the objective. Major Scott's men thrust directly against the centre of the German resistance, a thick-walled farmhouse with out-buildings, which spat fire in all directions. The company was pinned down but their commander snatched a Bren gun from a dead man and raced in, firing as he ran. Struck again, he went down, but was on his feet at the head of his Gurkhas when he fell riddled within ten yards of the enemy. His men surged over the farmhouse and wiped out the garrison. A heavy enemy shoot compelled a temporary withdrawal, but other companies immediately moved up and retook the position.

The stage was now set for the master assault on Monte Chicco. At

2200 hours on October 13th, 2/6 Gurkhas passed their start line with "D" Company leading. The tiny hamlet of Monteguzzo, built on a knife-edged ridge, was overrun after a stiff resistance. "B" and "C" Companies pushed through, and savage fighting developed among the bare hummocks of the narrow crest.

Swept from the crown of the hill, the Germans rallied and infiltrated along the slopes clinging tenaciously to every yard of ground. Bomb squads crept up to toss grenades into groups battling their way forward on the summit above them. For a mile behind the fighting enemy artillery searched the ridge top, so that supplies and reinforcements ran the gauntlet of incessant shellfire. By dawn, 2/6 Gurkhas had reached Monte Chicco, to be held up by furious assaults from three sides. Both 2/8 and 2/10 battalions sent companies forward, and the struggle mounted in bitterness throughout the day. Fighter bombers from the Corps "Cab-rank" intervened with well-timed and accurate dive attacks on enemy mortar teams. Major C. W. P. Head, artillery liaison officer, followed the thick of the battle. As the day wore away, he embodied more and more artillery in his fire plan. By evening all the Divisional gunners were enrolled in a box barrage programme which protected the flanks and front of the heavily engaged hillmen. When night fell a heavy shoot by spandaus and mortars seemed to presage a continuation of the tense struggle, but it turned out to be deception fire, under cover of which the Germans withdrew. By dawn the fighting had died away, and the Gurkhas walked freely along the high ground above the deep valley of the Savio.

On the parallel ridge system, 4/10 Baluchis, who had been held up in front of the Soara Valley, likewise found their front empty next morning. They pushed on until at Monte Reale they could see above the diminishing ridges the spires and turrets of Cesena, less than three miles away. Cesena by now was almost in the grasp of the Forty-Sixth British Division, advancing from the south-east in the plain below. On the night of October 16th a Baluchi assault at battalion strength sent the last enemy rearguards scurrying from Monte Reale. A few hours later 3/1 Punjabis passed through and seized Aquarola, a mile nearer Cesena. The battle was not yet over. In San Demetrio, on a lower and intermediate ridge, the enemy stood at bay. For fourteen hours the battle ebbed and flowed around the church and square. Two platoons of Punjabis infiltrated during the night, and having established themselves, beat back assault after assault. A German tank moved up and shelled them at point blank range. Even then the panzer grenadiers could not close. At dawn the Punjabis emerged from their battered refuges to find the Germans gone.

Tenth Indian Division had accomplished its mission. In this skilful and bitter fighting it had doubled the width of the front through which Eighth Army might advance on to the plains. Its next directive called for an abrupt change of direction. With British troops converging on its immediate front at Cesena the axis of advance wheeled from north into the west, where beyond the Savio Valley the enemy lay entrenched in a series of strong hill positions. Even before the close of the Monte Chicco-Monte Reale fighting, patrols of both 25th and 43rd Brigades had explored the eastern banks of the Savio, mopping up rearguards and selecting crossings. There were no roads leading from the ridges into the valley below, and the main lateral road (Route 71) followed the enemy's side of the river. It was essential that the Savio should be crossed at once. As ostentatiously as possible (in order that the enemy might be led to believe that the full strength of the Indians was arrayed on the eastern bank), 2/6 Gurkhas, from 43rd Brigade, and 3/18 Garhwalis from 25th Brigade, sent strong fighting patrols to probe the river line. The Garhwalis effected a lodgement on the far bank at San Carlo, five miles south of Cesena, and the Gurkhas with less difficulty crossed some three miles further up the river.

The careful reader may have noted that 20th Brigade disappeared from this narrative after relief at Monte Farneto. During the bitter fighting on the saddlebacks, Central India Horse had been exploring the upper Savio in search of fords. At Cella, well to the south of Montecodruzzo, a shallows was discovered. On October 20th, 20th Brigade with three field regiments under command, unobtrusively and without opposition crossed the stream at this point and turned into the north. Moving rapidly through the hills, by the evening of October 21st the patrol screen was approaching Monte Cavallo. the first of the fortified positions west of the Savio. The Brigade was ordered to attack three hours after a similar assault was launched by 25th Brigade upon Tessello, two miles further north.

At 1700 hours on October 21st, 25th Brigade began to cross the Savio through San Carlo. King's Own in the lead immediately deployed, and moved up a broad spur leading into the hills. 3/18 Garhwalis infiltrated on to high ground along a narrow re-entrant, while 2/4 Gurkhas headed directly up the slopes towards Formignano, a village prominently perched on the crest of the ridge. Concurrently 20th Brigade closed up from the south against Monte Cavallo, less than a half-mile south of Formignano. 2/3 Gurkhas led the latter advance, with 3/5 Mahrattas in close support.

The night was dark and weather conditions appalling. Everywhere the dogged infantry slogged through squelching mud. Before midnight all five leading battalions were committed to stubborn fighting. Situation reports at dawn showed no objectives gained. King's Own and Garhwalis had been thrown back by a savage counter-attack from a newly arrived assault battalion. 2/4 Gurkhas were no more than halfway to Formignano. On the slopes of Monte Cavallo 2/3 Gurkhas and 3/5 Mahrattas were pinned down.

An episode during the counter-attack on the Garhwalis deserves to be recorded. The Indians ran out of ammunition and the over-bold enemy closed in for the kill. Naik Trilok Singh, with his section's last round spent, told his men to sit tight. He would go and fetch an enemy machine-gun. He stalked a spandau crew as they crept forward, killed them in hand-to-hand fighting, and brought back gun and ammunition in time to beat off the next counter-attack single-handed. Unfortunately this fine soldier died later in the day while covering the withdrawal of his section.

During October 22nd 1/2 Punjabis moved up to reinforce the fighting line, while 2/6 and 2/10 Gurkhas crossed the Savio to fill the gap between 20th and 10th Brigades. That evening for the first time in Italy, 20th Brigade staged a set piece attack behind a heavy shoot. 10,000 shells were cast on the enemy positions; a general assault went in all along the line. On the slopes of Monte Cavallo, 2/3 Gurkhas crept forward; a swift rush out of the dark won home everywhere. Strong parties of the enemy were mopped up; a havildar engaged in clearing houses flushed nineteen Germans with smoke grenades and took all prisoner. 3/5 Mahrattas passed through the hillmen and after bitter and confused fighting closed upon the crest of Monte Cavallo. The defenders struck back in reckless counter-attacks, during which the Mahrattas held their fire until the Germans were silhouetted on the skyline above them. At first light on October 23rd Monte Cavallo was captured. The exhausted Germans for once failed to muster sufficient strength for the customary counter-attack.

Indian Sappers and Miners working at top speed had thrown two Bailey bridges over the Savio. Supplies and support weapons now reached the fighting men in the hills. 43rd Brigade retrieved the two battalions loaned to 20th Brigade, and began to leap-frog into the north-west. 20th Brigade thrust in the same direction on a slightly different axis, and likewise made ground rapidly. 25th Brigade turned due north, to cleanse the broken ground above the west bank of the Savio. By the sad irony of war, in the course of an advance in which little except bickering occurred, three outstanding personalities of Tenth Indian Division were killed. The O'Neill, commanding North Irish Horse, was struck by a shell. Major Anandrao Kadam, a highly esteemed Mahratta company commander and athlete, who had risen from the ranks, fell, together with Captain "Tim" Hodge of 68 Field Regiment, one of the best-known artillery officers in the Division.

The enemy had dropped back everywhere to the line of the Ronco, which paralleled the Savio ten miles further west. The river was in spate, a turbulent torrent twelve feet deep. The weather had broken completely, and every valley bottom was aswirl with storm water. 43rd Brigade on the night of October 25/26 closed up on the Ronco to the north of Meldola, and pushed a patrol across. Simultaneously

Naba Akhal Infantry, which had rejoined 20th Brigade on October 23rd, reached the river, about the same distance south of Meldola. Two companies crossed and seized a position on the western bank. Here they were isolated, without support weapons; but they immediately despatched strong fighting patrols which contacted groups of 15th Polish Cavalry Regiment, thus closing the front.

Although resistance along the Ronco was spotty, the enemy was known to hold substantial forces in the neighbourhood of Forli, a few miles away. The Divisional sappers at once set to work to bridge the river. An aerial ropeway was slung over a two hundred foot gap, and the remainder of Nabha Akals rode in slings to the west bank. Next day 43rd Brigade discovered a damaged aqueduct to the north of Meldola, which was made into a bridge by knocking down the side walls of the channel. The Gurkhas crossed and consolidated a shallow bridgehead. Tenth Division established advanced companies for two and a half miles on either side of Meldola, and the forward brigades immediately despatched strong forces to deepen the perimeter. On October 28th Nabha Akals drove enemy rearguards off the height of land between the Ronco and the Rabbi, the next river to the west. A rapid stroke by 43rd Brigade followed. In a thrust into the north 2/6 and 2/10 Gurkhas advanced across the open fields towards Forli. Both battalions after sharp fighting broke through the enemy defensive cordon, taking forty-five prisoners and killing many more. By now the Germans had had enough. On October 30th a wireless intercept revealed them to be retreating everywhere. Forty-Sixth British Division, Tenth Indian Division and Third Carpathian Division were all converging on the Forli airfields, and the Indians in the centre were squeezed out of their front. First the Gurkha Brigade, then 20th Brigade was withdrawn. Finally 25th Brigade handed over to British troops, and the Indians went back to well-earned rest.

These operations among the eastern spurs of the Apennines revealed Tenth Indian Division in its most adept role. Concealment, unobtrusive infiltration, followed by a violent pounce upon enemies taken unawares—so ran the tale of attack after attack. General Reid's slogans inculcated his divison with a dominant idea in terms sufficiently simple to be understood, sufficiently explicit to serve as a standing guide and instruction. With vile terrain and abominable weather fighting half the enemy's battle, the Division refused to be held up, or even slowed down, in its relentless march across ridges and rivers. As has been pointed out elsewhere, the narrative must follow the fortunes of the infantry, and it is only on occasion that a "Shabash" can be given to the other half of the Division—the gunners, sappers, and men of miscellaneous services who shared in full the rigours of every occasion. The lot of artillery in mountain warfare is not a happy one, yet the British gunners throughout found means of intervening effectively on every call. Their losses were commensurate with their activities: during the advance along the Tiber Valley, 68 Field Regiment had more casualties than some of the infantry units which it supported. The sappers likewise were full partners in every enterprise. Without their clever improvisations and endless hours of work in the mud and rain, the enemy could not have been brought to battle. Colonel Datt's medical units achieved an astonishing level of efficiency, not only in the handling of casualties, but in field hygiene and in the prevention of ordinary illnesses. The anti-tank and anti-aircraft regiments, in lieu of regular employment, became maids of all work. In the course of the advance 13 Anti-Tank Regiment raised mines, manned mortars, maintained smoke-screens, built Bailey bridges, and provided crews for field guns and howitzers. Between the Savio and the Ronco this regiment had rafted their guns, had winched them up cliffsides, had slung them across ravines on aerial ropeways, hand-hauled them through shallows, and towed them with oxen across the hills. 30 Light Anti-Aircraft Regiment had been equally versatile: a field poet catalogued its enterprises in a blithe parody of "IF", the last stanza proclaiming:

> " If you can drive a tractor in the darkness,
> Along a road that winds both up and down,
> If you can winch a Bofors up the starkness
> Of some foul mountain feature without frown;
> If you can lay a line, or spot a mortar,
> Or organize the traffic on its way,
> If you know how to be a ration porter
> Then you'll know why you joined the Light A.A."

It was the spirit behind this versatility that broke the Nazi grip on Italy.

CHAPTER SIXTEEN

EIGHTH DIVISION—FIFTH ARMY'S FLYING SQUAD

THE NARRATIVE must now retrace its steps, both in place and in time, and cross the mountains to Florence in mid-August. With order restored and public services functioning, Eighth Indian Division was again available for sterner employment.

After 21st Indian Brigade had been relieved in the city, the Division moved twelve miles to the east, into the Pontasseive area. Here the River Sieve flows down in a great bend along the foothills of the

Apennines. Within this bend the enemy held a series of high spurs which constituted the outworks of the Gothic Line, barring entry into the narrow valleys by which the main roads climb over the crests of the mountains. Due east of Florence the first contours of this high ground are rounded and gracious, tree-clad and heavily cultivated; but as the ridges fuse into the foothills they tend to become sharp, rugged and irregular. The Indian front covered the intermediate stage of this transformation, in which thickly wooded hills rose about thirteen hundred feet above the river, and in which the rolling countryside had begun to yield to narrow summits and little crooked valleys.

The Supreme Commander had planned that when the attack upon the Gothic Line had been launched by Eighth Army, and the expected withdrawal in the Adriatic sectors had begun, Fifth Army would mount a massive assault across the Apennines with Bologna and the Po Valley as its objectives. Should this stroke succeed, all German forces south of the Po would be trapped against the Adriatic Coast. The main Fifth Army attack was deputed to Second U.S. Corps, while Thirteenth British Corps protected the right flank of the Americans and conformed with their advance over the mountain. Thirteenth Corps at this time consisted of First British Infantry Division, Sixth British Armoured Division, and Eighth Indian Division, and was deployed with the Indians in the centre of the Corps area.

Beyond the intermediate high ground on Eighth Division's front stood the great wall of the San Benedetto Alps, whose crests rose to more than five thousand feet above the valley of the Arno. This barrier the Indians must penetrate. From a height of land not more than thirty miles to the north-east of Florence, a profusion of streams flowed down to the Adriatic bearing through parallel valleys into the north-east. The roads naturally followed these valleys, and for the advance over the mountains a number of alternative routes diverged from the great centre of Florence. For convenience these roads will be described in this narrative by their code names, and the graph on page 124 will show their relationship to each other. Route 67, a main highway which followed the Arno to the east before turning north-east along the valley of the Sieve, was known as Star Route. It debouched from the mountains at Forli. The second main road from Florence to the Adriatic followed a parallel course to the crest of the Apennines at Marradi from whence it forked into the valleys of the Lamone and the Senio. Sword Route lay in the Lamone Valley and Arrow Route in the Senio Valley, five miles further west. The grain of the ground was such that lateral roads were almost non-existent on the eastern slopes of the Apennines, and this circumstance was responsible for the early committal of Eighth Indian Division to battle. Less than fifteen miles above Pontassieve the only cross-road in the mountains linked Dicomano on Star Route with Borgho San Lorenzo on Arrow Route, and further west, both these routes with the main Florence-Bologna highway. This lateral road permitted the enemy to move his reserve troops from one sector to another, and afforded him alternative lines of communications through the mountains. It traversed the Sieve valley immediately under the outworks of the Gothic Line, and was regarded by both adversaries as a military property of first importance.

On arrival at Pontassieve, General Russell was warned by the Commander of Thirteenth Corps that Eighth Indian Division probably would be called upon to establish a bridgehead over the Arno. Investigations began immediately. 17th Brigade deployed in the hills south of the river, and fighting and sapper patrols began their search for approaches, shallow fords, and exits on the northern bank surmountable by vehicles. The river rose rapidly after rain storms, sometimes by as much as five feet in a night. This circumstance made it difficult to decide upon suitable crossings. On August 21st, 47 Field Park Company, after several unsuccessful attempts by other units, succeeded in raising the sluice gates at Le Sieve, which controlled the level of the river. This operation was carried out under enemy mortar and small arms fire.

The next move was to bring 19th Brigade further east in order to organize a Divisional front. By August 24th Eighth Division was disposed south of the Arno on a sector of not more than two and a half miles, with 17th Brigade on the right, 19th Brigade on the left, and 21st Brigade in reserve. It was a tight fit, and General Russell's greatest need was elbow-room. The enemy fortunately solved his problem. During the night of August 23/24, Royal Fusiliers heard transport moving to the north-east along Star Route. It was the first indication of enemy withdrawal from outpost positions north of the Arno. On the following night, patrols reported the ridges above the northern bank to be clear. On August 26th both brigades forded the stream, establishing a bridgehead five miles broad and three miles deep. 7 and 69 Field Companies, Indian Engineers, went to work at once on bridges. 26 Light A.A. Regiment, which in the absence of the Luftwaffe devoted themselves to a miscellany of duties, laid down a smoke screen to cover the sites and the sappers. By August 27th in spite of incessant shelling, three bridges had been completed. Thereafter the supply services functioned without interruption. Beyond the river mule trains came forward to give the infantry freedom of manœuvre and assurance of supplies across the broken ground and over the trackless spurs.

Both forward brigades now began to probe into the hills. The countryside was not unlike many parts of India, and the sepoys, accustomed from early childhood to hill climbing and a strenuous open air life, were completely at home. Sometimes by day, and always after dark, British, Indian, and Gurkha patrols worked forward through the narrow cobbled streets of the hilltop villages. Perhaps the enemy was gone, and the villagers, creeping cautiously from their cellars, would encounter strange men who gave them friendly grins and enquired after the Boche in queerly-accented but quite comprehensible Italian. Elsewhere a sharp challenge and a crackle of tommy gun fire might break the silence of the night before the German rearguards disappeared into the darkness. Sometimes sad tragedies awaited the liberators, as in the hamlet of Pervecchia, where a Royal Fusiliers patrol found the bodies of thirteen hostages who had been shot as reprisal for the killing of a German anti-aircraft gunner by the Italian partisans.

Early opposition was encountered near Tigliano, about six miles north of the Arno. Here a battalion of Seven Hundred and Fifteenth German Infantry Division occupied a ridge and showed no disposition to leave. The commander of 17th Brigade sent forward 1/5 Gurkhas with instructions to secure Point 526, south-east of the German position. Thereafter Royal Fusiliers would pass through and working along the crest would clear the ridge. At 2100 hours on August 28th, "A" Company of the Gurkhas crossed the start line, closely followed by "B" Company. Two hours later both companies silently closed on the enemy's first positions. Under heavy fire the Gurkhas overran the outposts, killing the garrison and sweeping through to the battalion objective. The Germans counter-attacked immediately, and fierce hand to hand fighting followed. A platoon of "A" Company, under Major Benskin, who had been hit three times, was forced back, but its comrades dourly held on in spite of raking fire and lack of cover. The left forward company had barely beaten back one assault when the next rush came. Out of ammunition, the Gurkhas in traditional fashion leapt with their knives to meet the enemy. Lance-Naik Raimansingh Rana found himself confronted with three adversaries. He struck down the first, but the blade of his kukri stuck in his opponent's skull. He snatched a spade from the ground and slew a second German. Two instant deaths unnerved the third Boche, who dropped his machine-gun and fled into the darkness, with the Lance-Naik in close pursuit, spade in hand.

By 0530 hours on August 29th, the Gurkhas firmly held all objectives. Royal Fusiliers passed through, and with them a squadron of 14th Canadian Armoured Regiment. By 1600 hours, the enemy had been chased from their positions in disorder. The British infantry's story is that the Canadian armour did the job. Firing at trees in order to obtain air bursts over the slit trenches, and setting fire to the woods by means of incendiary shell, the tanks hunted the Germans from their bolt-holes until the position was seized with only slight losses.

1/12 Frontier Force Regiment thereafter took up the running, and at first light on August 30th passed through Royal Fusiliers. During the preceding night the Germans had reoccupied a number of positions, and early in the day the Frontiersmen were pinned down by heavy machine-gun fire. As dark fell a heavy enemy shoot crashed down, followed by a counter-attack approximately a half-battalion in strength. The weight of the drive overran the Indian outposts, and for forty-five minutes confused fighting followed. The Germans were first held and then ejected. When morning broke, quiet reigned with no enemies in the neighbourhood. Whereupon the Frontiersmen advanced and occupied Poggio Cerrone, an intermediate ridge snuggling against the haunches of Monte Giovi, which towered to a height of 3,000 feet to the north-east.

On the left, 19th Brigade also had been busy. When morning broke on September 1st Argyll and Sutherland Highlanders had worked up to the village of San Brigida, a little more than a mile west of Poggio Cerrone. As the Argylls moved towards the thickly wooded slopes, the quiet of the pastoral scene was shattered by the fierce staccato of machine-guns. The Scotsmen were pinned down. 6/13 Frontier Force Rifles came forward on the left in an endeavour to turn the position. Monte Calvana, commanding Arrow Route and protected by twin escarpments with precipitous approaches, barred the way. Thick groves of oak and walnut afforded excellent cover to the defenders. Before the Piffers could close, artillery fire caught them at a crossroads. The battalion mule train encountered a heavy concentration shoot which caused substantial casualties and consequent disorganization.

At first light on September 2nd, two companies of Argylls began to work their way through the thick undergrowth on the right flank of the position where they had been pinned down. A blaze of machine-gun fire greeted them; as they bored in, they were met by a billowing curtain of flame from a flamenwerfer. No further advance was possible. Similarly, on the opposite flank, 6/13 Frontier Force Rifles found obstinate and unyielding enemies blocking the way to Monte Calvana. The day's fighting yielded no gains. That night 3/8 Punjabis advanced to their start line through heavy shell fire. (One of the casualties was Major Wright, who will be remembered for his adventures in crossing the Gari.) A thunderstorm broke, and rain poured in torrents. Wireless communications broke down; in the undergrowth sections and platoons lost touch. Individual groups which adhered to the line of advance found themselves at dawn in contact with the enemy's main positions, but without the strength to attack. Reorganization became necessary. At 0800 hours the gunners laid a smoke screen behind which the Punjabis withdrew.

This tenacious resistance changed Thirteenth Corps role from auxiliary to partner in the main attack. Instead of conforming to the American advance on the left, orders were now issued for an individual attack on the Gothic Line. The immediate objective for Eighth

Indian Division was the most prominent mountain in sight—Monte Giovi—which stood half-way between Star and Arrow Routes, dominating both valleys. Three thousand feet in height, the steeply rising upper slopes of the mountain were bare, with open grassland upon which sheep grazed. A winding path offered the only track to the crest. The planners turned to their maps and began to arrange dispositions to deal with this formidable obstacle, but before the attack could be launched the enemy obligingly settled the matter. The fierce resistance in front of Monte Giovi had been a temporary manœuvre designed to protect the lateral road during a period in which German forces were being regrouped to meet Eighth Army's offensive on the Adriatic front. When the trans-Apennine transfers of troops had been completed, Wehrmacht High Command decided to abandon all terrain ahead of the main battle positions of the Gothic Line. On September 8th, civilian refugees reported that the enemy had left Monte Giovi, after driving back all available cattle and sheep. Patrols pushed forward from both Indian brigades, and confirmed the news. The front was open.

21st Brigade now closed up on the right of 17th Brigade, and the Divisional front moved forward, covering the oblong between Arrow and Star Routes. By September 11th patrols from 1/5 Mahrattas had crossed the Sieve on its western reaches. Without pause the Indians continued to work up against the ever-rising ground broken by innumerable small valleys feeding down to the Sieve. Three miles north of the river, strongly wired and entrenched positions were found abandoned. Immediately behind stood a series of imposing heights which barred the way—high defiant crests which proclaimed that here was the real thing at last—the Gothic Line itself.

The mountains basked in the summer sunshine, and save for the endless streams of mules and jeeps which stumbled and bumped along the mountain tracks, the scene denied the imminence of battle. As the troops went by, Italian husbandmen paused as they trained their vines, and their women leaned on their hoes to scan the columns. On the unscarred slopes, cattle and sheep grazed peacefully. (The imperturbability of cows while fighting raged about them was a subject of endless controversy among the troops. Some said cows had no hearing; some said they had no nerves; all agreed that they had no sense.) The groves and the cloak of undergrowth showed no scar, yet carefully collated intelligence had reported these summits to be raddled with trench systems, revetted and camouflaged, studded with elaborate bunkers and strongpoints. Trees had been felled unobtrusively to give better fields of fire. Concrete machine-gun posts were roofed and casemented. Soil from the trenches had been carried away lest the fresh earth betray the positions to aircraft. Headquarters were deep underground, with buried cables radiating to forward sectors. Belts of concertina wire, ten yards and more in width, skirted the accessible approaches. Mines were sown everywhere.

On Eighth Indian Division's front, three principal bastions barred the way. Le Scalette on the left, Alpe di Vitigliano in the centre and Femina Morta on the right, stood high above the countryside, approached only by bare, rocky spurs, with narrow crests and precipitous slopes. Following the grain of the ground from south-west to north-east, these spurs joined up with the parent features well below their crowns, so that any attack along the ridges would be completely commanded from the summits. The crests were trackless, with rocky winding footpaths as the only means of communication and supply.

General Russell planned to lead off with 21st Brigade in an assault upon Monte Citerna and Monte Stiletto, two feeder ridges intruding into the Alpe di Vitigliano buttress. 1/5 Mahrattas were briefed to seize the approach ground, with 3/15 Punjabis passing through to secure Monte Citerna. Thereafter the Mahrattas would push on to the north-west against Monte Verruca.

At dusk on September 12th the Punjabis began their arduous advance. Just before dawn they made contact with the enemy at Point 632, south-west of Monte Citerna. Day broke upon a thunderous bombardment which ran for miles along the Apennines, as Thirteenth and Second U.S. Corps moved to the assault. Punjabi Mussalmans under Major Nairne scaled an almost vertical cliff and cut through a belt of wire. Machine-gun fire pinned them down on two occasions, but thrusting with splendid dash they swept over Monte Citerna and destroyed the garrison. Without pause the battalion drove for the central buttress of Alpe di Vitigliano, and shortly after noon, after climbing always along the reverse slope of the spur, Lieut.-Colonel Macnamara's men, in a great-hearted effort, routed the garrison on Point 1015, about half-way between Citerna and the main objective. The Punjabis had climbed one thousand feet since dawn and had stormed two positions. They were now halted by concentrated fire from Monte Stiletto on their right rear and Le Scalette on their left front. It was impossible to run the gauntlet of two flanking fires by daylight so the doughty Indians dug in and waited for night. An officer wrote truly: "The Punjabis have opened with a magnificent innings."

During the same hours 1/5 Mahrattas had swung to the left, for the assault on Monte Verruca. The attack was led by "C" Company under command of Major N. J. M. Pettingell, M.C., and was watched by General Russell from a vantage point on a spur 1,000 yards below. Major Pettingell, who has been met previously in this narrative, had reconnoitred his line of attack intimately, and had arranged an ingenious artillery programme in support of his assault. It was impossible to deploy more than two sections of infantry at a time, and therefore it was necessary to draft a detailed time-table for each individual objective. The leading platoon crossed the start line at 1620 hours, and headed for a pin-pointed nest of machine-guns. The Canadian tanks gave close fire support on a system of pre-arranged signals, and plastered the first objective until the Indians were within fifteen yards of the strong-point. As the last shell fell the Mahrattas leapt in, killing four and capturing fifteen defenders. On the tick the next platoon passed through, to be held up short of their objective by machine-guns dug in in defilade, where the tank cannons could not reach them. Naik Nathu Dhanuwade dived into the scrub, clambered like a chamois, and reappeared above the German redoubt, upon which he showered grenades until resistance ceased. The third platoon followed through as though upon exercise. Divisional artillery wreathed smoke over Monte Verruca to blind the defenders, and a sniping gun which had been manhandled up the mountain smashed the German emplacements with direct hits. Once again with the blast of the shells the Mahrattas sprang to the close, finishing off an operation carried out in text-book fashion. The Divisional Commander was thrilled. "I wish His Majesty had been here to see it," he said. As soon as night fell a strong fighting patrol climbed to the crest of Monte Verucca. Only a handful of enemies remained and they scuttled away as "A" Company reached the summit. A German captured three days later carried an unmailed letter which read:

"September 13th was my birthday, and I shall never forget this one. Tommy attacked and I had a hairsbreadth escape from capture. I have never run so fast as I did then, and up a mountainside. I had received two parcels from home, but everything was left behind...."

From Monte Verruca the Mahrattas bore into the north-east for the climb to Le Scalette. A bitter struggle was anticipated, but fortune smiled. For some reason that is yet unknown, this extremely strong position which might have defied a brigade fell with only scattered resistance. By noon on September 14th the first of the Gothic Line strongholds was the prize of the hard-fighting Mahrattas. Even better news was to come. After bitter resistance on the lower slopes of Alpe di Vitigliano 3/15 Punjabis had spent the day in reorganization. The assault was renewed at 2230 hours that evening. Enemy artillery and mortar fire searched their line of advance, and when they closed up on their objective at midnight it was in anticipation of a grim struggle. The narrow approach compelled attack on a single company frontage. As the leading platoons clambered towards the black skyline they were greeted by heavy small arms fire. Dauntlessly they flung themselves at the crest. A few enemies remained to die in the weapon pits, but more scuttled to safety in the dark. The emplacements were mopped up, and a second bastion of the Gothic Line had fallen.

Of the three main objectives on the Indian front, only Femina

Morta remained in enemy hands. On September 16th, 1/12 Frontier Force Regiment passed through the 3/15 Punjabis' positions on Vitigliano. A Gurkha officer had carried out a daring and skilful reconnaissance, and had found a path up the side of a precipice. This narrow footway was too precarious to negotiate by night, so the attack went in at first light. Two companies scaled the cliff and took the Germans completely by surprise. The garrison was destroyed and fifteen prisoners taken. The enemy for the first time in the Gothic Line battle struck back—fiercely and swiftly—but the ridge was so narrow that only twenty to thirty men could join in the assault. The Frontiersmen broke every rush. On September 17th they pushed on and mopped up Point 1084, an adjacent razor-backed ridge which had been selected as start line for the assault on Femina Morta.

Simultaneously 3/15 Punjabis had sallied from Alpe di Vitigliano to do some useful tidying up. Pushing into the north, two ridges on the western approaches of Femina Morta were cleared of the enemy. This operation gave 1/5 Gurkhas, who came forward to pass through 1/12 Frontier Force Regiment for the main attack, a secure western flank. At noon on September 18th the gunners plastered Femina Morte with a concentration shoot which pinned down the defenders. Under cover of a smoke screen the Gurkhas scrambled ahead over rough rising ground. For nearly three hours they forged slowly upwards against heavy harassing fire. As they drew towards the summit, opposition weakened, and at 1500 hours the bastion was won. Twenty-five German bodies were found, and forty-seven prisoners winkled out of dug-outs and emplacements. The garrison had been substantial, but the flank threat, together with the artillery programme and the unrelenting approach of the hillmen, led to half-hearted defence and early flight.

In seven days Eighth Indian Division had broken through the Gothic Line. It is no detraction from the superb leadership and outstanding fighting ability of the Indian soldiers to record that the ease with which this defensive zone was pierced came as a surprise to everybody. It is difficult to understand why positions of such strength, fortified with such care, should have been entrusted to such meagre garrisons. The German troops did not fight particularly well, but they were much too thin on the ground to make an effective stand against well-mounted attacks. Captured officers attributed the disaster to loss of contact between Tenth and Fourteenth German Armies, which were heavily engaged on both sides of the Indians. Other German prisoners stated that battle reserves were on their way forward and had not arrived. It seems possible that the real answer lay in the paucity of lateral communications and that with the Air completely under Allied control the enemy found it impossible to move reinforcements into the threatened area.

The brief, bright record of the assault troops is by no means the full story of Eighth Indian Divisions assault on the Gothic Line. Behind the indomitable infantry that clambered and won the peaks, the entire Division worked in high gear. The smoothness of the ancillary services was the yardstick of the speed of the attack. Next to the battle line, both literally and in priority, came the mule trains, the patient animals and the indefatigable drivers who followed wherever the fighting men went. They fetched food, water, ammunition and blankets, and took back litters of wounded. Day by day Indian sappers drove jeep-head deeper into the hills. Winding up the mountain slopes for mile after mile, the narrow tracks looked like threads of cotton against the brown mountainsides. The Divisional provosts in an unbroken tour of duty policed these routes in order that the traffic might flow steadily and without jam. Signallers laid hundreds of miles of cable; no sooner had the infantry dug in than the telephones began to buzz. At vehicle-head the stretcher-bearers lifted the wounded from the litter mules and laid them carefully on specially fitted jeeps which edged cautiously down the mountain side. The "Q" Services worked twenty-four hours in each day, replenishing sub-dumps from main dumps apportioning and delivering supplies by jeep, mule, and man pack. In a general order General Russell summarized these exceptional performances.

"To-day, the 24th of September, the Division completes a year in Italy. Much has happened during this period. The Division has reason to feel proud of its achievements. Our major battles have been concerned with river crossings. We can cut notches for the Biferno, Trigno, Sangro, Moro, Rapido and Arno rivers. There are more ahead. Between these obstacles, led by our reconnaissance unit, our success has been largely due to rapid reduction of transport, maintaining pressure by skilful patrolling and by hitting really hard when an attack was necessary. Junior leaders have played a great part in preparing for the kill. Our artillery, machine guns and mortars have always made it possible for our infantry and armour to administer the *coup de grâce*.

"Sappers, Signallers and Services have played an important part in maintaining the momentum of the advance. The untiring efforts of Sappers and Miners, bridge-building, mine-laying, improvising, have ensured our place well up in the hunt. Without the very high standard of communications, maintained with such cheerful energy, little could have been done. Those who worked behind the scenes in the Services tending our sick and wounded, fitting and replenishing, maintaining and recovering our hard-worked transport, have had a great share in this successful year.

"Many have performed tasks for which they are not primarily intended. Ack-ack Gunners have made excellent traffic control police, and as a smoke-producing unit they have saved many casualties at considerable risk to themselves. Anti-tank gunners have performed valuable pioneer work. The spirit of 'Is there anything we can do to help?' makes it easy for a commander.

"This retrospect is pleasant, the prospect is inspiring. Keep right on to the end of the road."

In the opinion of many who fought in this battle, the decisive contribution was that of the Air. Never have the Allied air forces intervened in greater strength and with greater effectiveness. All day long the sky above the mountain peaks was filled with the thunder of aircraft, sallying and returning, with never an enemy machine to challenge them. Along the narrow valleys, as on the bare crests, the fighter bombers, the mediums and the heavies, struck devastating blows. The enemy lived like a beast in this hole, in terror of what awaited him. By day he dared not move. After dark when his horse-drawn transport dashed along the roads, with urgent supplies, the night bombers swooped with destruction in their maws. As prisoners marched back they often glanced overhead, where the sky traffic roared ceaselessly. Bitter words came to their lips and they cursed Hermann Goering as the author of their downfall.

Everywhere Fifth Army's assault had gone well. The American attack in front of Florence, under a massive air umbrella, had broken through the Giogi Pass and was thrusting for Firenzuola, twelve miles northwest of Marradi. First British Division on the Indians' left had made good gains against heavy opposition. On the extreme right flank of the attack Sixth British Armoured Division had stormed Monte Peschiena, a key position in the Gothic Line, and the tank men were working up Star Route as rapidly as demolitions and road blows would permit.

Eighth Indian Division now inherited the thankless task of bifurcating into two flank guards, and of continuing its march over the trackless mountains between the two main roads. These moves represented little in blood and danger, but in terms of transport the new duties imposed a critical strain upon the Division. Two brigade groups each requiring two thousand vehicles and five hundred mules were obliged to operate on diverse axes, using roads and tracks crammed with the vehicles of the flanking divisions.

During the Femina Morte fighting, 19th Brigade had moved up on the right of 17th Brigade to cover the flank of Sixth British Armoured Division. Led by 1st Jaipur Infantry, a recently arrived states forces unit, the Brigade turned into the east and occupied a commanding height above the village of San Benedette in Alpe, from whence a lateral road, now fallen into disuse, had led across to Marradi. It was necessary quickly to restore this track to working order. To cover the road sappers 6/13 Frontier Force Rifles pushed off on a long march through the heart of the mountains and seized commanding ridges near Monte di Gamogna, to the north-east of Marradi.

In similar fashion 17th Brigade began to work from peak to peak above Star Route, the main axis of advance of First British Division. On September 2nd, 1/5 Gurkhas left the Lamone valley and followed a rough track up the hillside on to the high ground to the east. After a sharp clash with a rearguard at Monte Scarabattole, Royal Fusiliers passed through and thrust against Monte Castelnuovo, where two German battalions were found to be in garrison. 1/12 Frontier Force Regiment came forward to reinforce the Fusiliers. Castelnuovo was a strong position, but the enemy preferred not to fight on even terms, and withdrew. With this height secure, Marradi was not longer menaced, and the reconstruction of the much needed lateral road proceeded apace.

A gradual shifting into the west began. After the storming of Monte Battaglia on September 27th, the American advance veered from north-east into the north, in a drive for Bologna. To conform, First British Division took over more ground to the west, and Eighth Indian Division followed suit. By October 1st, 17th Brigade was deployed to the west of Sword Route north of Marradi, with responsibility as far as Arrow Route in the valley of the Senio. On the right flank, 19th Brigade was similarly spread out over a sea of mountains as far as Star Route. This increase in frontage coincided with the arrival of the fresh and vigorous Three Hundred and Fifth German Infantry Division, which included many men who wore the eidelweiss badge awarded only to accomplished mountaineers. But no matter what front or what opponents General Russell's instructions were to continue offensive operations with the utmost vigour. Over the mountain crests on stilly nights came the sullen grumble of guns as Eighth Army smashed its way across flaming ridges on the enemy's left flank rear. Sooner or later, the Germans would be compelled to relinquish their grip on the mountains. The task of the Indians was to speed that hour.

During the first days of October a fresh advance began. On the right flank, 3/8 Punjabis immediately detected new mettle in the enemy. Attempts to occupy a nearby feature, Monte L'Alto, led to brisk scrimmaging, in which Jemadar Anant Ram and his men dashed across the open against spandau fire and destroyed a number of outposts. Two days later Argyll and Sutherland Highlanders fought their way up Monte Cavallara, and hurled the enemy from its summit. The way was open for a bid for Monte Casalino, a steep tree-clad hill a mile to the north-east. This height barred the way to Monte Gaggiolo, three miles further north, which rose above the gut of high ground where Sword and Star Routes converged to within five miles of each other.

On October 7th, 3/8 Punjabis established two companies on the lower slopes of Monte Cassalino. Two nights of intensive probing preceded the assault. Soon after first light on October 10th "B" Company smashed at the German positions. Heavy fighting followed and the resistance proved to be beyond a company's strength to break. When the Punjabis fell back the enemy followed down the slopes, launching a heavy attack in the middle of the forenoon. After a grim struggle the Germans in turn abandoned the battle and returned to their strongholds on the crest of Monte Casalino.

To the west of Sword Route, 21st Brigade, on the evening of October 13th, found a similar obstacle in its path. Monte Pianoereno rose to two thousand three hundred feet, almost exactly between Sword and Arrow Routes, and dominating both highways. The only approach lay along a narrow ridge which tapered into the north, barren and windswept, with rocky knolls and huge boulders punctuating its crest. At 2030 hours on October 17th, a heavy shoot was laid down on the approach spur. 3/15 Punjabis advanced and after two hours' hard fighting had swept the enemy from Point 711. Two companies then turned against Croce Daniele; after two repulses, in which serious casualties were sustained, a third furious charge won home. Another company pushed through Point 711 towards Point 768, but were beaten back three times with heavy losses. The Mahrattas closed up in close support to continue the assault, but once again the Germans had had enough and disappeared when darkness fell.

Beyond Monte Pianoereno enemy groups continued to hold clusters of farmhouses covering Monte Romano. Before dawn on October 20th two companies of Royal West Kents went forward to deal with these detachments. The first company to attack was pinned down, and had to be extricated under cover of a smoke screen; but Major Gunsey by a clever manœuvre worked his men into the rear of the German positions, destroyed the garrison, and took thirty prisoners. Another smoke screen was laid, this time over Monte Romano. Behind it the 3/15 Punjabis raced up the slopes. Again the gallant Indians encountered furious fire which halted them, and again under cover of night, the Germans slipped away.

This time the enemy withdrawal was fairly general along Eighth Army's front. The Americans had smashed through to Monte Grande, a key position of which more will be heard, only seven miles south-east of Bologna. On the Adriatic front, Forty-Sixth British Division had entered Cesena. The enemy could feel the breath of one Army on his right cheek, of another behind his left ear. Yet the obstinate foe dare not weaken his mountain positions since they constituted the hinge on which his front swung both to east and to west. The withdrawal in front of Eighth Indian Division was more of a realignment than a retirement, and patrols found the enemy to be in strength on a series of buttresses between Star Route and Arrow Route, which commanded strong lay-back and covering positions. There was now elbow room for deployment and for the first time in the Gothic Line fighting, all three brigades of Eighth Indian Division could be brought into the battle line. On the right the Jaipurs closed up on Monte Campaccio, the southernmost bastion of the new positions. Next door 1/5 Gurkhas after three attempts ejected the enemy from Monte Casalino, where the Punjabis had been held up for two weeks. 1/12 Frontier Force Regiment moved on Monte Gaggiolo, covering the key buttress of Budrialto. Royal Fusiliers carried the line down to Maragnano, on Sword Route. 19th Brigade worked up the Lamone valley along the main axis of Sword Route. Further west 21st Brigade was deployed with 3/15 Punjabis facing Monte Giro, and the Mahrattas opposite Monte Colombo. To the joy of the Indians their old friends of 14th Canadian Armoured Regiment came barging up the roads into close support, on the first tankable terrain encountered since the mountain battle began.

The advance had no more than been resumed when such appalling weather supervened that the commander of Fifth Army ordered the offensive to be suspended. Regrouping of American forces led to another Divisional shift. 21st Brigade sideslipped across country to take over a sector astride Arrow Route. In turn the other brigades widened their fronts until Indian responsibilities extended over ten miles of mountainside. The peaks and high ridges were now behind; on the eastern slopes of the Apennines, the uplands swelled in softer contours, with vegetation and patches of shrubs replacing bare rocks and heavy timber.

No sooner had General Russell deployed his men to the west than they were needed in the east. Second Polish Corps had moved up through the gorges of the Apennines into the gap between the Adriatic and the Central Italian sectors, much in the same manner as Fourth Indian Division had come forward to open the Gothic Line battle. The left flank of the newcomers rested on the broken and precipitous ground to the right of Star Route, where Sixth British Armoured Division had been relieved. In the No Man's Land between the Indians and the Poles, a high ridge stood to the west of Star Route, between two roads converging at Modigliano, a pleasant mountain resort some miles ahead of the battle line. 17th Brigade therefore was obliged to sideslip to the east, much as 21st Brigade had extended to the west, for the purpose of dealing with this high ground on the flank of the Polish advance. Three crests, Mosignano in the south, Pompegno in the middle, and Monte Bartolo in the north, marked the summits of this ridge system.

On the night of November 5/6th, 1/5 Gurkhas raided Montsignano to test the defences. A sharp clash followed, but next morning the Germans were gone. By the evening of November 10th the Gurkhas had closed up on Pompegno, and once again the enemy, perhaps because of Polish pressure from the east, did not stay to fight. 17th Brigade was now only two miles short of the last obstacle, the small grassy knoll of Monte Bartolo. General Russell regarded this feature as no more than another crest which the enemy in due course would evacuate. The Polish commander, however, rated it more highly, declaring that his attack could not be launched until this ground was secured. General Russell immediately assured his colleague that there would be no delay, and deployed 17th Brigade against Monte Bartolo.

On the afternoon of November 11th a Gurkha fighting patrol, investigating the lie of the land, detected a group of Germans well dug in on the slopes of this position. Ahead of the patrol moved two scouts, one of whom was Rifleman Thaman Gurung. By skilful fieldcraft these scouts worked their way unseen into the midst of the Germans. Thaman Gurung spotted a nest of German machine-gunners in the act of swinging their weapons on to the main body of the fighting patrol. He sprang to his feet and charged. Taken by surprise the Germans surrendered. The intrepid Gurkha then crawled upwards to the lip of the ridge, and from there engaged other well dug-in posts on the reverse slopes. From flank positions German machine-gunners brought fire to bear on the fighting patrol. Standing in full view, this lone figure on a bullet-swept hilltop held back the enemy single-handed until his comrades had extricated themselves. He then fell mortally wounded, and in death joined the immortal band of heroes who have earned the Victoria Cross.

Other fighting patrols probed Monte Bartolo to encounter a similar reception, but each brought back something to be fitted into the general picture of the enemy's dispositions. On November 13th, artillery searched the knoll with harassing fire throughout the day, while a troop of Canadian tanks worked forward on the left flank. As it grew dark, the eerie glow of artificial moonlight cut through the gloom, and two companies of Gurkhas advanced to the assault. Enemy machine-guns clattered into action, and a group of spandaus near a white farmhouse on the summit seemed invulnerable. For six hours the Gurkhas edged forward cannily, avoiding casualties but never giving ground. By midnight the investment of the knoll neared completion and the garrison was in straits. Before dawn the Germans melted away into coverts in the broken ground below the ridge. Twenty-four hours later, 6th Lancers entered Modigliano.

While 17th Brigade tidied the right flank, the weather worsened. Driving rains, turning to snow storms on the summits, pelted the mountain sides. Thick mists followed, reducing visibility to nil, and limiting the usefulness of patrols. The ground hardened in the grip of sharp frosts. Life in the open resolved into a series of miserable failures to keep either dry or warm. Roads collapsed, jeep and mule tracks became impassable; sappers worked night and day. Supply lorries were never off the roads except when they were in the ditches. The enemy was in better case, for the foul weather grounded the Allied Air Force, and so gave respite from incessant attack; moreover, on the crumbling mountain roads horse transport functioned better than wheels. In the face of such inclemency it was well-nigh impossible to seize new ground, and completely impossible to provision and munition further advances. The attack gradually slowed to a standstill.

During this lull, organization for the battle to come continued apace. Once again Eighth Indian Division was asked to widen its front in order to allow heavier concentrations elsewhere. Repeated sideslips had carried the Divisional flank west of Sword Route. A further extension now took 21st Brigade across Arrow Route. By November 19th, 3/15 Punjabis were guarding the western flank of the Division at Monte Battaglia—the scene of fierce fighting by U.S. Second Corps at a time when Eighth Indian Division held a lesser frontage than that now held by 21st Brigade.

On November 26th, the enemy forces began to give ground on the right flank. 17th Brigade conformed to a turning movement by Second Polish Corps, and the axis of advance veered into the north-west. Far across at Arrow Route the same movement was in progress; behind a screen of rearguards the enemy dropped back on Veno Del Gesso escarpment—a peculiar earth fault which rears a high chalk ridge so precipitous on its southern face that only a trained mountaineer can negotiate it. The Senio and Santerno rivers cut narrow gorges through this barrier. Should the enemy elect to stand this sheer wall provided an unequalled rampart for defence. 21st Brigade with Punjabis and Mahrattas leading began to clear the ground up to this formidable obstacle.

The advance had scarcely begun when fresh complications arose. 19th Brigade was last reported as moving up Sword Route in the Lamone Valley. Progress had been slow, less because of enemy resistance than because of the weather and the difficulties of deployment. The western swing of the Polish corps now promised to reach the Lamone further to the north, making 19th Brigade's operation unnecessary. At this juncture new and urgent employment emerged for Brigadier Dobree and his men. On December 1st, General Russell was ordered to despatch a brigade with all speed to reinforce First British Division on Monte Grande, ten miles to the north-west of the Divisional flank at Monte Battaglia. Here a mountain buttress towers to a height of two thousand feet above the valley of the Sillaro River. Route 9, the main lateral highway of Northern Italy, passes less than five miles to the north; on a clear day the towers and domes of Bologna can be clearly seen.

Monte Grande had been the scene of bitter fighting during the

American drive, and the enemy had never acquiesced in its loss. A sure sign of its importance was the appearance in this sector of First German Parachute Division—the men of Cassino. These fanatical and highly trained troops were never entrusted with holding roles. Wherever they stood, they struck. As soon as the paratroopers appeared, First British Division was the recipient of unwelcome attention. Savage raiding thrusts tested sensitive sectors, and revealed the enemy to be conversant with the weaknesses of the position. As the resumption of Fifth Army's offensive depended on possession of this key sector, it was wisely decided to strengthen the garrison.

For 19th Brigade to travel fifteen miles as the crow flies necessitated a two days' journey. The weather was windy, wet and cold. Skidding and sliding, the troop carriers negotiated the wintry mountain roads: over the crest of the snow-girt peaks, down the multiple switchbacks along the western slopes, thence to turn back uphill at Borgho San Lorenzo, to grind slowly forward over the summits again, and along a second class track into the valley of the Sillaro. On steep inclines it was sometimes necessary to winch uphill, while the troops warmed their chilled and cramped limbs by pushing behind. Only a mule track led from the Sillaro to the battle positions on Monte Grande; in its mudholes even the seldom-beaten jeeps bogged down. Trudging doggedly, the Indians clambered upwards and by December 6th, 19th Brigade had relieved 2nd British Infantry Brigade. All three battalions were covering the main Monte Grande positions. On the right, the Argylls held Frasinetto Ridge; in the centre Frontier Force Rifles occupied Monte Cerere; on the left 3/8 Punjabis were astride Monte Grande itself. In each position the crest was narrow, and defence in depth impossible. Anywhere a sudden rush might win home, and sudden rushes were the speciality of the paratroopers.

An Argylls officer in a private letter gave a description of this ominous sector.

"I know how my grandfather felt at Majuba Hill. We had the high ground and it was of little use to us. Our positions were under constant observation. We had to sit tight all the time, just like old Bill in Flanders. A bitter wind whistled up the valley and curled over the crests, adding one more misery to sitting in a slit trench all day and all night, with a drizzle gradually soaking clothing and blankets, and freezing the bones. A heavy mist would come down; if the paraboys could not see us, neither could we see them. It was rather eerie this being hunted through the fog, and we grew very quick on the trigger."

The only positions for artillery and dumps lay in the Sillaro valley, under intimate enemy observation. The fog which the Argylls officer mentions was a blend of natural elements and smoke from the canisters, released to screen traffic movements and gun positions on the lower ground. Short of the impossible, supply difficulties achieved on all-time nadir. The journey from jeephead to Frontier Force Rifles, a distance of under two miles, occupied five hours. Even the surefooted mules sometimes failed to negotiate the slimy mud of the hillsides, crashing to death on the rocks below, with wounded men in their litters.

The enemy was spoiling for trouble. The quiet of the day was broken regularly by the weird moans of the nebelwerfers, heralding short fierce mortar shoots on the advanced Indian positions. At night men slipped from their holes to patrol forward, to lay traps and ambushes, to stalk on sound and to kill the unwary. The Argylls were no sooner in position than they were assailed. On the night of December 6th a fighting patrol of paratroopers sprang out of the darkness, and after a savage melee managed to snatch three prisoners. On the same night after vicious mortaring forty Germans closed from all sides on a house which sheltered a combined post of Punjabis and Gordon Highlanders, at the junction of the British and Indian positions. Setting fire to the building with a bazooka, the paratroopers sought to flush the garrison into the open. The Punjabis blew back the rush after suffering twelve casualties; the Gordons lost an officer and eight men as prisoners.

These scrimmages were prelude to the main assault on Monte Grande. On the morning of December 12th, after a half hour's intensive mortar and artillery fire, the enemy laid a smoke screen over Argyll and Frontier Force positions at Frasinetto and Monte Cerere. Behind this cover a battalion of paratroopers surged to the close. On the right of the assault, the Argylls were waiting and as one of the men put it, "gave them everything". The attack disintegrated. On the inner flank of the Frasinetto position, the Argylls were caught on the wrong foot, half-way between their day and night stations. Leaping through the smoke and fog, the adversaries grappled in deadly hand to hand fighting. No quarter was asked or given. The impetus of their rush carried the Germans over the advanced posts and the Scotsmen were overrun, save for two bonny fighters—Lieutenant and Sergeant Reid—who dived into a ditch and in Wild West shooting matches accounted for a number of enemies before scrambling to safety in the fog.

In the centre of the position the paratroopers thrust with equal vehemence against Frontier Force Rifles. The right forward platoon was overrun, and the Germans burst into the main battle positions. A reserve company of Frontiersmen doubled into action, and their weight decided the melee; the paratroopers sullenly gave ground. Whereupon the storm troopers who had won ground from the Argylls decided to join the fray. It was their last and worst decision; as they raced from flank across a hundred yards of open ground, the Mahratta machine-gunners caught them at point blank range. Within seconds the hillside was strewn with dead and dying Germans. Few escaped.

Everywhere except on the inner flank of the Argyll position, 19th Brigade had broken the assault. At 1100 hours First British Division picked up a dispairing enemy intercept, pleading for reinforcements. This good news stimulated the Argylls, who prepared to put paid to the remaining intruders. After a half-hour's bombardment with every available weapon, the Scotsmen charged. They swept over the lost ground, and by noon were re-established in their original positions. Under cover of a Red Cross flag German stretcher bearers moved amongst them, picking up many dead and wounded.

Thirteen prisoners were taken—surly ruffians all, and bitterly garrulous over their failure. Much interesting information was proffered. These statements were implemented when an extremely drunken paratrooper, sent forward on a one-man patrol to ascertain the fate of his comrades, was snared in front of the Indian positions. This old sweat declared the assault to have been planned by the battalion commander against the advice of his officers. "He was set on fighting," said the tosspot, "because of the tickling of his throat." The startled interrogation officer was about to enquire further into this interesting subject of thirsts, when he remembered the Wehrmacht idiom. The battalion commander had wished to feel the ribbon of an Iron Cross upon his neck.

By December 23rd the threat had passed. 19th Brigade was relieved and set out to rejoin Eighth Indian Division. This time it meant more than going down one mountain road and up another. A far call had come for Fifth Army's flying squad, and Eighth Division was on its way far across Italy. But before relating the diverting episode of Serchio, it is necessary to return to the Divisional front between Star and Arrow Routes, where 21st and 17th Brigades battled forward slowly and precariously against tenacious rearguards, abominable weather and all but unsurmountable terrain.

The wheel of the Polish attack into the west continued to constrict the front and to limit the responsibilities of 17th Brigade between Star and Sword Routes. As a result Royal Fusiliers were loaned on December 10th to Seventy-Eighth British Division. They migrated in their troop carriers to a ruined uplands village south of Monte Grande in the Sillaro Valley. On December 17th the remainder of 17th Brigade crossed to Arrow Route and relieved 21st Brigade, in order to slog towards the cliffs of Veno Del Gosso. The Poles had in plan an operation against the eastern extremity of that barrier. Eighth Indian Division were folded into this scheme, and its role defined as penetration of the Senio gorge in the chalk escarpment, thereafter wheeling left in line with the Polish attack, and seizing the watershed between the Senio and Santerno rivers. Patrols began to search the eastern cliffsides for scaleable chimneys, only to find the enemy exceedingly alert. On Christmas Eve heavy snow fell. A bitter wind swept across the crests, and the roads were blocked with drifts. The Polish attack, originally timed for December 29th, was set back, and the Indian brigades settled down to routine duties in a most uncomfortable locality.

During this wait, events took shape elsewhere. Ninety miles to the west, in the sectors adjacent to the Gulf of Genoa, there had been little serious fighting. Both the enemy and Fifth Army held wide stretches of the Tuscany uplands with sparse forces. Yet the area was of vital importance to American formations, which drew most of their material from Leghorn, a port less than forty miles behind the loosely held front. From Pisa the supply route turned inland, running eastwards to the picturesque walled city of Lucca in the Serchio valley, fifteen miles behind the battle zone. A comparatively limited advance by the enemy in this sector might disrupt the main American communications.

In early December intelligence reports revealed an undue muster of enemy forces in the upper Serchio valley. From this concentration area, it was possible either to strike down the coastal roads towards Pisa, or across the equally easy terrain of the Serchio valley towards Lucca. The latter sector was guarded by comparatively weak forces of Ninety-Second American (Negro) Division. Early appreciations did not cause anxiety, but later information suggested that something was afoot. On the evening of December 22nd, an urgent instruction flashed to General Russell's headquarters in the Apennines. Eighth Indian Division, less one brigade, must move with all haste to Lucca.

Fifty-two miles of winding icebound roads, with two high passes deep in snow, separated Eighth Indian Division from the Arno valley. Another fifty miles must be traversed before concentration at Lucca. To gather up a Division scattered for miles on peaks and in canyons, and to start all units on an organized trek to another front, called for feverish staff work. By Christmas Eve marching orders were out and the Indians under way. As late as Christmas morning Fifth Army professed to view the move as precautionary; but Brigadier Dobree, arriving at headquarters of U.S. Fourth Corps that afternoon, was informed that an enemy attack down the Serchio valley would be launched within twenty-four hours. As General Russell had not yet arrived, he was entreated to take charge, and to organize a support line. As rapidly as Indian units arrived, they were deployed in defensive positions.

The Serchio valley is wide, easy and well cultivated. A railway and two highways follow the line of the river, a quiet stream which averages one hundred feet in width. The area is heavily populated, with clusters of farmhouses and small hamlets scattered along the roads and in the glades among the beech woods. The countryside exhibited no signs of devastation, and the gracious contours and pleasant expanses delighted the Indians, fresh from a nightmare existence in the gale-swept valleys of the winter Apennines.

One Hundred and Forty-Eighth German Division, reinforced by

elements of three Italian Fascist Divisions, held the front between the Serchio valley and the seacoast. All were troops of second quality. The German division contained many Poles and other impressed groups of non-German birth, who had lost any enthusiasm which they might once have had for the Feuhrer. The morale of the Italian divisions was even lower, with an average desertion rate of forty daily.

Nevertheless, U.S. Fourth Corps had correctly assessed the situation. Early on Boxing Day three battalions of 286th German Infantry Regiment, after a short bombardment, launched an attack down the Serchio valley. It succeeded beyond all expectations. The front crumbled and two parallel enemy columns thrust into the south. Mobile artillery in close support pumped a few shells here and there and the infantry stolidly followed up and took possession. By noon it was evident that the line was open, and that Ninety-Second Division was not competent to offer organized resistance.

General Russell arrived to find 19th Brigade deployed as a blocking force. Making the best of his handfulls, Brigadier Dobree arrayed his men in the localities least easy to by-pass. Slightly south of Barga, 3/8 Punjabis found a strong position, dug in, and waited. On their left, 6/13 Frontier Force Rifles covered the winding road, and prepared to take the shock. South of the river, under cover of some wooded spurs, Argyll and Sutherland Highlanders spread out and scanned the north for first sight of the advanced elements of the enemy.

They never came. Either the Germans were too surprised by their success to exploit it, or the operation had been no more than a bluff. By the morning of December 27th, General Russell, who at the request of the American corps had taken command of all troops in the Serchio valley, felt the situation to be under control, and proceeded to tidy up. The negro battalions were withdrawn through 19th Brigade, and the flood of Italian refugees diverted on to side roads and into the fields. On December 28th, 21st Brigade arrived and came up on the right of 19th Brigade. Next day 6th Lancers threw an armoured car screen across the valley and began to probe forward. The first patrols into Bagno di Lucca found the Union Jack flying, and a Scottish UNRRA officer, who had hidden under his bed for a few days, nonchalantly reorganizing his work. A certain amount of outpost bickering followed, but it was apparent that the Germans had bolted back to their start line. By New Year's Eve the operation had reached a sufficiently lighthearted stage to allow a company of Frontier Force Rifles to relieve the Argyll and Sutherland Highlanders, in order that the Scotsmen might celebrate with all due ritual their sacred occasion of Hogmanay.

After the rigours and deadly encounters of the mountains, this excursion into the west had proved to be something of a frolic. It was a different enemy and a different sort of war. When all ground had been regained, General Russell's mind turned to 17th Brigade, which had missed the fun. He suggested to the American corps commander that if granted his full division, he would be pleased to chase the Boche for any stated distance. But something even better was in store. Early in January a general relief began, and the Division dispersed at rest in the Pisa area.

So ended a remarkable tour of duty, which began with a static role for Eighth Indian Division between two assaulting armies; to be followed by commital to battle in the critical task of breaking into the Gothic Line; thereafter a steady extension of responsibilities, with aid first to the Poles at Monte Bartolo and afterwards to First British Division at Monte Grande; finally, a long jaunt into the west and a bit of light relief in the way of war.

HIGH APENNINES

(GURKHA PATROL IS FROM THE PAINTING BY CAPTAIN HARRY SHELDON)

GURKHA SNOW PATROL

SIKH RAIDERS

JAIPUR GUNNERS

SIKH SKI-MAN

GURKHA SIGNALMAN

SAPPERS AND MINERS—LAMONE RIVER

HARDY MUSSALMANS

MAHRATTAS STORM FLOODBANK

ARK BRIDGE

RAIDERS UNDER ARTIFICIAL MOONLIGHT

(THE ABOVE IS FROM THE PAINTING BY CAPT. HARRY SHELDON)

DUKWS LOAD GUNS

GUNS ACROSS

JEEPS ACROSS

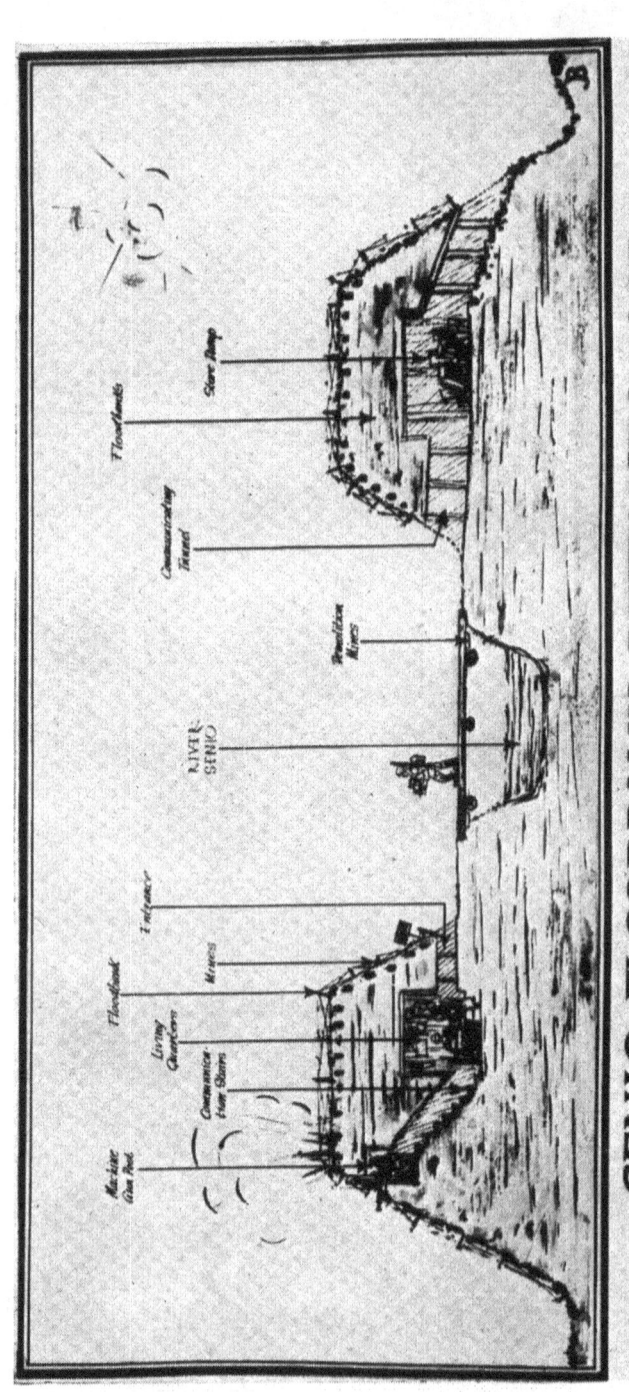

5. THE LAST CAMPAIGN

CHAPTER SEVENTEEN

THE FLOODBANKED RIVERS

THE CAMPAIGN IN THE MOUNTAINS was over. The enemy still clung to Monte Grande and a few similar strongholds, but his forces had been backed against the escarpment above the plains and could be ejected at any time. From assaults on rounded ridges, from the storming of precipitous summits, from infiltration along valleys and ravines, from the forcing of brawling streams, the Indian Divisions now turned to another sort of warfare.

The Emilian plain beyond the Apennines was by no means a strategical and tactical paradise. This low land in centuries past had formed a great marsh. When the snows melted on the Apennines each spring immense torrents poured down through clefts in the foothills, seeking the Adriatic. This spate spread across the plain, engulfing large areas. As the countryside became populated it was found possible to contain these seasonal floods by raising the river banks with ramparts of earth. The turbid water moved sluggishly to the sea, tending to silt rather than to erode. No deep channels were cut, and the levels of the river rose rather than fell. To confine the spring freshets the banks were built higher and higher, until to-day the line of each river is marked by great dykes standing above the plain.

These floodbanks are military works of first importance. They transform each river into five successive obstacles—the fortifications of two outer banks, of two inner banks, and the river itself. The soft ramparts lend themselves to burrowing, so that these high mounds may be converted into elaborate fortifications. When the threat to the Gothic Line became imminent, the German military labour organization swung into action. The floodbanks were scooped out, and underground accommodation provided for substantial garrisons. Longitudinal tunnels were built and revetted with stout timbers. Leading off these galleries, vertical and horizontal shafts opened on to the sides of the flood banks like portholes in a ship. From these portholes protruded the ugly muzzles of scores of guns. The plain was usually so flat that a weapon pit only a few feet above its level would command the approach for hundreds of yards. The lazy meanders of the river made the successive posts mutually supporting, and allowed them to sweep a wide front with converging and enfilade fire.

A river line was a fixed zone of defence. Being without outworks attacking forces were kept at a distance by means of belts of wire and aprons of mines. The near floodbank was breached in places, with a view to flooding the approaches when necessary. All bridges were destroyed; the garrisons of the near bank crossed on foot bridges which when not in use were swung back against the far bank. The northern floodbank for some inexplicable reason was usually slightly higher than the south bank. These few extra inches improved the observation of the defenders.

Other factors complicated the problem of attack. The narrow dykes offered a meagre target for artillery, and even less target for bombs. Without bridging they were impassable for tanks or vehicles, and bridges could only be built on the site of former bridges, since the slopes of the banks were too steep for tracks or wheels to surmount without approach ramps. Thus to reach these floodbanks with mechanized arms presented a problem of extreme difficulty; to storm them, a grim task indeed.

Every device breeds its anti-device. Not only the Germans but the United Nations had given a lot of thought to floodbanked rivers. The problem of attack was threefold—to approach, to effect a lodgment, and to cross. It was obvious that the approach must be made in small numbers, as anything resembling a massed assault would incur sufficient casualties to weaken the assailants, and so endanger the second stage of the operation. On the other hand, there was no assurance that isolated posts and small detachments when established on the near floodbank would be able to bring the river line under sufficient control to effect a crossing. Basic tactics therefore had to be determined by the empirical method of trial and error. It speaks volumes for the resource of Eighty Army planners that after a few weeks of experiment the problem of approach had been solved. Artillery was deployed in such fashion as to cast shells within a few yards of the men whom the guns supported; it became possible to bombard the inner slopes of a floodbank without undue risk to troops dug in ten yards away on its outer bank. Supplementing the artillery, the weapon of fire was enlisted. Crocodiles and Wasps, fire-throwing vehicles great and small, and Lifebuoys (manual flame-throwers) were mobilized to burn out the warrens of the defenders. While billows of blazing oil smothered the banks, jets of flame would be injected into the portholes, rendering the tunnels uninhabitable and driving the garrison into the open.

For crossing these narrow high-banked rivers the sappers devised an ingenious variation on the "Ark" bridge. Instead of a full span the bridge was little longer than the tank. With the tank resting in the river bed the span could be lifted hydraulically and placed in position. Should the river be deep, the superstructure was so designed that if the bottom "Ark" carrier was submerged, a second tank complete with bridge could drive on to the top of the sunken vehicles and so construct a crossing two tanks deep. Other ingenious equipment included new and strong types of aerial cableways, on which not only men but guns and vehicles could be slung rapidly across the narrow troughs of the rivers.

A battle group organized for assault on floodbanked rivers incorporated a wide range of specialist formations. Armour was important, because the high dykes gave considerable cover to tanks closing up in close support of the infantry. Anti-tank guns, particularly of the self-propelled variety, were of value for sniping into port-holes and for reducing enemy posts on the near bank. Machine-gun companies firing from flank could hold the floodbank under a lash of steel until the infantry had closed to within a few yards. Flamethrowers would lead the way, with Kangaroo armoured troop carriers in close support. Special assault companies of sappers would move forward with the infantry, and would begin work on crossings while the battle raged about them.

Yet in spite of all technical assistance and mechanical device, the issue remained between man and man. Had the enemy been able to oppose the Allied advance with troops of commensurate courage and endurance, the strength of his fortifications might have decided the day. Fortunately the German divisions which manned the floodbanked rivers had been mauled and battered for month after month, thrust headlong from position after position. The cream of the German armies had been destroyed. No troops could endure such punishment without realization of the futility of fighting on. A rising proportion of German troops were no longer battle-worthy. Disillusion had reacted on the relationships of officers and men until a slow but incurable depression clouded all but the most fanatical minds. Its recurrent motif was that no battle lost or no battle won could affect the final result. The Germans continued to fight, but they fought as doomed men.

Their adversaries of the United Nations moved from strength to strength. The front had been broken in Normandy, and seven armies were thrusting into the vitals of Germany. The Russian avalanche rolled remorselessly towards the Reich. In Europe the end drew near; in the Pacific the ring closed around Japan. In Italy, despite all hardships and dangers a dominant thought rang like a bell in soldiers' minds. "We too shall be in at the kill."

CHAPTER EIGHTEEN

TENTH DIVISION CLEARS THE WAY

AFTER RELIEF ON THE RONCO, Tenth Indian Division rested for a bare fortnight. During this period Fifth Corps had swung into the west. On Novermber 9th, after a fierce battle, Fourth and Forty-Sixth British Divisions stormed Forli. A fresh attack was immediately planned with Faenza, the next important town on the main transverse highway, as the principal objective. Tenth Indian Division was ordered to establish a bridgehead over the Montone through which the assault divisions might deploy on their start lines.

On November 19th 10th Indian Brigade relieved a brigade of Fourth British Division on a front of four miles near the Montone river. The ground was monotonously flat, intersected by a network of drainage rhines, and heavily cultivated. Vineyards, orchards and farmhouses dotted the countryside. All bridges had been blown, the roads cratered and the paths mined. The river proper, a sludgy stream thirty feet in width, was no great obstacle, but inside the flood walls a soft mud bottom flanked the watercourse, extending the gap to two hundred feet. The enemy had breached the banks, and the countryside was flooded for one thousand yards east of the river. The only approaches were along built-up roads covered by machine-guns and artillery.

On November 22nd, 43rd Gurkha Brigade took over a sector on the left of 10th Brigade. Two nights later 20th Brigade came up on the left of 10th Brigade, and Tenth Division was aligned for its attack. 10th Brigade brought forward assault boats and with the Durhams leading prepared to force a crossing. The enemy was alert and laid down a fierce shoot on the line of the river. The advance was held up for several hours until 3/5 Mahrattas, accompanied by tanks of 6th Royal Tank Regiment, could advance laterally from the left flank and engage the enemy. With the aid of this distraction the Durhams rapidly built up a bridgehead force of two companies. By noon both 10th and 20th Brigades were represented in an expanding perimeter to the west of the Montone.

For the next phase First Canadian Corps entered the line on the right of the Indians, and the New Zealand Division relieved Fourth British Division on the opposite flank. The Indian brigades by nibbling tactics began to edge towards Albereto, a village a mile east of the Lamone, the next water obstacle to the west. This village proved to be the core of the enemy defences, and bitter fighting ensued when twin attacks closed in from opposite sides. A confused close-quarters free-for-all raged until the enemy slowly and sullenly withdrew. Forty German dead were picked up among the ruins of the village.

At 0545 hours on November 20th, both Indian brigades attacked outwards from Migliara, the individual thrusts diverging like the spokes of a wheel from the hub. On the right 2/4 Gurkhas and North Irish Horse worked into the north-east. Their next-door neighbours, the Durhams, smashed through to their objective after sharp fighting at San Giorgio. Further west, 1/2 Punjabis broke into new territory and seized three hamlets. In the centre 3/5 Mahrattas with two companies of Nabha Akals, crashed through obstinate resistance. On the extreme left 2/3 Gurkhas captured Pianetto and La Gessa, taking 56 prisoners. By midday all Indian battalions were well established in the main German positions. An enemy wireless intercept declared "Defence plan completely broken". With such encouragement the attack was pushed home, and with the New Zealanders making equal headway on the left all territory east of the Lamone was mopped up.

This local scrimmaging cleared the battlefield for the stroke to follow. Four corps struck at the wavering salient which incessant assaults had gouged in the German defences. The Canadians attacked to the north-east towards Ravenna. Second Polish Corps mounted an all-out drive on the last high ground held by the enemy in the Apennine foothills, along the dwindling ridges between the Lamone and the Senio valleys. Thirteenth Corps moved at right angles to the Poles, with the objective of pinching out enemy formations east of the Senio. Fifth Corps drove on Faenza. Leading the attack, Forty-sixth British Division on December 3rd battled its way after wild fighting across the Lamone five miles south-west of Forli.

At the outset of this great assault Tenth Indian Division's role was restricted to "noises off"—deception shoots and bridge-building clamour behind smoke screens. Beyond the Lamone Forty-Sixth Division became involved in some of the stiffest fighting of the war. For a week this hard-hitting British formation exchanged hammer blows with a veteran and ever-dangerous opponent—Nineteenth Panzer Grenadier Division. It then became necessary for someone else to take over the slogging match. On December 11th Tenth Indian Division moved up and relieved Forty-Sixth Division. The bridgehead over the Lamone was slightly less than two miles in depth, and the danger point lay around Pideura, in the centre of the position. Here 25th Brigade came into the line. 3/1 Punjabis and King's Own immediately became involved in bickerings which flared up from time to time into heavy fighting. No less than five enemy counter-attacks were thrown back in the first twenty-four hours of the tour. These quick venomous jabs were designed to dislocate the timing of the main assault of Fifth Corps, which was near at hand. Such tactics failed: when zero hour struck at 2300 hours on December 23rd, five Indian battalions advanced against the enemy to give the New Zealanders a firm flank for their drive to the Senio.

At point of junction with the Kiwis, the Durhams of 10th Brigade smashed at Pergola. The North Countrymen encountered one misfortune after another. Defensive fire caught them on their start line. The leading troops walked on to an uncharted schu-minefield when approaching their preliminary objective. A frontal assault failed to shake the enemy, and when the Durhams swung to flank, they found themselves in the midst of another minefield. These tough globetrotters were loath to admit failure, and fought on throughout the day; but Pergola was beyond their grasp.

On the left of the Durhams, 3/1 Punjabis managed to establish a company on a low sharp-crested ridge. Once again haystacks played the villain's part. Fired by enemy tracer they silhouetted the gallant Indians as they charged. Even then the Punjabis might have held on had it not been for a serious deterioration on their left, where 4/11 Sikhs, after gallantly gaining their ground, were thrown back by a weighty infantry attack supported by self-propelled guns.

Beyond the Sikhs the King's Own fought along a hilltop to the north of Pideura. Farm houses which sheltered nests of machine-gunners took a heavy toll. A self-propelled gun knocked out the escorting Sherman tanks, and was in turn destroyed. All through the day the King's Own surged again and again to the assault; as evening fell they broke into Camillo, taking twenty-four prisoners. "C" Company, after having been in the thick of continuous fighting for upwards of twenty-four hours, had only one officer and twenty-six men standing.

On the extreme left 3/18 Garhwalis to some extent redeemed the grim picture on the remainder of the Divisional front. One company swung away on a march of three miles along a muddy track which brought it on to the rear of the enemy positions at Casa Zula and Monte Coralli. Concurrent assaults were launched from opposite sides. In bitter hand-to-hand fighting the enemy garrison was destroyed. The victors sweated over their spades, and when the counter-attack came they were well dug in. A wild hurly-burly followed. A white house surmounting a cypress-clad hillside changed hands several times. Spandau teams were detected in weapon pits sited under haystacks. This shortsightedness led to a series of incinerations as tracer fire ignited the hay. There were grim games of hide and seek; on one occasion an irate Garhwali rifleman, mounting a stack with his bayonet to winkle out a sniper, was surprised by his quarry, who emerged from beneath the hay, pulled the ladder away, and raced to fresh cover before he could be brought down. When the enemy finally abandoned attempts to oust the Garhwalis, sixty German dead and twelve prisoners remained in Indian hands.

In this assault Tenth Indian Division had failed for the first time to make its principal objectives. The grueling fighting, however, was not without reward, for the Indian assault had pinned down the enemy's reserves, and had given the New Zealanders a clear run to the Senio. With the Kiwis well ahead, on the night of December 14/15th, 4/10 Baluchis passed through the New Zealand front and turned south on the flank and rear of the Pergola positions. The enemy had foreseen this move and had pulled out. The line was open and that evening Indian patrols without resistance reached the tortuous meanders of the Senio between Renazzi and Tobano. The enemy was still reeling from the buffets dealt him, and without undue opposition Baluchis and Garhwalis crossed the river and established posts on the west bank. 2/4 Gurkhas moved up to stiffen the tiny bridgehead, and were told the astonishing but true story of the German tank which had attempted to approach the Baluchi positions with a Red Cross flag flying from its turret.

The Gurkhas immediately began to elbow their way forward, with the line of the railway running into Castel Bolognesi as their objective. The enemy recovered his breath, and the leading company of the hillmen became involved in a fracas sufficiently serious to require reinforcement. The bridgehead lay in one of the many loops of the river, and as resistance stiffened the Gurkhas found themselves with enemies on three sides. After increasing displays of truculence had indicated the arrival of enemy reserves, the Indian force was gradually withdrawn to the east bank of the river.

On December 15th, 43rd Gurkha Lorried Brigade passed under command of Second New Zealand Division, and under the description of Faenza Task Force, began to clear the Germans from that important centre. For the first time the Gurkhas were schooled in the peculiar technique of street fighting. The area was mine-infested and the Luftwaffe active. 2/10 Gurkhas entered the town from the east and encountered comparatively little opposition until the railway along Route 9 was reached. Thereafter resistance stiffened. 2/8 Gurkhas came forward to reinforce the attack. A German counter-attack with panzers in the van forced the hillmen back to the canal which parallels the Lamone. Here the adversaries glared at each other for twenty-four hours, while the sappers devised a crossing which would bear tanks. At 2100 hours Faenza Task Force moved to the assault with the Gurkha Brigade on the left of the Kiwis. Once again in the face of a set-piece attack the enemy had compounded with necessity and had cleared out. Little resistance was encountered except from road blocks and minefields. Faenza was liberated. The Germans fell back to prepared positions on the line of the Senio.

On Tenth Division's front wintry gales had slowed down operations to a standstill. Christmas and the New Year passed quietly, but early in January patrol clashes increased and raids became a nightly feature.

The loops of the Senio which thrust adjacent salients into the front exercised an inevitable fascination for patrols on the prowl. On January 12th the illfated members of Parliament who disappeared a few days later in a lost plane, visited the Division. The Germans chose this day to pester the Indians. A Garhwali sentry heard the sound of chopping and shrewdly deduced that trees were being felled for footbridges. The raiding party met a warm reception. Next morning the Garhwalis were interested spectators as the Germans buried their dead in full view on the opposite bank under the protection of a Red Cross flag.

On the following night an enemy detachment crossed the Senio and established itself in Chiarona. The Garhwalis accepted the challenge with alacrity and for variety's sake staged the ejection by daylight. Behind a smoke screen two platoons charged with tanks in the van. The Shermans pumped a hundred shells into the enemy's hideouts as the Garhwalis raced in from front and rear. The rear platoon literally caught the panzer grenadiers with their backs turned; twenty-five were killed and ten taken prisoner. That night a follow-up fighting patrol endeavoured to learn the fate of the Chiarona garrison. The Garhwalis were alert and few escaped.

Early in February 4/11 Sikhs had a bit of luck. Their raiders were closing on an enemy position when a false alarm distracted the German sentries. The schmessers and spandaus commenced to hose bullets to empty flank, while the Sikhs crept nearer. Undetected the Indians sprang upon the engrossed garrison, and destroyed it.

In a series of similar bickerings, which imposed a strain upon weakening adversaries, Tenth Division's tour on the river lines wore away. On February 9th Third Carpathian Division relieved the Indians along the Senio. Then followed a last look at the high mountains. The enemy still clung tenaciously to his strongholds in the upper Sillaro valley, including Monte Grande, which remained a key position covering the eastern approaches to Bologna. First German Parachute Division, in its customary uncompromising mood, continued to garrison this area, and Seventy-Eighth British Division after an extensive spell of duty was feeling the strain. On February 8th, 20th Brigade embussed at Faenza. By sky line Monte Grande was only sixteen miles away, but the road journey covered ninety miles and took two days. 10th Brigade arrived on February 12th to complete the occupation of the new Divisional sector.

The country was deerstalker's landscape, with high lookouts and deep scours. Everyone had an embarrassingly good view of everybody else. To cover supply movements in the Sillaro valley an American detachment maintained a continuous smoke screen near the San Clemente ford. The Divisional anti-aircraft gunners took over management of the canisters throughout the tour of duty. On the right of the Indians, Sixth British Armoured Division linked up with the Polish

Corps; on the left Eighty-Fifth U.S. Division carried the line to the west. From the beginning the paratroopers were bent on making nuisances of themselves. A smash and grab party, seeking to identify the newcomers, gave the forward company of Durhams a busy half hour, but the North countrymen mixed it so earnestly that the intruders finally fled, leaving a number of dead behind. Two nights later a keen-eyed Baluchi nobbled a paratroop observation officer, who was lying up close to the forward positions. Next morning four paratroopers dressed as stretcher bearers approached 2/4 Gurkhas. Despite protests they were arrested and packed off to the rear. The German commander thereupon despatched a note offering to exchange four Sikh stretcher bearers for his lost men. When the offer drew no response, the Sikhs were returned, revealing the ruse.

The Indians then got down to work. A patrol from 1/2 Punjabis crawled into the Germans' positions and mopped up three posts. When intercepted on the way home, their prisoners, anticipating rescue, threw themselves on the ground and refused to move. Having summarily dealt with the recalcitrants (first removing their jackets as identifications), the Punjabis charged with the steel and broke through, killing five at close quarters for the loss of one man killed and one wounded.

The same mettlesome and aggressive battalion despatched a roving patrol in the next night. A havildar and his section silently closed on a slit trench which covered a large house. Two Germans put up their hands; at the same time one kicked a signal wire. Flares and a red Verey light shot up; a machine-gun opened, and thirty Germans poured from the house. First putting paid to the prisoners, the havildar and his squad leapt into the slit trench, and raked their assailants with tommy guns. A dozen paratroopers fell. Three Indians were wounded, but all returned to safety.

A Mahratta patrol penetrated the enemy positions and lay in ambush in a copse beside a path which connected two German posts. An emergency flare signal had been arranged to call for covering mortar fire if required. When attacked the Germans by a remarkable coincidence fired the same signal. Down came the mortar shoot on the copse. With every licence to withdraw the Mahrattas stuck it for two hours. The shoot ended and patience paid a dividend. Fifteen Germans came trudging along the path. Eleven paratroopers were killed against three Indians wounded.

Finding the Indians more than their match in this grim hunting, the paratroopers tended to avoid front line clashes; instead, they specialized in deep penetration patrols. Detachments of two or three men would filter through, and would work back among the rear echelons. They dressed like civilians, retaining only sufficient vestiges of uniform to escape execution if captured. Each carried a few schu-mines, which they buried in well-trodden spots. They also carried miniature wireless sets; when concentrations of vehicles or personnel were encountered, fire would be directed upon them. If accosted they boldly tried to pass themselves off as Italians. Fortunately the sepoys' Italian was in many instances better than that of the Germans, and rigid security measures trapped so many of these audacious detachments that in self-defence they were obliged to increase the size of the patrols—thereby facilitating their detection.

On March 11th, 25th Brigade took over Monte Grande from U.S. Eighty-Fifth Division. For this task the Brigade was strengthened by an extra infantry battalion (2nd Highland Light Infantry), a squadron of Lovat Scouts, and "F" Reconnaissance Squadron, a volunteer Italian parachute formation of proven worth. The spring thaw had set in, and as the snow disappeared the bitterness of the fighting on this sinister summit was revealed. Many bodies of British, American and German soldiers were uncovered. One hundred and fifty dead mules were collected for burning or burial.

Throughout March all brigades continued to harass the enemy. Mahrattas, Nabha Akals and Punjabis found particularly good hunting; a strong patrol from the latter battalion on one occasion spent forty-eight hours in the rear of the German positions and emerged without casualty. 13 Anti-Tank Regiment, with no tanks to shoot at, themselves turned tank men, re-conditioned some derelict Shermans, and scouted enthusiastically.

As April began, and the great assault on the river lines grew imminent, the paratroopers apparently received orders to pin down the troops opposite them. When 2nd Loyals arrived to join 20th Brigade, the new hands were raided as soon as they entered the line. A forward platoon was overrun, but the remainder stood firm and blew back the attack. 4/11 Sikhs endured two attacks in one morning. As the Germans closed the grim bearded men leapt to meet them, and slew many on the lips of the slit trenches.

The master plan for the spring offensive called for Tenth Indian Division to participate in Eighth Army's drive by an advance down the Sillaro valley. General Reid was now six battalions over establishment; this permitted the wearers of the red and blue diagonals to be in two places at once. Lovat Scouts, Loyals, Highland Light Infantry, 4/11 Sikhs, Nabha Akals and Jodhpurs took charge of Monte Grande, while the remainder of the Division moved back across the mountains on the long up and down trek to the Adriatic. On April 9th the air was filled with thunder as Eighth Army smashed at the river lines in the climactic offensive of the war. A week later Tenth Indian Division was concentrated on the battlefield, waiting for the word to take up the running.

CHAPTER NINETEEN

EIGHTH DIVISION PUNCHES THE HOLE AGAIN

THIS NARRATIVE left the men of Eighth Indian Division, after their by-play in the Serchio valley, relaxed and enjoying themselves in the lovely countryside surrounding the old and charming city of Pisa. The jawans took their ease in good billets amidst a hospitable civilian population. Sprung from farming stock themselves, the sepoys revelled in the rich fields and pastures; they wrote home long descriptions of Italian tillage and husbandry. Six weeks passed quickly. On February 11th, the call came, and the Indians commenced to move back to Eighth Army. Some units travelled across Italy by cattle truck; rail transport was sufficiently novel to ameliorate the discomfort. Forty miles south of Ancona the Division mustered and turned towards the battle line. On February 25th leading units relieved elements of First Canadian Division north of Bagnocavallo astride Route 16, the main Adriatic highway.

On the left of Eighth Division 43rd Gurkha Lorried Brigade, who were last seen with the New Zealanders in Faenza, occupied an adjoining sector under command of Fifty-Sixth London Division. The Gurkhas had been in the line for a fortnight when Eighth Division arrived. They held five thousand yards, confronting intricate and elaborate defences. The Senio floodbanks, twenty feet high and six feet wide at the top, commanded the eastern approaches and made daylight reconnaissance impossible. Behind innocuous camouflage scores of tunnels in the near face of the floodbank housed observation posts, machine-gunners and snipers. Belts of wire and a heavy seeding of mines skirted the slopes. Farmhouses each in its small oblong field with pollarded boundaries stood along the river bank. Some of these buildings had been converted into outposts, the others abundantly booby-trapped.

The Gurkhas had been able to work forward to within a few hundred yards of the river, but thereafter every foot of distance harboured deadly menaces. Preparations for establishment on the near flood bank began immediately. 23rd Field Regiment deployed widely to flank and justified the Brigade's pride in its marksmanship by dropping shells unerringly on the inner banks, leaving the outer slope unscathed. Seventeen pounders were brought up to deal with enemy nests in the farmhouses, and to snipe the tunnel entrances. Delay action shell was issued to assure penetration bursts. Skinners' Horse moved its 75 millimetre tanks into close support.

At 2100 hours on February 23rd, Fifty-Sixth Division attacked on a two brigade front. All three Gurkha battalions swept forward, raced along paths cut in the minefields, wriggled through the wire, and reached the comparative safety of the outer slope of the floodbank. Furiously the hillmen dug, roofing their scanty niches in order that bombs rolled over the top of the bank might trundle by. Manual flame-throwers were rushed up and emplaced, individual cubbyholes linked into weapon pits. At dawn the sweating Gurkhas laid aside spades, picked up weapons, and waited. The first assault was thrown against 2/8 battalion at 1000 hours. Alert aircraft and artillery intervened to break up the attack. Thereafter except for showers of stick grenades, teller mines with time fuses cart-wheeling past and machine-guns from enfilade positions spraying bullets about, the day passed quietly. The Gurkhas went back to their spades and began to improve their positions. Saps were driven up to the lip of the bank. Counter-tunnelling commenced. Like two warring swarms the adversaries toiled in the same hive.

Night saw the footbridges stealthily swing over the river, and enemy raiders tiptoe across into the tunnel entrances of the inner bank. Here the assault groups organized, fingers on lips, for less than five yards of earth separated them from the men whom they had come to destroy. The Gurkhas waited also, tense in the darkness, tommy gun in lap, kukri loose in its sheath. When the rush came the quick-eyed and cat-footed hillmen seldom were second best. Often they leapt to meet their foes and beat them to the stroke. The death scream of a German cloven to the chine caused the man behind him to falter, and in that split second's delay the kukri took another life.

After three harassing days and nights, the Germans again struck in force. An intense mortar and artillery shoot crashed on the company of 2/8 Gurkhas holding the Bastion, a strong-point near a flood gap which the enemy had blown in the near bank of the river. Under the bombardment adjacent earthworks collapsed, burying part of the garrison. At 2100 hours enemy infantry swarmed across the river to mop up. With the Bastion secured, German detachments raced to flank to widen the breach. Within two hundred yards they were pinned down; on the left Subedar Jitbahadur Gurung and his platoon broke up attack after attack. Morning found the intruders penned in around the torn mound. The Gurkhas charged, snatched back the position, but were unable to hold it. Stroke and counterstroke followed rapidly, with the enemy clinging precariously to this tormented hummock. At the end of February, when the Gurkha Brigade was relieved, it handed over three miles of secure floodbank; but around the Bastion a hard-pressed handful of enemies still lurked in their burrows. The tour had cost the 43rd Brigade three hundred men.

Eighth Division's task of establishment on the Senio was in some degree less onerous than that of the Gurkhas. In a few sectors the outer slope had already been won by the Canadians. In other places vines and undergrowth permitted unseen approach. In still other places the Indian positions were on the plain a few hundred yards behind the river. Everywhere the infantry was under extreme and unremitting tension. The Germans employed great numbers of multiple mortars and a fearful new missile, a short range rocket with a two hundred pound warhead. Its inaccuracy was little consolation, for its blast was devastating. Night was hideous with the clatter of machine guns, the crash of mortars and the boom of grenades. On a battalion front of a few hundred yards, during the more or less static phase of the Senio tour, the average daily expenditure of ammunition amounted to eighty thousand small arms rounds, two hundred PIAT bombs, two hundred grenades, and eighty three-inch mortars.

In addition to more lethal ammunition, both sides bombarded with leaflets and pamphlets. The Allied literature did not argue; it usually took the form of a safe conduct, printed in three languages and signed by Field-Marshal Alexander. The Germans, on the other hand, waxed verbose and even lachrymose over the fearful risks attendant upon attack upon the river lines. One side of a leaflet would be printed in many colours, showing a land of corn and wine, with buxom maidens ready, willing and able in the fruitful Edens behind the German lines. The obverse, in stark black and white, portrayed thousands of British soldiers drowning under fearful bombardment, while a death's head grinned aloft. This propaganda served two unsuspected purposes. It commanded a souvenir's and collector's value; new issues were eagerly snapped up. In addition the frequency with which Urdu leaflets were fired into British lines and English pamphlets into Indian-held sectors indicated that German intelligence was not particularly up to date.

During the first weeks of the tour, immense ammunition expenditure summarized the activity on Eighth Division's front. Both adversaries were biding their time; the Germans against the massive shock to come, and the Indians because at this juncture it was not considered desirable to show undue interest in this particular sector. On March 13th, however, the Jaipurs with the support of a Wasp flamethrower destroyed an enemy outpost in a house to the east of the river. Twenty-seven Germans were killed for the loss of one Jaipur killed and ten wounded. A week later the Jewish Brigade, now under Divisional command, surprised ten Germans asleep in another house, and accounted for them all. An enemy force of company strength struck back at Frontier Force Rifles, but without success. The front remained quiet thereafter until April 6th, when a heavy and widespread shoot by German artillery raked the line of the Senio. An attack appeared to be imminent but nothing developed. It was afterwards learned that this artillery programme was general along Eighth Army's front, and that it had been planned as a deception shoot, to cover withdrawal to the line of the Santerno. At the last minute a direct order from Hitler's headquarters cancelled the operation. The instruction arrived too late for orders to reach the German gunners, who blazed away some hundreds of tons of ammunition to no useful purpose.

Spring was at hand. Once Hitler struck at the end of each winter; now a vast constricting circle had closed about Germany, and spring was handmaiden to the Allies. At the beginning of April the foliage had begun to break bud, and the flood water from the mountains was still some weeks away. The ground dried and the sky cleared. The hour of decision loomed.

The spring offensive of Eighth Army was part of the global plan to destroy the enemies of the United Nations. Four corps deployed for the assault. Under Fifth Corps Eighth Indian Division, Fifty-Sixth London Division, Seventy-Eighth British Division, Second New Zealand Division, 2nd Commando Brigade, 24th Guards Brigade, and the Italian Cremona Group prepared for battle. The plan called for Eighth Indian Division and the New Zealanders to smash the enemy's defences on the Senio and Santerno, establishing a bridgehead through which Seventy-Eighth Division would thrust for the Po valley. The Londoners and commandos were briefed for a flanking enterprise along the seacoast. The Guards Brigade and the Italians would enter the operation in its secondary phase.

When General Russell surveyed his front, a momentous decision confronted him. Experience had shown advance to the near flood bank to be an individual operation fraught with difficulties and often expensive in casualties. Should Eighth Division carry out this advance before the main battle began, or should both banks be stormed in a single operation? The Divisional objective was not only the crossing of the Senio, but the establishment of a bridgehead beyond the Santerno. Such task required the Indian infantry to force one major obstacle, to fight across six miles of easily defended country, and thereafter to burst through a second water barrier. On the other hand, to launch a preliminary attack against the near flood bank might attract unwelcome attention to the Divisional front, might result in augmented resistance, and might interfere with the timing of the main assault.

The problem presented delicate balances of advantage on both sides, but General Russell's faith in his men carried the day. He decided to regard the two banks of the Senio as a single obstacle. Training and detailed planning proceeded on this basis. At the end of February the Division held a front of eight miles. Bit by bit this unwieldy sector was reduced, until at the beginning of April, Indian troops were deployed over four and a half miles. Two brigades would head the assault, each supported by a heavy force of tanks, flame-throwers and mobile guns. Divisional engineers were instructed to provide five bridges over the Senio within eight hours of the capture of the far flood bank. The two leading brigades would continue up to the Santerno, and if possible would establish crossings. The reserve brigade would then pass through to secure and enlarge the bridgehead.

19th and 21st Brigades were selected to lead the attack. Plans in great detail for the crossing of the Senio were perfected and practised. Once over the river the assault battalions were given considerable latitude within the ambit of the general directive. It could scarcely be otherwise, as both flanks were open. No formation was attacking on the right, and on the left a gap of 4,000 yards, which included Lugo, a town of 25,000 inhabitants, separated 21st Brigade from the New Zealanders. On April 7th, General Russell stressed the basic necessity in an order to his commanders. He wrote:

"The Division must fight with one policy in mind. Keep 17th Infantry Brigade fresh for the Santerno. Only if there is danger that the Division will not be able to carry out its task will 17th Brigade be committed previously. All must plan to give the maximum support to 17th Brigade and to render the difficult tasks allotted to that brigade easier. Remember always that the Division's task is to secure a bridgehead over the Santerno river and that all our efforts must be directed to this end."

The first week of April slipped away in last minute adjustments and re-checks of the innumerable details attendant upon a major operation. The front was quiet—ominously so. A rigid wall of security measures immured the forward areas. Communications were restricted; correspondence, wireless and telephone calls were conducted in cipher or jargon. Movement of transport was reduced to a minimum, tents and bivouacs camouflaged, dumps carefully hidden among the vineyards. Brigade and unit signs disappeared. Eighth Army had gone to ground.

Neither secrecy nor deception measures could conceal from the enemy the imminence of the stroke. Above everything else, the high march of events made it the hour for the final reckoning. Against Fifth Corps, Seventy-sixth Panzer Corps could only array three divisions, with two panzer grenadier divisions the sole reserve force on Eighth Army's front. Beyond the Senio and Santerno other river lines existed, but they were not fortified. To avoid catastrophe the Allied attack must be contained on the present battlefield. Bravely but without hope the Germans made their dispositions, and waited.

April 9th dawned bright and clear. Few if any remembered it to be the anniversary of the tremendous Arras-Vimy Ridge assault in 1917. Under the warm sun and cloudless sky, the infantry rested among the vine trellises and along the pollarded ditches. At 1345 hours a dull drone grew in the sky. The troops sprang to their feet, scanning the south. Group after group of heavy bombers swam into view, sparkling silver in the sunlight. The earth shook as interminable clusters of bombs crashed home. For ninety minutes array succeeded array to smash at the enemy defences. At 1520 hours a tremendous artillery concentration took over and pounded the battlefield. At intervals the shoot would lift, and fighter bombers would swoop to pinpoint positions at which the enemy had manned his defences. The guns would re-open, battering the strong points and centres of resistance. Machine-guns played steadily with high angle fire on all cross roads, bridges, supply dumps and close support lines, in order to impede movement and to isolate the enemy troops in the forward positions.

For four hours this shattering bombardment continued. A vast cloud of dun-coloured dust rose and hung in middle air. At 1900 hours it caught and reflected the level rays of the setting sun. Twenty minutes later, long lines of tanks and flamethrowers surged out of the pastures and vineyards, with the first waves of infantry following in extended order. At that instant the guns ceased and the fighter bombers rocketed down on low level dummy attacks, to engross the enemy for the brief minute in which the fighting vehicles closed up. As they reached the flood bank the leading Crocodiles spurted sheets of flame. A wall of fire curtained the river, and black clouds of oily smoke piled above it. The guns of the tanks and enfilade machine-guns lashed the outer slope, and the leading companies of infantry charged home.

On 19th Brigade's front, Argyll and Sutherland Highlanders and 6/13 Frontier Force Rifles led the way. The Scotsmen encountered only minor resistance as they swarmed over the near bank and plunged into the river. Holding their rifles and machine-guns above their heads, they reached the far bank, mopped up and fell in behind the barrage as it began to march across the plain.

On their left 6/13 Frontier Force Rifles likewise carried the near slope in the first surge. But as they topped the bank, the trough of the river was lashed by a score of machine-guns, firing from portholes in both inner banks, and from enfilade positions on the left. The Frontiersmen dashed into the stream, where many fell dead and wounded. Then once more the hour bred the man. Sepoy Ali Haidar and two others were all of one platoon to reach the far bank. From thirty yards away a machine-gun nest spat death. Bidding his comrades give him covering fire, Ali Haidar lopped a grenade and followed in under it. Although wounded by a stick bomb he closed and destroyed the post. Without pause he charged the next weapon pit, from whence four machine-guns played on his comrades. He was struck twice and fell, but he crawled forward, pulled the pin of a Mills' bomb with his teeth, and hurled it into the spandau nest. Weak with loss of blood he pulled himself to his feet, staggered forward and threw himself upon the gunners. The two surviving Germans surrendered. It was the turning point. With the nearest weapons stilled the Frontiersmen made

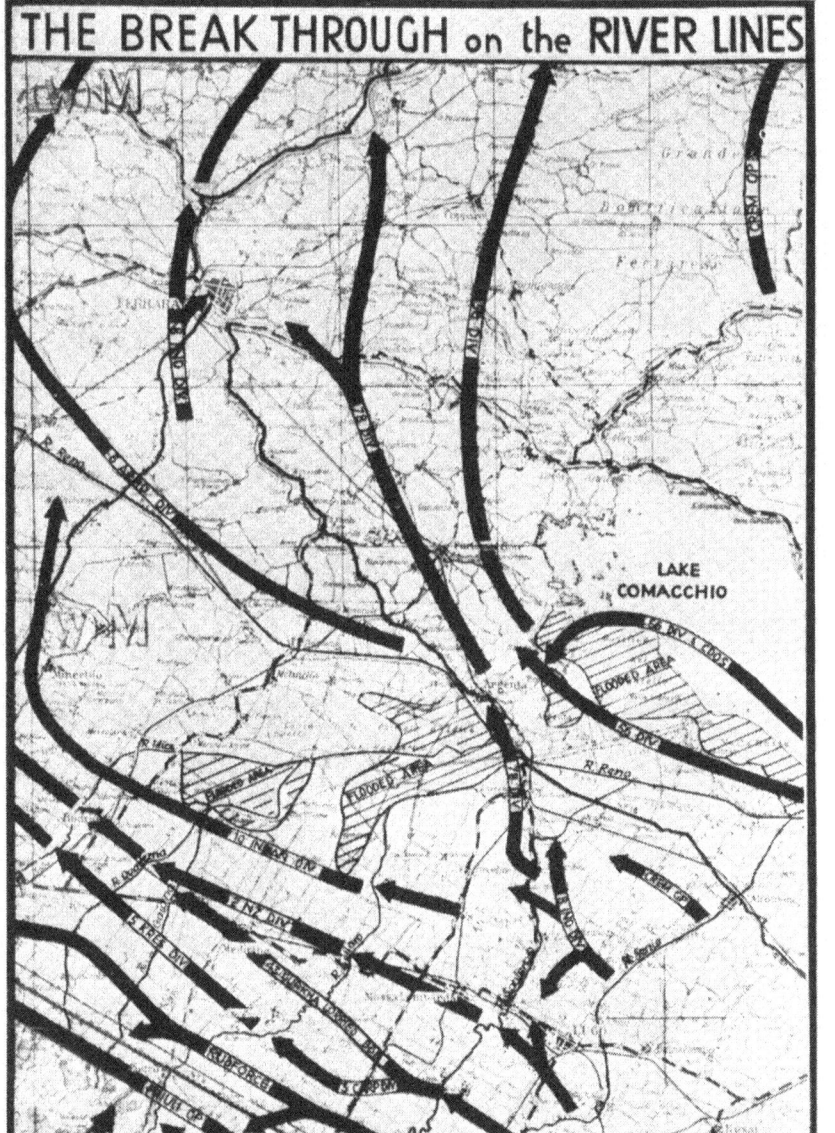

COMMANDER-IN-CHIEF'S THANKS

HISTORIC MOMENT

ARMISTICE DECLARED

their way across the river and took up the chase. Ali Haidar, sorely wounded, was carried back as his comrades swept forward. He eventually recovered to honour his regiment with its first Victoria Cross.

Thirty minutes after the advance began, the leading battalions of 19th Brigade were aligned and mopping up behind the barrage as regularly as though on exercises. By midnight they were two thousand yards beyond the Senio. Unfortunately they were in the blue, for their comrades of 21st Brigade had encountered misfortunes and were still fighting furiously in the forward enemy positions. This brigade attacked with 3/5 Mahrattas on the right, and 3/15 Punjabis on the opposite flank. The Crocodiles on the Mahratta front functioned, and the infantry worked up behind the cover of a bank of blazing oil. As with Frontier Force Rifles, the crest and inner slopes of the flood banks were flailed continuously by machine-gun fire; as the leading companies topped the bank, a hail of steel swept them to earth. The reserve companies closed up, dragging assault boats which proved too heavy to be hauled up the outer slope. With their commanders in the lead, the Mahrattas made a dash for it, leapt over the lip, plunged down the inner bank and into the stream. Small arms fire rose to a venomous crescendo as machine-guns opened from all sides; schmessers and spandaus blazed at the struggling sepoys from portholes, often within a few yards of the men endeavouring to make good their footing on the far bank. The leading companies were decimated, and the rain of bullets compelled the survivors to return to cover on the near bank of the river.

Sepoy Namdeo Jadhao found himself on the far bank with two wounded comrades. In the face of pelting fire, he half-dragged, half-carried the men back across the stream, struggled up the inner slope and deposited them in safety. These rescues necessitated three trips in full view of the enemy. Having saved his friends, Namdeo Jadhao resumed the battle single-handed. He dashed at the nearest machine-gun, and wiped out its crew. A bullet tore his hand, so he dropped his tommy gun and closed with bombs. Two more enemy posts were silenced in quick succession. Standing on the lip of the bank he shouted his war cry and waved his comrades forward. Three company commanders had fallen, but the Mahrattas, responding to such dauntless leadership, swarmed back across the river and ferreted the maze of boltholes, terrier fashion. With both banks clean they pushed on into the night, to deal with the obstinate garrisons of a number of houses in the flat fields adjoining the river.

Like Ali Haidar, Namdeo Jadheo received the Victoria Cross. These almost identical instances of superb gallantry, within a few yards and a few minutes of each other, made all the difference to the centre of Eighth Division's attack. The valour of two men had altered the fortunes of the day.

On the left flank of the Division 3/15 Punjabis shared in full the vicissitudes of the Mahrattas. Two of their four fire-throwers failed to flame. Led by "C" Company, the battalion charged. A hail of fire beat the sepoys into the earth, for the sector included a bend in the river, which allowed enfilade guns to wreak havoc. "C" Company followed up dragging assault boats which they managed to hoist to the crest of the flood bank; the craft drew such fire that the company commander ordered them to be abandoned. The Punjabis plunged into the river, swam or waded across, and found themselves amidst swarms of enemies, all very alive and full of fight. The preliminary bombardment had left this garrison unscathed; the Germans sprang from their pits and burrows and met the Indians at the water's edge. Men drowned in each other's grasp. Machine-gunners were yanked from their tunnels feet first and killed rabbit fashion. Naik Rangin Khan, oblivious to danger, charged post after post, destroying three before he fell mortally wounded. The Germans fought like beasts at bay, but they could not cope with such assailants. By midnight the warrens of the flood banks were empty save for sprawled dead, and the Punjabis were exploiting across the flat fields. At first light they were mopping up one thousand yards to the north-east of Lugo. Royal West Kents followed across, turned south and drew the flanking coverts. Up came the Jaipurs to garrison the flood banks, and to deal with any enemies who might have lain doggo in the hope of emerging to make trouble after the first waves of assault troops had passed.

Up came the sappers also, with their eyes on their watches, for hours were their enemies. In the midst of the flood bank fighting, the Mahratta Anti-Tank Regiment arrived to erect a steel cableway, on which jeeps and anti-tank guns were speedily slung across the river. On 19th Brigade's front, "Sterling" and "Selkirk" bridges were thrown over in less than the sparse eight hours allowed by the Divisional commander. At 0415 hours the first tanks crossed the Senio. 3/8 Punjabis had turned bridge sappers for the night, and under heavy mortar fire had constructed two Olafson bridges for foot traffic. 21st Brigade was equally expeditious; at 0540 hours a tank bridge was in position. Within the next ninety minutes three squadrons of 48th Royal Tank Regiment had lumbered across and had snorted off in the dim light in search of the enemy. 6th Lancers and North Irish Horse followed over, and when the battle began to sort out in daylight, a strong force of British armour was roving between the Senio and the Santerno, on call for the infantry.

Situation reports at dawn showed Eighth Division to be firmly embedded in the main enemy defensive positions and the battle developing according to plan. On the right Argylls continued to find easy going. 6th Lancers and a troop of Mahratta anti-tank gunners after seizing Maiella, exploited to the north as guardians of the open flank. Frontier Force Rifles had run into trouble, and were pinned down on the line of Schuolo Tratturo. In the left brigade sector, the Mahrattas had mopped up to the Lugo canal, while Jaipurs entered the town. This small market place, whose chief claim to fame is a monstrous modernistic statue of Mussolini, put on a brave welcome; the mayor advanced to meet the Jaipurs with a white flag in one hand and a bottle of wine in the other. On the extreme left, 3/15 Punjabis had brought forward their vehicles and were probing to find an opening through which they might exploit as lorried infantry—evidence of the optimism that was in the air. Unfortunately the quick bridging and the rapid closing up of the transport echelons led to a sad tragedy. From ten thousand feet one flood-banked river looks much like another. A number of flights of bombers briefed to smash enemy transport withdrawing behind the Santerno mistook their target and dropped their loads on the long columns waiting to cross the Senio. Heavy casualties resulted.

The Schuolo Tratturo positions had been prepared as a switch line to the Senio defences. In view of the extent of Divisional commitments it was not deemed wise to force the pace by day. That evening, after a short but intense bombardment 3/8 Punjabis, the reserve battalion of 19th Brigade, advanced to the assault. After mopping up rearguards the Punjabis found themselves in the open. Throughout April 11th, Mahrattas and Jaipurs likewise made steady progress on 21st Brigade's front, against disorganized resistance. During the afternoon the Mahrattas reached the start line agreed upon for 17th Brigade's jump off against the Santerno. Here they paused until the Jaipurs had come up on their left and had consolidated the Brigade position.

The Senio Line had burst; the terrain up to the Santerno had been mopped up. 17th Brigade moved up for the denouement, the climactic moment of the battle. Would another smash punch the hole, or would the sagging line hold? At 1730 hours a heavy concentration shoot crashed down on the enemy positions along the line of the Santerno. With an interval of twelve hundred yards between them (because of an intervening minefield), 1/5 Gurkhas and 1/12 Frontier Force Regiment advanced to the assault. It was an odd-looking battle array: an eye-witness said that it must have resembled an old-fashioned commando charge in the Boer war. A mass of vehicles rolled forward, led by flamethrowers. Armoured troop carriers followed, with groups of infantry interspersed on foot. Thereafter, pressing in upon the selvedges of the battle, came the miscellaneous transport of sappers, signallers and services, all intent upon speeding their functions and sharing to the full the risks and rigours of the decisive blow.

As the attack closed, the flamethrowers proved temperamental and accomplished little. The Kangaroos raced for the river; the infantry depouched within a few yards of the enemy and sprang into the fray.

(Some of Frontier Regiment's carriers ran on the minefield, and had to be extricated.) As the two battalions surged over the crest of the flood banks, the Senio struggle was re-enacted; groups of machine-guns from enfilade positions threshed the trough of the river, lashing the water with a hail of steel: one officer said it looked like a miraculous evening rise of fingerling. The sepoys gained the far bank to find it stiff with Germans. One company of the Frontier Force Regiment, two of Gurkhas, effected a lodgment; the enemy struck back with frenzy. Hour by hour the grim battle raged. Of the left flank platoon of Gurkhas only two men stood; on the right eleven men remained. Six counter-attacks were thrown in; each time sheer tenacity thwarted the enemy. At 0200 hours Royal Fusiliers came up and took over the battle, the Gurkhas pushing out at right angles to give flank protection. Simultaneously Frontier Force Rifles found resistance to be weakening, burst through in a soft spot, and fanned out across the fields.

A bridgehead had been established over the Santerno, but on the near bank 21st Brigade was still encountering fierce resistance. The crisis came when the Jaipurs, pushing up from Lugo, were thrown into the assault. In a fine rush "B" Company of the state troops reached the river. The enemy was slow in rallying on the flood banks; the Jaipurs seized their opportunity, and flooded across. They bore against a series of strong points in houses along the western bank. A heavy counter-attack forced them back, but after reorganization they surged forward again. This time the line broke; the defenders scattered and went to ground. The Jaipurs pushed on, leaving fifty dead Germans in the path of their advance.

This dashing advance completed the second breach in the Santerno defences. It now remained to make the bridgehead secure. At 0445 hours Royal Fusiliers pushed forward, working up a road running towards Mondaniga, marked on battle maps as "The Street". The Santerno was as yet unbridged, and the British battalion lacked support weapons. In a last desperate bid to block the hole German infantry with tanks in close attendance struck along "The Street". In the dim hour before dawn, the panzers roved freely. A forward Fusilier Company was overrun. Day was breaking as the enemy tanks prowled, seeking to close. On the other side of the Santerno, British armour chafed, unable to cross to the rescue of the precariously placed infantry, or to administer the *coup de grâce* to the shaken enemy. An engineer officer has supplied an exciting picture of the tense hours during which the sappers laboured all out at the all-important crossings. He wrote:

"At 0445 hours a bulldozer broke its track and partially blocked the near approach to our bridge site. Then the demolition charges in the flood banks failed to explode. A report reached us that a Tiger tank was waiting on the far side of the Santerno, two hundred yards away. Our near approach was widened around the disabled bulldozer, and the Sherman tank of the officer commanding the Armoured Engineer Squadron was positioned to take on the Tiger the instant the gap in the far bank was blown. No mistake was made this time: up went the bank. There was a lot of justifiable laughter when the only enemy in sight after the heavy charge exploded were two bomb-happy Germans who staggered out of a deep dugout not twenty yards from the crater. The dust of the explosion had scarcely settled when the first Churchills were over, and just in time to take on a troop of Tigers."

Had British armour been delayed for another hour, Royal Fusiliers might have been destroyed, and the bridgehead lost. The momentum of the attack would have suffered and the Germans might have rallied for one more stand. But before the heavy guns of the Shermans, the enemy panzers faded away. Seventy-Eighth Division came flooding through. The British troops had not been told of the second Indian bridgehead, and Royal West Kents, who came forward to relieve the Jaipurs, unwittingly assembled on Seventy-Eighth Division's line of advance. Forward elements opened fire on the Kentish men, who took refuge in some farmhouses. There followed the rather unusual spectacle of one British regiment hanging out a white flag to another.

Along the river lines which they had stormed the men of Eighth Indian Division rested content. They had punched the hole again with a speed and power which left the enemy reeling; their spearhead had gouged a gaping wound. Many German formations had been destroyed, and upwards of one thousand prisoners taken, at a cost of little more than 700 Indian casualties. The Army Commander and the Corps Commander said kind words and General Russell thanked his men in his own fashion. "Two rivers crossed in forty-eight hours," he said, "is not a bad achievement, even for Eighth Indian Division."

The end was in sight. Seventy-Eighth Division struck for the Argenta Gap, the slender isthmus of retreat between the salt marshes and Lake Comacchio. As the enemy, reeling from the mortal thrust, strove to block this bottleneck, Fifty-Sixth London Division and 2nd British Commando Brigade took to the Comacchio lagoons in "Fantail" amphibious craft and established themselves in the rear of the Argenta defences. The view halloo of a kill on the grand scale rang across the world. Two German armies were dying fast.

CHAPTER TWENTY

THE LAST PHASE

WHILE THE INFANTRY RESTED, their task accomplished, Eighth Divisional artillery and engineers had hurried forward to join in the battle of the Argenta Gap. It was a significant move, recalling Foch's triumphant summons in the summer of 1918. "The edifice begins to crack. All the world to the battle." The Wehrmacht had dropped its guard, and staggered dizzily under an avalanche of blows. Fifth Army had struck on a three corps front in Tuscany. Second Polish Corps was in the open. The New Zealanders were across the Senio, the Santerno and the Sillaro. No barrier remained to stem the tide.

Twenty-ninth Panzer Division, the remaining enemy reserve on Eighth Army's front, made a last unavailing bid to block the narrow gut of the Argenta Gap, only to crack under the unremitting assaults of Seventy-Eighth and Fifty-Sixth British Divisions. Tenth German Army began to break up. Many enemy formations dissolved overnight into groups of spent and broken men who sat by the roadsides and waited for the victors to dispose of them. Others retained their cohesiveness and dropped back with teeth bared, dying hard and extracting the full price of victory.

In the van of the drive into the north-west went 43rd Gurkha Lorried Brigade, serving its sixth master in six months of almost continuous fighting. (Previous commands had been First Armoured Division, Tenth Indian Division, Fifth Corps, Fifty-Sixth London Division and Second New Zealand Division). On March 8th the Brigade had been given two field regiments, two armoured regiments, sufficient Kangaroos to transport one battalion, and designated as the pursuit group of Second Polish Corps. On April 12th the Gurkhas joined in the hunt. Along the axis of Route 9, the main transverse highway of northern Italy, the Poles drove on Bologna. The right flank was open, and 43rd Brigade hurried to seize Medicina, an important crossroads through which a counter-attack from the north might be launched. At noon on April 13th, 2/8 Gurkhas, lorried infantry to the outside riding capacity of the tanks of the 14/20th Hussars, swept up to within three miles of the Sillaro river. A network of canals was encountered; although only lightly held by machine-gunners these rhines constituted serious tank obstacles. One after another they were cleared and bridged; but it took the best part of two days to cover the intervening distance to the Sillaro.

The remainder of the Brigade came up, and 2/10 Gurkhas forced the stream in the face of heavy and accurate fire. There was too much German artillery in the neighbourhood to bridge by day; rather than risk counter-attack before support weapons arrived, the Gurkhas withdrew for a few hours to the eastern bank of the river.

At 0400 hours on April 16th 23rd Field Regiment laid down a shoot and 2/10 Gurkhas recrossed the Sillaro. Within an hour the bridgehead was secure and the sappers at work. By noon a squadron of Hussar tanks with 2/6 Gurkhas in Kangaroos had passed through, heading for Medicina five miles away. Brushing aside rearguards and surmounting in one fashion or another the remaining canals, at twilight the tanks and armoured troop carriers swept up to the outskirts of the town. Brigadier Barker had been warned that paratroopers were in garrison and that enemy reinforcements were hurrying to their support. It was the occasion for a quick and unorthodox blow. A troop of tanks led by Major Browne, followed by fifteen Kangaroos bearing "B" Company under Major Greenwood, thrust for the centre of the town, where a large brick church with a Moorish-looking dome stands above the square. Major Browne's tank led the way around the corner of the piazza into the main street.

The next ten minutes gave everyone a good deal to remember. One hundred yards away in the narrow street a self-propelled gun squatted against a wall, its crew working furiously. Fifty yards further back two 88 millimetre guns stuck their long noses out of cover. It was a death trap—neck or nothing. Major Browne charged with his troop at his heels. His cannon gunner beat the German crew to the lay, and pumped two rounds into a point blank target. The self-propelled gun slewed sideways, on fire with its crew strewn over the limbers. Sweeping past, the lap gunner dispersed the crews of the 88 millimetre guns with squirts from his Browning at a range of ten feet. At the end of the street Major Browne swung round the corner to confront a German recovery tank twenty yards away, tugging an upended panzer on to even keel. In the same instant a German cyclist stepped from behind a building with a bazooka and hurtled a bomb at touching distance into Major Browne's tank. Within seconds the self-propelled gun blew up, bringing down several buildings and trapping the remainder of the troop. The Gurkhas had depouched and were racing on the trail; diving through the dust and clambering over the rubble Subedar Raghu Gurung arrived first. He slew the bazooka man as he fitted a second missile. Having dragged Major Browne from his tank badly wounded, his crew armed only with their pistols charged the German panzer.

By now the battle was general. Twenty-two paratroopers, standing at bay in a broken building, died under showers of grenades. In another section of the town the fighting resolved into a foot race, with the Germans outdistancing their pursuers through the streets and into the open countryside. Of forty paratroopers who held the communal school only one elected to fight it out. But in cellars, in alleys, in lofts and even on the rooftops, grim individual grapples ensued as the Gurkhas hunted to the death. Major Greenwood, bare-headed, carrying a stick and wearing a bright red scarf for identification, moved about the streets in a supervisory role. He reached the German recovery tank with its engine still running. He climbed in and tested the wireless. It came through loud and clear. He shut off the wireless, for it was wasting battery.

Eight o'clock struck in the church tower. An ammunition dump went up in a nearby field with a colossal crash. The Gurkhas continued to put paid to desperate enemies in lairs and hideouts. German tanks arrived outside the village but thought better of coming in. Towards dawn a bazooka man stole up to the vehicle park in the piazza and sent up a Hussar tank in flames. When morning broke six guns, two tanks, one hundred shaken prisoners and dead Germans everywhere were all that remained of the war in Medicina.

The tide of battle swept on. That same day, Tenth Indian Division joined the hunt. The breakthrough tended to develop at right angles, with Fifty-Sixth and Seventy-Eighth Divisions advancing to the north, while the Poles and New Zealanders thrust into the west. A quick move brought 13th Corps out of the mountains. 10th Indian Brigade was placed at the disposal of the New Zealanders, and took up a position on the Kiwis' right flank, with instructions to extend the breach and to exert the utmost pressure. On the line of the Sillaro the Durhams crossed the river through the front of 5th New Zealand Brigade, and cleared the west bank. There was a holiday air in the countryside. Wherever the Indians paused they were fed and wined. 4/10 Baluchis and 2/4 Gurkha Rifles passed through with most of the infantry riding on tanks. On April 17th the progress was somewhat slower, and on the line of the Quaderno the New Zealanders were held up by violent resistance. With their world falling paratroopers and panzer grenadiers fought on.

Pushing beyond Medicina, 43rd Brigade reached the line of the Gaiana. Here 2/6 Gurkhas took a nasty crack. In a gallant attempt to sustain the momentum of the pursuit this battalion endeavoured to carry that river by storm. Both flanks were open, and the paratroopers were well dug in. Advancing under intense fire, small parties of the hillmen managed to gain the western bank where bitter hand-to-hand fighting followed. One platoon was reduced to seven men. The havildar of another, although wounded four times, killed five Germans singlehanded and brought four survivors out of action. When the leading company had been reduced to forty men, the attempt to cross the river was abandoned.

That night the New Zealanders came up on the right flank of the Gurkhas and again took 43rd Brigade under command. Twenty-four hours later a set piece assault was launched on the Gaiana defences.

A monumental barrage of astonishing accuracy marched forward. One hundred and fifty thousand shells were fired to provide a moving shield of steel. Wasp flamethrowers followed and drenched the river banks in torrents of burning oil. The infantry advanced with 2/8 and 2/10 Gurkhas on the left flank of the Kiwis. It was the end of the road for the arrogant desperadoes of Fourth German Parachute Division. A half mile beyond the river 2/10 Gurkhas mopped up a regimental headquarters, killing a senior officer. 2/8 Gurkhas cut down mortar squads while they still served their weapons. Across open country the pursuit veered into the north towards the Idice, the last water barrier before the Po.

On the right of the New Zealanders, the remainder of Tenth Division now came into the picture. On the night of April 19th, 20th Brigade forced the Quaderno and took over the running from 10th Brigade. With 1/2 Punjabis on the right and 2/3 Gurkhas on the opposite flank, the Indians pressed ahead, mopping up scattered pockets of the enemy. On the afternoon of April 20th, advanced patrols reached the Idice, to be confronted with floodbanks thirty feet high, and to find the near bank covered by a wide irrigation ditch at the bottom of the slope. The position was held in force; and for the last time Tenth Division encountered Germans of the type they knew so well—fanatically brave fighters, skilled in battle, contemptuous of death. Contact had been broken with the New Zealanders, and neither air nor artillery support was on call. 1/2 Punjabis moved forward to storm the defences, and plunged into its bitterest fighting of the war.

With great gallantry two platoons of Dogras of "D" Company reached the far bank. While mopping up a German who had already surrendered shot the only remaining officer. British armour arrived, but the tanks either bogged down in the irrigation ditch, or were destroyed by mines and enemy fire. Two platoons of "B" Company, rushing to the aid of the dwindling garrison on the west bank, lost twenty men in ten minutes. "A" Company was trapped against a belt of wire and pelted by machine-guns. Major Sharma fell dead; Subedar Sainchi Singh, in spite of dangerous wounds, led the company until he dropped unconscious. An Australian, Lieut. Lawrence, headed "B" Company in a desperate bayonet charge which destroyed the remaining enemy posts on the eastern bank. A South African artillery observation officer, Lieut. Spiro, took over command of "A" Company and at the same time continued to direct the fire of his guns. On the far bank the Dogras fought to the last man, ringed by implacable enemies who asked and gave no quarter. Seldom in this war have so many died by the steel; when found the Dogras lay in groups clutching their bloody bayonets.

This ferocious fighting marked the end of organized resistance on the front of Thirteenth Corps. When morning broke any Germans who survived were gone. The remainder of 1/2 Punjabis crossed the Idice without opposition. 3/5 Mahrattas and 2/3 Gurkhas with Skinners' Horse in the van, thrust into the north-east. It was a notable day everywhere. The Poles were entering Bologna and on the right the advanced screens of Fifth and Thirteenth Corps had reached the Po.

On this same day (April 21st) Eighth Indian Division moved out of rest joyfully. Each British soldier and each sepoy was gripped by the exciting knowledge that the end was in sight. 19th Brigade led, passed through the Argenta Gap and struck for Ferrara, city of classical swordsmen, and for the main Po crossings. 3/8 Punjabis brushed aside light opposition, and at noon on April 22nd closed up on the outskirts of the town. 6th Lancers and Argylls forged ahead to mop up small groups of infantry and armoured cars which sought to delay the pursuit. 21st Brigade joined the hunt, clearing Ferrara airfield to the south-west of the city. A group of panzers in Ferrara station held back the Mahrattas; rather than resort to house to house fighting it was decided to by-pass centres of resistance. 19th Brigade pinned down the defenders, while 21st Brigade swung to the left. Royal West Kents escorted by Churchill tanks of North Irish Horse reached the Po to the north-west of Ferrara on the afternoon of April 23rd. The Jaipurs followed through, and British and Indian infantry spread out along the high bare banks of the mightiest river in Italy.

Prisoners began to be a problem. Along the Po stragglers of hundreds of units waited disconsolately to be picked up. A motley assembly wearing the insignia of many divisions, they cluttered the roads and overflowed into the fields. Some were shaken and even hysterical, but most sat dumbly with blank faces, their courage and manhood exhausted.

21st Brigade swung sharply to the right behind Ferrara to cut the German line of retreat. Six tanks and a strong force of infantry blocked their advance in factory buildings opposite I Gorghi. As the Jaipurs came hustling forward six enemy tanks emerged from two large storage sheds five hundred yards ahead. Four moved off while the others lumbered towards the Indians. The Jaipurs scattered and went to ground. Above them anti-tank guns and North Irish Horse took over the battle. One panzer went up in flames. Thirty German infantry following the tanks raced in full flight over the open fields under a hail of fire.

Next morning the three miles of industrial suburbs and open fields between Ferrara and the main Po crossings were clear of the enemy. Concurrently 21st Brigade pushed into the city from the south-east. Argyll and Sutherland Highlanders searched street after street until they reached the mediæval moated fortress in the centre of the town. Eighty-five prisoners and a number of tanks in working order were taken. Ferrara was relatively undamaged, only the road ramps approaching the city having been bombed. The inhabitants were in good heart, well dressed, well fed, and full of enthusiasm for their liberators. Here for the first time appeared the neo-partisans, who were to become nuisances afterwards—brassarded young men with shiny tommy guns which had never seen the light of day until the enemy was gone. These intrepid patriots roved the streets upon vague errands not unconnected with private scores.

The principal Po bridges at Ponte Lagoscuro were more than 200 yards in length. Their crumpled ironwork lay in the bed of the river. As the first to arrive, Eighth Indian Division inherited the task of constructing crossings. The banks were precipitous, the river swift, and time pressed. The great width put an immediate Bailey bridge out of the picture. (Later, South African sappers built a triple Bailey bridge over 1,000 feet in length on this site—perhaps the longest on record.) It was therefore a case of aerial cable-ways, pontoons or amphibious craft. The latter were nearest at hand. Through the endless lines of traffic pushing up to the river came tank carriers bearing Fantails, DUKWS, amphibious Shermans, and quick-moving storm boats.

April 25th will long be remembered by men of Eighth Indian Division as a day of almost lunatic confusion. Traffic jams blocked every approach to the Po. Bulldozers broke down on the launching ramps. German guns accurately shelled the embarkation sites. Nevertheless the time table was preserved and at 2200 hours two companies of Royal West Kents were waterborne to lead the crossing. They landed against negligible opposition. Before dawn 3/15 Punjabis also were over the river. A squadron of 6th Lancers rafted their armoured cars across and explored the countryside for five miles ahead. On the left, 17th Brigade began a similar crossing soon after midnight, with Royal Fusiliers leading. The amphibious Shermans followed with infantry clinging to the tanks. Support arms followed, and the Indian brigades pushed into the north in full cry.

Everywhere groups of Germans stood along the roadside, shoulders drooping, hands held aloft. A low-flying screen from Desert Air Force searched the countryside ahead of the armoured cars and tanks. By the evening of April 27th patrols from 6th Lancers, 1/5 Gurkhas and 1/12 Frontier Force Regiment had reached the Adige, fifteen miles beyond the Po. This substantial river, even swifter than the Po, ordinarily would have been regarded as a serious obstacle. But the pace was ever quickening, and the exciting procession of sights and sounds—deliriously happy Italians, girls with flowers and old gentlemen with wine, the vast debris of a broken army everywhere, the long columns of dead-faced enemies trudging into the south—had galvanized all from commander to sepoy with a single urge—to be in at the death. General Russell had ordered his men to hurry, and he also issued a set plan for the crossing of the Adige. The two instructions did not coincide, so the first took precedence. 19th Brigade swarmed over the river on anything that would float—rafts, rowboats, even on battens and spars. When the amphibious tanks arrived sepoys who could not swim took a firm hold and were towed across. Thus Eighth Indian Division passed over its last river in Italy.

Glittering prizes gleamed ahead. Twenty-five miles to the north of the Adige stood the ancient university city of Padua. Beyond, fifteen miles of autostrade stretched to the end of the causeway which ran across the lagoon to Venice. General Russell rose in his stirrups. 19th Brigade group with 6th Lancers was ordered to dash through in lorries. A company of Frontier Force Rifles mounted on amphibious tanks of 7th Hussars raced forward by another road. 68 and 69 Field Companies, working at top speed, threw a bridge across the Adige on the night of April 28th. The armoured screen of 6th Lancers tore into the north, covering fifty-two miles in a morning. But there were other runners, and in inside positions. Fifty-Sixth London Division had scrambled across the Po to the west of Ferrara. Still further west the New Zealanders, ever in the van, were thrusting from the south-west at full speed. With the Kiwis came 43rd Gurkha Lorried Brigade, hurdling rivers, brushing aside opposition and oblivious of everything except that the end was near.

As the advance neared Padua, transport conditions became incredible. Mile upon mile of vehicles crawled nose to tail. 43rd Brigade turned aside to secure Este, while the Kiwis barged on. In this mad traffic scramble Tenth Indian Division reached the end of the road. After the bitter fighting at the Idice crossing 25th Brigade had passed through 20th Brigade, and had thrust swiftly northwards. By the evening of April 22nd Skinners' Horse was in screen far ahead of King's Own, 3/1 Punjabis and 3/18 Garhwalis. But even armoured cars could make little headway, and Tenth Division found itself in the centre of a vast cone of traffic converging on Ferrara and the Po crossings. Trapped between these tides of transport the Indians were crowded off the roads in the triangle between the Bologna-Ferrara highway and the single road which ran into the north through the Argenta Gap. On the banks of the Reno, at the small muddy village of Malabergo, their advance ceased. Hope revived when Thirteenth Corps, with perhaps more pessimism than the situation warranted, briefed Tenth Division for assault should the enemy stand along the picturesque ridges of Collei Eugenei, high ground studded with castles and monasteries to the south-east of Padua. Before the stricken quarry could reach this covert, the kill came.

Eighth Division likewise found no roadroom beyond the Adige. 21st Brigade never crossed the last river. The privateering expedition of elements of 19th Brigade was abandoned in endless traffic jams around Rovigo. Farthest ahead, the Frontiersmen riding as outside passengers on 7th Husaar tanks were obliged to relinquish their seats to the south of Padua, and to give up the chase. Yet such are the fortunes of war that Eighth Indian Division was vouchsafed the opportunity of adding a postscript to its great record in the Italian campaign. While German emissaries were presenting themselves at Allied headquarters to accept a victor's terms, a squadron of 6th Lancers moved northward on escort duty, through Trento into the Italian Alps. Far up on the road to Austria, partisans brought word of a German division dug in on a rocky hillside under the snow-clad peaks, and determined to fight to the death. The armistice was two days old when Lieutenant Conisbee, with two Sikhs and six Jats, went forward to investigate. In an eyrie well-nigh as impregnable as Cassino he found what survived of the men who had held Monastery Hill and Snake's Head Ridge—the First German Parachute Division. He was bluntly informed that the German commander would only surrender his force if met by an officer of his own rank. General Russell was far away, and an American general close at hand. Yet it was some consolation to know that Eighth Indian Division was represented by this small patrol at the capitulation of such formidable adversaries.

Of the Indian forces, only 43rd Gurkha Lorried Brigade remained on the move. Carried forward by the irresistible swoop of the New Zealanders, Brigadier Barker and his men stood a fair chance of seeing the curtain fall from a front row in the stalls. On April 30th the citizens of Padua stood all day in the rain, lining the streets to cheer madly as the fighting vehicles flashed past into the north. But as they arrived, the lorries bearing the crossed kukris were diverted into the main square. In the Paduan suburbs a certain amount of bushwhacking was in progress, as Fascist snipers sought belated martyrdom. Red-scarfed bandoliered youths began to celebrate liberation by summary executions, by shaving women's heads and throwing collaborationists into the river. Padua needed a garrison. The Gurkha Brigade took charge and when Cease Fire blew, the city had regained its staid and civilized tradition.

In the fields, around the village fountains, in the billets of the towns, the sepoys told the civilians, "Guerra è finita". The volatile Italians cheered and cried and celebrated; the Indians were kissed and embraced and wined and fed. They took it all gravely. It had been such a long road that it was a little difficult to realize that the march was over. It was hard to believe that a man might walk upright and openly in the daylight without death seeking him. That night hereafter would be a time for sleep instead of for bitter marches and grim encounters—this too seemed a strange thing. The dim years in Eritrea, Syria, Iran, Iraq, Western Desert and Tunisia blended with the bright yesterday in the common crucible of battle. Now in a trice something had supervened. The job was finished, the vocation of the acolyte withdrawn. There was satisfaction yet some disquiet, in the knowledge that it was all over.

CHAPTER TWENTY-ONE

POSTSCRIPT: MACEDONIA AND THE JULIAN MARCHES

IT WAS NOTED at the beginning of this narrative that the business of war had grown progressively technical, and that the demands upon the private soldier and his officer alike had steadily increased in complexity. Nor had these calls been restricted to the needs of the battlefield. War as waged by the Nazis absorbed the civilian population in the military regime. When German power was broken, it was essential to establish an interregnum during the which the civilian population, displaced, regimented, cowed and starved, could be nursed back from neurosis to health, and persuaded to reshoulder the responsibilities of free peoples. This task of intermediate control and guidance inevitably devolved upon the soldiers.

Nowhere was the problem more acute than in Greece. This unhappy country, after more than twenty-five years of political and social turmoil, had gallantly sprung to arms when the jackal imitated the wolf, and Mussolini staged his unprovoked attack. In the mountains along the Albanian boundary the Italians were easily contained until Hitler struck in aid of his henchman. Then followed the tragic campaign in the spring of 1941 in which inadequate British and Dominion forces, rushed from Western Desert, were driven back against the sea. The Royal Navy intervened to save the remnants, and Greece passed under the conqueror's heel.

The jackboot weighed heavily. Without food to plunder for the fat fraus at home, and without industries to feed the German war machine, Greece possessed no saving grace in Nazi eyes. Its civilian population was treated abominably; only the Poles suffered more. To reckless and desperate men the mountains offered sanctuary. Soon after the occupation, the first guerilla bands began to muster in the less accessible highlands. Daring British officers arrived by parachute to advise, to organize, and to arrange for supplies. Thus the Greek resistance movement was born.

Unfortunately the fatal schism which had tormented Greek political life for decades soon appeared in the camps in the mountains. Greek hated Greek more than Greek hated German. From non-co-operation the guerilla bands passed to active hostility. From hostility the next step was treason. Certain Greek organizations aligned themselves with the German invaders in order to promote their internecine feuds. British liaison officers brought despairing report to Middle East; whence the principal guerilla leaders were flown for conference. No reconciliation was effected. As years passed the rival groups tended to coalesce into two main bodies: ELAS, the left wing partisans, and EDES, the right wing party. This clarification simplified the task of negotiation, and when the defeat of Germany loomed, another effort was made to secure Greek unity. At a conference at Caserta in September, 1944, a measure of success was achieved. Leaders of the respective groups agreed to sink their differences during the period of reconstruction, to accept orders from the Allied High Command during the liberation of Greece, and thereafter to obey the dictates of the provisional government until such time as it was replaced by more representative authority.

By this time ELAS had established a measure of control and even of government in many parts of Greece. Only in the north-west did EDES hold sway. It was obvious that the Caserta resolutions alone were not sufficient to ensure an orderly liberation, nor indeed to prevent civil war. As signs of German withdrawal multiplied, British commando forces, operating in the Ægean islands, began to step up towards the mainland. With the consent of both principal factions British troops were entrusted by Allied High Command with the task of reoccupying Greece. Definitely limited objectives were set: "to eject the enemy, to maintain law and order, to repair communications, to distribute civil relief and to remain strict political neutrals". In mid-October, 2nd Independent Parachute Brigade and 23rd Armoured Brigade landed near Athens, the leading battalion under the command of Lieut.-Colonel Lord Jellicoe. The British troops received a tumultous welcome. On October 19th the British Commander of Land Forces, Greece, Lieut.-General Scobie, the Greek Prime Minister and his Government entered the capital. Three weeks later, Salonika, the principal port of Macedonia, was occupied. This short interim period had been sufficient to allow ELAS to establish a makeshift authority in Macedonia, but the British paratroop advance guard was received with manifestations of friendship.

On October 20th, Fourth Indian Division, at rest in the Perugia area, received orders to proceed to Greece. Brigadier Lovett of 7th Indian Infantry Brigade and his staff officers flew to Greece on the same day. The plan called for Fourth Division to be dispersed in three widely scattered areas. 7th Brigade with Divisional troops were allocated the troublesome cockpits of Macedonia, Thrace and Thessaly, with instructions to keep watch on the borders of Yugo-Slavia and Bulgaria. 11th Brigade would garrison the principal towns of Western Greece and the Ionian islands. 5th Brigade would take over the

Ægean area and the Cyclades, and would move into Crete when the enemy garrisons in that island capitulated.

In the second week of November, 7th Brigade and Divisional headquarters arrived at Salonika. On debarkation the troops were welcomed by the civilian population, and the attitude of the local ELAS forces likewise remained friendly. While monarchist and other factions existed in Macedonia, ELAS was preponderant in strength, organization and arms. Civilian administrations were controlled by the ELAS formations; if opposition developed, strong-arm tactics prevailed. In addition, ELAS had adopted from the Germans the odious hostage system. It is well to remember, however, that for a thousand years the history of Macedonia has been characterized by massacre, pillage and the rule of force, and that new-found freedoms were bound to excite rather than to stabilize such a volatile people as the Greeks. Nevertheless, the first week passed pleasantly, with the ELAS commander correct in his attitude and the general public appreciative and co-operative.

The quiet was short-lived. It now seems probable that whereas in the first instance ELAS had been content to wait for a general election and to come to power by constitutional means, the arrival of prominent royalists in the train of the new Government created the suspicion that the King of the Hellenes might turn up at any moment, to rally all anti-communist and anti-socialist elements to his standard. A number of subsidiary developments led to tension. British commanders refused to hand over political prisoners and ELAS offenders against the peace. When EDES and ELAS bands clashed, British troops intervened to restore peace. The first draft of National Guard officers arrived at Divisional Headquarters for training. This body was designed to replace the guerilla forces, and had been recruited as non-partisans. Unfortunately there were no neutrals in Greece, and many recruits had an anti-ELAS background. ELAS felt its predominant position in Macedonia to be challenged, and agitators at once gave tongue. Guerillas occupied the Salonika airfield, refused to hand over local barracks, and cut the country roads, isolating Fourth Division detachments in the hinterland.

These manifestations mirrored similar developments in Athens, where it would appear that a trial of strength had been decided upon. Towards the end of November, a steady infiltration of ELAS forces into the capital began.

11th Brigade arrived at Patras during the third week of November and commenced to distribute detachments among the outposts of the Gulf of Corinth. The situation in Patras differed from that in Salonika, in that the British commandos had landed on the heels of the retreating Germans, and ELAS had had no opportunity to install local governments. In outlying points, however, ELAS forces at once began reprisals against the German-organized "security battalions". Any attempt to protect these wretched impressees was bitterly resented. In Patras the "security battalion" had surrendered to the first British forces to land. Protection of these prisoners afforded an excuse for an aggressive and intimidating attitude upon the part of ELAS. In the course of 11th Brigade's deployment a tragedy occurred. A ferry carrying troops into Missolonghi hit a mine and sank with a loss of seventy lives, in a fairway known to have been clean a short time before. Two days later a landing craft blew up in almost the same spot.

Meanwhile in Athens events rapidly moved towards a crisis. On December 3rd the ELAS members of the Greek Government resigned. A general strike was declared, and police opened fire on demonstrators. British troops were not involved. On the next day ELAS troops attacked British and Greek Naval Headquarters in Piraeus, the port of Athens. General Scobie ordered all ELAS formations to leave the capital by December 7th, under penalty of being declared hostile.

In Italy Fourth and Forty-Sixth British Divisions hurriedly prepared to embark. Ahead came 5th Indian Infantry Brigade, diverted from the Ægean islands. On December 8th Brigadier Saunders-Jacob arrived at Athens. British headquarters had been constricted behind a tiny perimeter in the centre of the city, and was under fire. Beyond the perimeter a number of detachments were isolated. At Piraeus, ELAS forces pressed on Naval Headquarters from all sides. The immediate need was to clear the harbour area.

The Piraeus peninsula is two miles long, stretching from south-west to north between Faliron Bay and Leonidas Harbour. The northern tip is dominated by Lofos Castella Hill, which rises steeply to a height of three hundred feet. A waterside district of tenements and unpaved streets stretches to the south. The Greek Naval College stands on the western neck of the peninsula. Here 139th British Infantry Brigade covered Naval Headquarters, and here on the night of December 9th 1/4 Essex led the Indian reinforcements ashore.

Two days later 3/10 Baluchis and 1/9 Gurkhas landed under fire. On December 12th, 5th Brigade went into action. In their first advance the Essex severed the neck of the peninsula separating the double harbour. Thereafter day by day the three battalions fought their way through the streets, pushing back the ELAS besiegers and enlarging the perimeter. On December 15th, 1st Field Regiment arrived, but the guns were used sparingly because of shortage of ammunition. 1/9 Gurkhas encountered strong opposition on the slopes of Lofus Castella, where German-built concrete emplacements were manned by obstinate detachments. For political reasons the hillmen were denied the use of their kukris, but in a night attack they overran the area with modest losses.

On December 19th, 5th Brigade was relieved on the southern

harbour front, and three days later landed on the quays at Dhrapetsona, in the northern harbour. With tank and air support available fierce but sporadic resistance was beaten down. Rocket firing aircraft and sniping by tank cannon did much to discourage the defenders. From an island in the harbour, 1st Field Regiment, ample ammunition having arrived, averaged 100 rounds per gun per day. By the end of the month the Piraeus dock, power and petrol installations had been recovered, and over one thousand prisoners taken for total Brigade casualties of 166 of all ranks.

The strife in Athens naturally reacted on relations elsewhere. In Macedonia demonstrations and threats became so prevalent that outlying detachments were called in. 7th Brigade established a defended perimeter on the outskirts of Salonika, while a strong force garrisoned the dock area. Impudent and provocative incidents followed. The civilian population were incited to obstruction, and only the high morale and steady patience of the Indian troops prevented clashes. There is reason to believe that coincident with the outbreak in Athens, ELAS ordered their Macedonian commander to attack in Salonika. That officer with great good-sense preferred to wait and see what happened in the capital. When the *coup d'état* failed, the tension in the north tended to relax.

Similarly, events in Athens resulted in repercussions in the south. On the night of December 3/4th the newly formed National Guard battalions which were to assist British troops in policing western Greece, was surrounded and disarmed by ELAS forces in Patras and Pyrgos. A cordon was established around these centres to prevent British and Indian troops from patrolling the country districts. On December 14th at Krioneri three British officers, including one proceeding on a special mission under a white flag, were seized as hostages and imprisoned. Next morning ELAS forces attacked the small British detachment at this outport. Naval fire dispersed the half-hearted assault. Considerable tension continued and during the New Year celebrations a British outpost was destroyed in treacherous fashion at Zakhinthos, seven soldiers being killed. The sorely tried British and Indian detachments, enraged by such murderous incidents, walked more lightly, with quicker trigger fingers: a senior officer, exasperated beyond measure by the insolence and double dealing of an ELAS emissary, slammed him into a chair, bounced him around the room, and demonstrated in no uncertain fashion that the time for nonsense was over. Thereafter the belligerence of the ELAS formations in Patras oozed. On January 9th the glad tidings arrived that 11th Brigade might now proceed to mop up the countryside. Two days later Camerons, Gurkhas and Frontier Force Regiment sallied in three columns. After a long night march 2/7 Gurkhas closed at dawn on ELAS positions near the village of Klaus. Fighting ensued in which

ELAS sustained 134 casualties for the loss of two Gurkhas killed and two wounded. This sharp lesson cleared the air; four German officers and sixty-nine men, serving under ELAS command, surrendered as soon as it became apparent that the British meant business. On January 25th a British brigade arrived to take over the 11th Brigade concentrate i for transfer to Salonika.

On January 15th a truce had been concluded in Athens, by the terms of which ELAS undertook to withdraw from the capital and Salonika and to occupy rural concentration areas. Except for isolated incidents this truce ended the phase of active operations in Greece. Hostages began to return; eleven hundred British nationals were brought in, many showing evidence of abominable ill-treatment. Victims of summary execution were exhumed and given decent burial. The task of Fourth Indian Division ceased to be military and became tutelary. 5th Indian Brigade left Athens for Volos, an important supply centre on the east coast, through which much of the entrepôt trade of the Greek islands passes. In Volos ELAS were in complete control, but the Brigade landed without incident. The port served as a clearing station for the ELAS garrisons of the Ægean which were being withdrawn to a concentration area near Larissa.

5th Brigade remained in Volos for two months. Relations in this hostile outport evolved in characteristic fashion. For the first few days the Greek press—blatant windy inflammatory broadsheets which passed for newspapers—ignored the Indian garrison, and gave themselves over to scurrilous abuse of Mr. Churchill. When this drew no response, alleged atrocity stories from returned ELAS prisoners of war were played up, with flaring wood block headlines and a wealth of gruesome detail. Once again the lethargic British displayed no interest. This apathy was unendurable. Delegations began to pester the Brigade commander with every conceivable complaint, fortified by the most impudent falsehoods. The Greeks talked and talked; British officers listened and listened. Towards the end of January, fatigue set in and wronged parties grew less plentiful. A newly recruited battalion of the National Guard arrived in time to save the situation. In a trice the alleged abominations of Indians and British were forgotten, in a spate of venom directed against the Greek soldiers who sided with law and order.

The induction of National Guard battalions became one of the chief duties of Fourth Indian Division. This sponsorship imposed a dual task—to persuade the National Guardsmen that they must act impartially, and to convince the Macedonian villagers that the new formations must not be regarded as enemies. In a countryside addicted to vendettas, where every man is a politician and raw hate the substance of his conviction, it was difficult to inculcate such a simple and reasonable attitude. Men whose kin have been butchered do not forget overnight, and the arrival of National Guard units in some areas coincided with regrettable reprisals.

Some of the National Guard battalions had received limited battle experience in Athens and were reputably under discipline. Before installing them, however, it was thought best to see that the terms of the truce were being observed. Indian troops were despatched to occupy the principal Macedonian villages and towns. This move introduced Fourth Indian Division to the country people, and served to convince all but the most bigoted ELAS supporters that they had nothing to fear. The reception of these occupying forces varied from sullen hostility to hysterical acclamation, but such is the strength of tolerance and good humour that except for a few cantankerous centres, the hostility quickly dissipated. If a carrier patrol passed through a town where the population lined the street defiantly chanting "Zito KKE", with clenched fists raised, the troops cheerily responded, also with clenched fists raised, and perhaps with bursts of ELAS songs. In lighthearted fashion they were prepared to be all things to all men. The return of hostages in pitiable condition, together with the singularly uninformed comment of some sections of the home press, aroused resentment among British troops. But their anger was directed against ELAS forces, and not against the civilians who through fear and ignorance parroted the farragos upon which they had been fed.

When voluntary recruiting for the Natonal Guard was succeeded by a draft system, the time had arrived to install Greek forces on a wider basis. British liaison officers were attached to each National Guard unit. On induction, British and Indian troops accompanied the Greek detachments, remaining with them for a trial period. In spite of the efforts of politicians, and of a singularly irresponsible section of the Greek press, incidents were fewer than might have been expected. The ways of the National Guard were not British ways, and on occasion they exceeded their authority and reverted to practises indistinguishable from those of ELAS. But fortunately the earlier formations came from Athens, with no hereditary interest in the Macedonian feuds. Before long even the most fear-bound villages began to yield a few friends. Some were informers of the most loathsome type, but others reacted to the hope of peace and liberty. Village secrets began to emerge; that there were arms stored here, and ammunition there; that so-and-so had not delivered up his weapons; that someone else moved from place to place creating trouble. These contacts simplified the task of tidying up. On the whole the National Guard did not betray their mentors, and bit by bit the Indian squads were withdrawn and directed to other duties.

Such duties were manifold, for it was urgently necessary to repair the shattered economy of Macedonia. The roads were in woeful state, and nearly every bridge was blown; in a pastoral land where flock migrations are essential, the first task was to reopen communications. Divisional Sappers and Miners went to work with a will. Ferries were devised and operated by Indian personnel. As Bailey sections arrived, the principal streams were bridged. Under Divisional guards, UNRRA convoys began to move into the hinterland. It became possible to bring in welfare workers and medical supplies. Communications were established with the Bulgarian and Jugo-Slav frontiers, and detachments of the Division moved up to investigate the endless spate of charge and counter-charge concerning boundary violations. An exchange of dispossessed persons with the neighbouring states began. Bit by bit sources of irritation were ironed out. Sections of the Greek press, with a magnificent disregard for the truth, continued to spread any tale which suited their book. Politicians ranted. Some people could not forget. But when the carrier patrol rolled up to the village, the children swarmed about it, for the sepoys usually had sweets in their pockets. The officer sat in the shade with the headman, listened to his troubles, made notes, and proffered advice. When business was over, and the ceremonial glasses of wine had been drunk, sturdy Macedonian wenches came crowding with garlands, and the carrier moved off amid salvos of "Zitos", and sometimes with an embarrassing number of simple presents.

Fear had gone or was going. Security had arrived, or was on the way. Some of the mercurial Greeks felt prosperity to be just around the corner. It was not as simple as that. There were thirty-nine recognized political parties in Greece, and each had its own articles of faith. The Greek nation had been through fire, but had not burned out its dross. There was a limit to what friends could do, and in the long run the Greeks must save themselves. But throughout 1945 British and Indian troops continued to serve the stricken northern provinces, allaying apprehensions, preventing abuses, and steadily restoring normal intercourse. When in January, 1946, the wearers of the Red Eagle gathered at Salonika to take ship for home, it was with the knowledge that they had put the feet of the Greeks in the path which might lead to ordered life thereafter.

Fourth Indian Division, first to arrive, was last to leave the Mediterranean theatre. After the collapse of Germany Eighth Indian Division quickly mustered to transfer to India, as it had been selected for employment against Japan. Tenth Indian Division and 43rd Gurkha Lorried Brigade were due to follow when a sudden crisis loomed in Trieste. Istria and Venetia Guilia, provinces snatched by Italy from the disintegrating Austro-Hungarian empire after the last war, contained a large Yugo-Slav population. Marshal Tito's valiant troops, having expelled the enemy from their homeland, pursued the Germans to the north and west. When the surrender came, the Yugo-Slavs held Italy to the line of the Izonzo river, and had effected a considerable penetration into Carinthia, the playground province of southern Austria.

It had already been decided in high conclave that these areas should form part of the British zone of occupation. Unfortunately Russian forces which had overrun part of Carinthia at first showed little inclination to hand over. When a big man succeeds, a little man tries. The Second Yugo-Slav Army occupied the Julian Marches up to the Izonzo, reinforced their token force in Carinthia, and stood fast.

More than disputed provinces were at stake—the integrity of inter-Allied agreements and the authority of the Supreme Allied Command. In terse terms the Russians declared their views on Carinthia; the Yugo-Slavs at once took the roads towards home. They were more loath to relinquish Italian territory, and Field-Marshal Alexander was obliged to reinforce his unmistakable declaration with troop movements. 43rd Gurkha Brigade was already covering the bottleneck into Trieste, where the New Zealanders nonchalantly trafficked with the somewhat truculent Yugo-Slavs. Tenth Indian Division and Eighty-Fifth U.S. Division crossed the Izonzo, and moved up to take station along the roads leading to the Tarviso and Caporetto passes through which the three British divisions in Austria were maintained. Fifty-sixth London Division followed, and a strong corps stood ready to reinforce the dictates of the Allied High Command.

Fortunately force was not necessary. The Yugo-Slavs stood their ground but sedulously avoided incidents. There were many opportunities for friction in this double occupation: the common use of crowded roads; different curfews (Yugo-Slav time being two hours ahead), contiguous billeting areas, incessant propaganda in which the Italians participated, an abundance of pretty girls and harsh wines. British commanders refused to allow villages to be searched for Fascists and alleged enemies of the state. British medical officers insisted upon a standard of field hygiene with which the Yugo-Slavs were unfamiliar. At times these irritations prickled, and hot-headed local commanders bluffed. Mortars were mounted to command British airfields. An 88 millimetre gun was trained at point blank range on a park of British tanks in a village piazza. But always good sense prevailed and the spectacle was witnessed of men deployed to thwart each other mounting double guards, chatting over handfuls of cherries, kicking a football together in the village streets, and side by side examining with horse-lovers' eyes animals lately "requisitioned" from White Cossack prisoners. This forbearance in the first days of impact bore bountiful fruit. Second thoughts succeeded first impulses, and the two forces settled down in amity to the joint occupation.

On acquaintance both British and Indian troops learned to respect the hardy Yugo-Slavs who had fought so well, and who seemed able to operate a division on less transport and equipment than required by a single British battalion. Tito's forces (about one-quarter of the army were women) proved to be cheerful folk, good at games, and within the narrow range of their resources, invaringly hospitable. They carried their drink well for the local wines were bodiless beside the wild plum brandy of their homeland. They were fond of music, men and women harmonizing in folk songs replete with immemorial Slavonic nostalgia. They saluted British officers with a punctiliousness which it is hoped that British other ranks reciprocated. These pleasant characteristics fortified the tendency to leave political questions to those who must settle them, and meanwhile to make the best of the impasse.

In pursuance of such resolve, Tenth Indian Division devoted itself to a series of "Jug" parties which did much to cement growing friendships and mutual appreciation. A single entertainment may be described as characteristic of a score of similar functions. To the east of the Montfalcone-Gorizia road 25th Indian Brigade moved into a solidly Yugo-Slav area. The craggy village which served as Brigade headquarters was crammed with Tito's troops. A house-warming seemed to be indicated so an invitation was extended to all Yugo-Slavs in the neighbourhood. They turned up in hundreds. At a buffet supper to the officers a Yugo-Slav commissar and a Gurkha subedar major baited each other in fluent and cheerful Italian and effectively laid the foundation for animated and amiable conversation. After supper Brigadier Arderne led out a woman adjutant, formidable of form but beaming, for the first dance. In a natural amphitheatre behind the village, hundreds of British, Indian and Yugo-Slav soldiers sat down together to al fresco entertainment. That greatest of cosmopolitans, Mickey Mouse, received the same belly laughs from all. Newsreels of the German prison camps were received by all with the same shocked silence. On the flood-lit floor of the amphitheatre, Durham Light Infantry produced a beauty ballet that was both vulgar and hilarious; the Yugo-Slavs rolled in mirth. Indian dances, culminating in the wild Khattak of the North-West Frontier, drew round upon round of applause. Everyone knew "Lily Marlene". At the end, all streamed home together, comrades undivided.

The tension relaxed, agreement over Trieste was reached, and the mission of the Indians fulfilled. 43rd Gurkha Lorried Brigade was first to go. The New Zealanders regarded the hillmen as their own, and when the Gurkhas took ship they sailed from the midst of their greathearted comrades. The bands of the New Zealand Division played each battalion aboard, and Sir Bernard Freyburg stood by the roadside, and later by the shipside, to give all godspeed. The Kiwis lined the streets as the columns swung past. "Good-bye, Johnny," they called, hands flung high—a soldier's farewell between men diverse in colour, creed and culture, yet who in service of the same cause had compiled records of skill and valour unmatched in the history of battle.

Tenth Indian Division crossed Italy for a tour of duty in the Milan area. In December the Indian units took the roads to a southern port. Then came the wrench of parting, for the British formations, infantry, artillery and services, were left behind. Indian and Briton alike felt emptiness, for each in his heart knew the Indian Army to be an indissoluable partnership, in which the old concept of subject and dominant castes has disappeared, and in which all races are now brethren in arms.

Across the high seas, toward India, the ships bore many thousands of fighting men. They were not the raw recruits, the simple peasants, who had fared forth three, four, or five years before. They had travelled thousands of miles; they had seen diverse peoples: they spoke foreign languages; they had matched their manhood against the greatest aggressor and had not been found wanting. Now they were going home. Many wondered what home would mean. Proud of their service, keen and eager for the opportunities of to-morrow, it rested with India to fit them into service in a newer, better world.

NAIK AND BRIGADIER

EVERYBODY HAPPY

GENERAL FREYBERG'S FAREWELL

HOMEWARD BOUND

www.ingramcontent.com/pod-product-compliance
Lightning Source LLC
Chambersburg PA
CBHW022004220426
43663CB00007B/959